Malinowski in Mexico

International Library of Anthropology

Editor: Adam Kuper, University of Leiden

Arbor Scientiae
Arbor Vitae

A catalogue of other Social Science books published by Routledge & Kegan Paul will be found at the end of this volume.

Malinowski in Mexico

The economics of a Mexican market system

Bronislaw Malinowski
and Julio de la Fuente

Edited and with an Introduction by
Susan Drucker-Brown

Routledge & Kegan Paul

London, Boston, Melbourne and Henley

*First published in 1982
by Routledge & Kegan Paul Ltd
39 Store Street, London WC1E 7DD,
9 Park Street, Boston,
Mass. 02108, USA,
296 Beaconsfield Parade, Middle Park,
Melbourne, 3206, Australia and
Broadway House, Newtown Road,
Henley-on-Thames, Oxon RG9 1EN
Set in Press Roman 10 on 12 point by
Columns, Reading
and printed in Great Britain by
The Thetford Press Ltd, Thetford, Norfolk*

Library of Congress Cataloging in Publication Data

*Malinowski, Bronislaw, 1884-1942.
The economics of a Mexican market system.
(International library of anthropology)
Bibliography: p.
Includes index.
1. Markets – Mexico – Oaxaca Valley.
2. Oaxaca Valley (Mexico) – Rural conditions.
I. Drucker-Brown, S. II. Title. III. Series.
HF5473.M6203956 380.1'0972'74 81-23416*

ISBN 0-7100-9197-4 AACR2

Contents

Editor's acknowledgments ix
Glossary xi
Malinowski in Mexico: introduction 3
Susan Drucker-Brown
The economics of a Mexican market system 53
Bronislaw Malinowski and Julio de la Fuente
Prefatory note and acknowledgments 55
1 The actual problem of fieldwork in Mexico today 58
2 General aspects of trade in the Valley, and a visit to the market place of Oaxaca 70
3 The Valley markets; their cultural and economic interdependence 82
4 A brief survey of the surrounding district and townships 93
5 Problems and methods in the analysis of market transactions 107
6 Economic background of the market place 115
7 Market transactions under the microscope 137
8 Concrete data on selling and buying 154
9 The maize market 174
10 A comprehensive look at the market 182
Appendix 193
Notes 196
Bibliography 203
Index 211

Illustrations

Plates between pages 114 and 115

I The ethnographers

1 Bronislaw Malinowski with friends

2 Julio de la Fuente at the periphery of a market

II The approach to market

3 Procession en route to market

4 Ox-carts entering the market

5 Pack mules stabled in the main hostelry of Oaxaca City

III Forms of dress in the Oaxaca market

6 Zapotec woman

7 Zapotec man

8 An old woman wearing a *huipil*

9 A woman wearing a Mije Indian style of blouse

10 Mixed styles of women's dress

IV Market products

11 Clothing

12 *Rebozos*

13 Salted meat

14 Cooked food and cheese

15 A client examines an earthenware pot

16 *Ixtle* fibre products

17 Brooms

18 Firewood

19 Votive offerings

20 Iron machetes, knives and hoe blades

21 Oxen for sale in the livestock market

22 Sugar skulls, etc. sold for the Day of the Dead

V From maize kernel to maize bread

23 Maize

24 Lime

25 Maize dough being prepared for tortillas

26 Metates on sale

27 A decorated *metate* for a bride

28 Earthenware griddles

29 Sale of tortillas

VI Aspects of market transactions

30 The *almud* used to measure maize

31 Scales used to measure chile

32 A barter transaction

33 A *regatona* sorting eggs

VII The Oaxaca City market, new and old

34 The clothing section

35 Woven baskets

36 Woven baskets in the Benito Juarez market, 1941

Maps

		page
1	Mexico, showing the state of Oaxaca	71
2	The state and districts of Oaxaca	72
3	The Valley market system	92

Editor's acknowledgments

My greatest debt is to Mrs Helena Wayne *nèe* Malinowska, who provided me with the English typescript of *The Economics of a Mexican Market System* and a commentary on the text by Julio de la Fuente. Mrs Wayne also made available to me letters and memoranda written by her father. In addition she read and patiently helped me to edit the manuscript. Changes in the manuscript have been made for the sake of clarity but we have tried to retain the flavour of Malinowski's English. Somc additions of substance have been made in editor's notes and for these I am entirely responsible.

I am indebted to the publishers Routledge & Kegan Paul for financial aid which allowed me to travel in Mexico during August 1978. I would particularly like to thank Dr Gonzalo Aguirre Beltrán for his help at that time and for the hospitality he extended to me when I visited him in Jalapa. His description of the interest aroused by *The Economics of a Mexican Market System*, and of its use by the Instituto Nacional Indigenista, as well as his recollections of his friend and colleague Julio de la Fuente, were invaluable.

In August 1978 I tried to locate copies of the original field notes from Oaxaca which belonged to Julio de la Fuente. Although I was unsuccessful, many people helped in the search. I would like to thank Don Antonio Pompa y Pompa of the National Museum Library in Mexico City, Dr Javier Romero Molina of the Instituto Nacional de Antropología e Historia, Dra Evangelina Arana de Swadesh, and especially Professor Luis Reyes García and Alfonso Muñoz.

In Oaxaca, Manuél Esparza, of the Regional Office of the Instituto Nacional de Antropología e Historia, arranged for my introduction to the Administrator of the Oaxaca Market, Sr Marcos, and his assistant, Sr Sanchez Cruz, who kindly answered my questions. Mrs Jean Ames sent me the newspaper clippings referred to in 'Malinowski in Mexico'.

At an early stage in this work Professor Sir Raymond Firth sent me copies of letters relevant to the history of the Malinowski papers dealing with Mexico. These papers now belong to Yale University and are at present in the possession of Professor Ronald Waterbury of Queens College, New York. Professor Waterbury sent me a missing section of the de la Fuente commentary from this collection. He also made the original photographic negatives available to Mrs Józefa Stuart *née* Malinowska. Mrs Stuart made prints from the negatives, some of which have been chosen to illustrate the text, often following indications in the original manuscript.

In 1969 Professor Michael Coe of Yale University received Malinowski's papers dealing with Mexico from Valetta Malinowska. I have never had direct access to these papers, nor to the notes written by Julio de la Fuente also contained in the collection. I am grateful to Professor Coe and Professor Waterbury for providing me with the specific materials I have requested.

I have prepared the maps and diagrams which illustrate the text. In addition to photographs from the original collection, I have used photos kindly provided by Bodel Christensen (nos 5 and 6), María de los Angeles Romero (no. 22), and Manuel Esparza (nos 34 and 35). Mrs Jean Ames sent me newspaper clippings and a description of the new Oaxaca City market. Dr Guillermo Bonfil, Salomón Nahmád, Professor John Murra and Professor Sir Edmund Leach made bibliographic material available to me which was difficult to obtain in England. Professor Meyer Fortes, Dr Audrey Richards and Professor John Murra read the introductory essay 'Malinowski in Mexico' and made helpful suggestions. I had valuable conversations with Polly Hill and André Beteille. My thanks go to Adam Kuper who tactfully kept reminding me that research is not an end in itself. To all those who have so kindly offered aid and encouragement I am grateful. I would like to point out that they are not responsible for the finished product. Finally I thank the Department of Social Anthropology of Cambridge University for providing me with space in which to work.

Glossary

Acaparador Bulk buyer, particularly of foodstuffs; one who acquires and retains sufficient goods to fix market prices.
Alfarería Earthenware.
Almud A dry measure, roughly 5 litres in volume.
Atole Thin maize porridge made with boiling water or milk and maize flour.
Barrio Section or neighbourhood of a villagc (*pueblo*).
Bolita A species of maize with a rounded kernel.
Cal Lime, quick lime
Cántaro An earthenware jug for carrying water.
Cantina Tavern.
Carga Literally 'burden'; a standardized weight carried by pack animals.
Chicharrón Pork skin, prepared by boiling in fat.
Comadre Literally 'co-mother'; a term used reciprocally by the sponsor of a child and the mother of the child sponsored at Catholic life-cycle rituals.
Comál Round, earthenware griddle used for heating maize bread (tortillas).
Compadrazge Co-parenthood established through Catholic ritual.
Compañía deslindadora Surveying company.
Copãl Resin used for incense.
Correctos 'Respectable people'; used to refer to those who follow the models of behaviour assumed to be Spanish rather than those assumed to be indigenous.
De pilón A quantity in excess of the measured amount, given by a seller to buyer, generally of foodstuffs or drink.
Ejido A unit of land held in collective ownership.
Fánega Dry measure consisting of 24-5 *almudes*, or 120-5 litres.
Fonda Small eating place or restaurant, usually within or near a market.
Gringo Derived from 'angle'; used in Oaxaca to refer to fair-skinned foreigners.

Hacienda Farm or ranch; normally used in Mexico to refer to enterprises which cover a large area of land in the possession of a single family.

Huaraches Sandals.

Huipil Type of blouse or dress worn by Indian women.

Ixtle Cord made from the fibres of the agave.

Marchante Buyer or seller in a routine market transaction.

Mayordomía Feast held to celebrate a saint's day, usually one of a set of such feasts celebrated in a particular village (*pueblo*) or village section.

Medianería Customary form of land lease in which crops are shared between the owner and the cultivator of land.

Mercería Haberdashery, ribbons, lace, combs, mirrors, etc.

Meson (pl. **mesones**) Hostelry.

Metate A low, three-footed rectangular grinding table made of stone which is carved to slope downwards, away from the user. Normally, only women use the *metate*. Grain, chocolate, fruit, vegetables and spices are ground against the low table using a cylindrical stone pin which is held in both hands in the manner of a European rolling-pin. The grinding pin is called 'the *metate*'s hand' (*el mano del metate*).

Mezcal A distilled alcoholic liquor made from the upper portion of various species of liliaceous plants popularly called 'maguey' in Mexico.

Montaña Mountain region; highlands below the peaks.

Montañés One who lives in the mountain region.

Natural Native; term used to refer to Indians.

Nixtamal Maize which has been soaked in a mixture of water and lime, then ground to produce a wet flour with the consistency of bread dough. It is used to make the tortilla and other cooked foods.

Palenque de contrabando Illegal distillery.

Propio One who sells his own produce or manufactured items.

Pueblo Village.

Puesto Market stall.

Pulque Fermented drink made from juice drawn from the heart of the agave.

Rebocero Seller of shawls.

Rebozo Shawl warn by Mexican women. It may be used to cover the chest, head, and shoulders in a variety of ways. It is also used for carrying children.

Regatona Female haggler, intermediary in bulk-buying (*regatón* male haggler).

Serrano Inhabitant of the high mountain peaks.

Tontos Literally 'the foolish ones'; term used by *los correctos* for those whose customs are considered to follow indigenous rather than Spanish models.

Tortilla The carbohydrate food staple; a round, thin pancake of soaked maize dough, baked rapidly on an earthenware griddle.

Vigilia Fast, particularly that which precedes the celebration of Christmas or Easter.

Zócalo Central square of a town which is the location of state offices and a cathedral.

Malinowski in Mexico: editor's introduction

by Susan Drucker-Brown

I Introduction

In June 1940 Bronislaw Malinowski, his wife Valetta Swann, and a young Mexican ethnologist, Julio de la Fuente, began research in the Valley of Oaxaca. Malinowski spoke fluent Spanish which he had learned in the Canary Islands as a young man.[1] Julio de la Fuente spoke fluent English which he had learned during four years' residence in New York City. *The Economics of a Mexican Market System*, subtitled *An Essay in Contemporary Ethnography and Social Change in a Mexican Valley*, resulted from the collaboration of these two men.[2]

The men were in sharp contrast to one another. Malinowski was 56 years old and at the height of his fame when he arrived in Mexico. Julio de la Fuente was 35 years old and had only begun his career as an anthropologist.

Malinowski was profoundly apolitical in the sense that he had no allegiance to any political party. Born in Poland, educated there and in Germany and England, he had grown to maturity in that multinational state known as the Austro-Hungarian Empire. He had travelled in Mediterranean countries and lived in Australia, the Trobriand Islands, Great Britain and the USA.

Like most Poles he was, until the end of the First World War, a reluctant subject of the Habsburgs. Briefly and with enthusiasm he had been a Polish citizen, and finally in London, a British subject. He thus had a complex personal experience of a wide variety of political systems.

Julio de la Fuente came from a small village in Mexico, and was educated in the provincial state capital of Veracruz and in Mexico City. He had worked as an artist and at a variety of other jobs. He had been a student of Marxism and active in mass political organizations for most of his adult life. His commitment to anthropology marked an end of this kind of involvement in national politics. But he saw anthropology as contributing to the political development of Mexico.

The Economics of a Mexican Market System addresses the question: what is the function of the numerous small markets scattered throughout the Valley of Oaxaca?

We have, in response, the first description of some of these markets and an initial step towards an analysis of the socio-economic interdependence of the communities the markets serve.

The essay was originally intended for students. Malinowski's contribution is dominant but De la Fuente brought to the work a greater ethnographic knowledge of the region and an awareness of the social concerns of Mexico in this period. As a description of the Oaxaca Valley in 1940 *The Economics of a Mexican Market System* is now a remarkable historical document. In 1940 it was a pioneering work: one of the earliest studies of markets in the ethnographic literature and the first in a series of studies to deal with market systems in Mexico.

The fact that the essay was a co-operative effort is of particular interest. Collaboration of this kind appears to be rare in anthropological literature. It is unique among Malinowski's writings. One aim of this introduction is to place the collaboration of Bronislaw Malinowski and Julio de la Fuente in its historical context; another is to introduce the work of Julio de la Fuente which is little known outside of Mexico. Finally, the contents of the essay, their place in Malinowski's work and in the existing literature on Oaxaca, deserve comment.

During the winter and spring of 1941 Malinowski and Julio de la Fuente wrote the essay at Yale University where Malinowski held a professorship. The two men appear to have discussed each paragraph. Malinowski then dictated the text in English to a shorthand-typist who then prepared a draft from the dictation.

When De la Fuente returned to Mexico the two men continued to correspond. Among the papers found after Malinowski's death were two detailed commentaries on the text sent by De la Fuente from Mexico. The present edition of *The Economics of a Mexican Market System* incorporates De la Fuente's comments in the fashion of a dialogue.

Although neither author revised the text before it was first published, another note found with the manuscript indicates that Malinowski intended *The Economics of a Mexican Market System* for publication. He expressed the hope that publication of research on the market system of Oaxaca in 'two phases . . . would serve a didactic purpose'. The first phase, represented by *The Economics of a Mexican Market System*, was to illustrate the procedures of fieldwork. A second phase would provide a definitive study of the market system.

Clearly then, *The Economics of a Mexican Market System* was conceived by Malinowski as part of a larger research project. Malinowski did return to the Oaxaca Valley in the summer of 1941.[3] When he died suddenly in May 1942, he had already completed preparations for what would have been a third field trip to Oaxaca in the summer of that year.[4]

The Economics of a Mexican Market System was first published in 1957, some fifteen years after it was written. It appeared then in a Spanish translation, published by the Students' Society of the National School of Anthropology and History in Mexico City. Thus it was in Mexico that the essay's 'didactic purpose' was first served.

An introduction to the Spanish translation was provided by a student editorial committee. In this introduction Malinowski's major publications and his earlier work on social change and 'culture contact' were approvingly mentioned. The authors of the introduction also apologized for errors in the text. There are indeed numerous minor errors in the typescript which were unfortunately translated into the Spanish version. Some are the result of typing mistakes, others were minor factual errors (many of which were corrected in Julio de la Fuente's commentary). There were also ambiguities and errors of English grammar. English, after all, was neither authors' native language. One interesting problem of translation was caused by Malinowski's special use of the English word 'charter' for which there is no simple Spanish equivalent.

Nevertheless, when it was finally published *The Economics of a Mexican Market System* became the first work by Malinowski available in Spanish to students in Mexico. In 1957 the major works of Malinowski, Radcliffe-Brown and their students, which had been published in Great Britain and the USA during previous decades, were still little known in Mexico and virtually unobtainable.

Between 1954 and 1960 I was a student at the National School of Anthropology and History (Instituto Nacional de Antropologiá a Historia) in Mexico City. I completed my degree in ethnology there in 1960. Like other students of my generation, I was soon aware of the importance of *The Economics of a Mexican Market System*.

By 1957 the essay had already made a contribution to research and teaching. The authors themselves had made provision for their research to be used in Mexico before they began fieldwork. In June 1940, Malinowski and De la Fuente signed a memorandum, together with members of a committee which had been set up to sponsor their research. In this memorandum the authors agreed to place a copy of research materials destined for publication at the disposal of the Inter-American Indianist Institute. Complying with this commitment, Malinowski sent copies of the typescript of the text to members of the sponsoring committee. One of these copies served as the basis for the Spanish translation. (See Appendix I.)

In 1953 Alejandro Marroquín, working under the auspices of the National Indianist Institute, with students from the National School of Anthropology and History, began a study of Tlaxiaco, a market centre in the Mixtec Highlands. The Marroquín study, published in 1957, is explicitly based on the earlier work of Malinowski and De la Fuente.

As a student at the National School of Anthropology and History, I took part in two brief field studies of markets which were organized in conjunction with courses given at the school.[5] These field trips were presented as an introduction to the type of fieldwork advocated by Malinowski and also as an introduction to the study of the particular type of relationship which exists in Mexico between the Indian and non-Indian populations.

In 1956 Julio de la Fuente and his colleague Dr Gonzalo Aguirre Beltrán taught a course at the National School of Anthropology and History which dealt directly with the social, economic and medical needs of Indian communities. I was fortunate that my experience as a student brought me into further contact with Julio de la Fuente. In 1957, on behalf of the National Indianist Institute, he commissioned me to carry out research in the coastal region of Oaxaca. He supervised this work between 1957 and 1960.

I visited the main Oaxaca City market with Julio de la Fuente in 1959 and revisited the market in 1978 when I was able to interview the market administrator and his assistant. Because I have worked in rural Mexico I am familiar with some aspects of market organization. However, it is not as a student of market systems that I approach this essay. My own interest in presenting *The Economics of a Mexican Market System* to an English reading public emerged from the contrast between my experience as a student in Mexico and my subsequent experience as a student of social anthropology in Cambridge, England.

When I arrived in England in 1961 I discovered, of course, that Malinowski's work had long been taken for granted as part of the general study of social anthropology. *The Economics of a Mexican*

Market System was, however, practically unknown. I felt that the essay, described in its Mexican context, would be of interest to students who encountered anthropology as an academic discipline and Malinowski's work primarily as part of that tradition. *The Economics of a Mexican Market System* was regarded in Mexico less as a guide for academic research than as a device for organizing the study of practical problems.

Between 1956 and 1960 the National School of Anthropology and History was training students for work in government agencies, both for research and for the administration of community development programmes. *The Economics of a Mexican Market System* was directly relevant to these interests.

In 1948 the Mexican government had created the National Indianist Institute (Instituto Nacional Indigenista, or INI). Dr Alfonso Caso, a member of the committee which sponsored Malinowski and De la Fuente's research, was the first director of the INI. Julio de la Fuente became director of research at the INI from 1951 until the illness which led to his death in 1970 made work impossible.[6]

The INI was committed to planning and administering a programme of community development for the Indian regions of Mexico. The creation of a separate agency, with both administrative and planning responsibility for the social, economic and medical problems of Indian communities, met with some opposition. At one extreme were those who claimed that pro-Indian action was a form of racist discrimination. This opposition argued that community development programmes should be directed to the rural population as a whole. Opposition of another sort came from those who were concerned to maintain the *status quo* in rural areas (see De la Fuente, 1958b).

The debate about a 'pro-Indian' policy dates from the sixteenth-century inception of Spanish colonial administration in Mexico, after the Spanish conquest. The history of later anti-colonial, and ostensibly pro-Indian, legislation could be seen clearly after 1943 (Chavez Orozco, 1943) to have resulted in a dramatic erosion of the political autonomy and financial viability of the Indian communities. In the colonial period these 'communities' constituted nations, tribes, indigenous states – a vast range of differing cultures and polities. The fate of different groups varied throughout the four centuries of colonial rule, as it continues to vary at present. However, some indigenous polities held the status of 'republics' in Spanish colonial law. Throughout the colonial period Spanish, and later independent Mexican, administrations, were to reinforce one another in policies which led to the destruction of properties held corporately (in land and currency) by these 'republics'. The legal basis of the Indian republics was destroyed by legislation which followed Mexican independence. Likewise, educational institutions for Indian students maintained by Indian funds were expropriated after independence (Chavez Orozco, 1943; *Memorias del INI*, 1954).

The defence of an Indianist policy after 1940 was informed by recognition of this past history. A new policy was to be based on the view that careful study of Indian communities would enable special programmes of 'co-ordinated change' to be developed which would protect rather than destroy the Indian population. The goal of Indianist policy was to 'integrate' the Indian into the modern nation. Thus Villa Rojas writes (1976, p. 26),

> The integrationist thesis aspires, as a final goal, to extend the conception of 'nationhood' (Spanish – *Patria*) to all human groups, Indian and Mestizo, who live in the national territory in such a manner that mutual understanding and solidarity will make effective the essence of common nationality which should unite all Mexicans. (Trans.)[7]

It was obvious that modernization of the Mexican economy, to which the national government was committed, would increase contact between Indians and non-Indians. It was considered obvious, from the social and economic conditions in these communities, that the Indian populations were unable to defend themselves within the laws meant to protect or 'advance' the rural population generally. Basic to the goal of controlled, co-ordinated change in Indian communities was a theoretical concept of the Indian community as a total social system existing in a state of equilibrium. It was argued that a change in one aspect of social life implied others. By providing a 'multilineal approach' to change, it was hoped that the 'equilibrium' of these communities could be preserved, and simultaneously that the standard of living could be improved.

The 'multilineal approach' was supposed to contrast with both uncontrolled change and change of a 'unilineal' kind. Uncontrolled change proceeded, as it had in the past, with little regard for the welfare of the Indian communities. Unilineal change was characteristic of early pro-Indian action focused on a single aspect of community life, e.g. education, health, agricultural techniques. Such programmes had not been notably successful and were dispersed in different government agencies. A 'multilineal' approach was meant to deal simultaneously with related problems. The thesis advocated by Malinowski, that all aspects of social life were interrelated, lay at the base of this conception. Theoretically, it was argued, only a programme of change which took this interrelationship into account could be successful. The success of such a programme might lead Indian and non-Indian populations to merge. Thus 'The Indian' would disappear, or become 'integrated'. However, as an initial policy the 'multilineal' approach would allow changes in one area of community life to be compensated for by others and need not imply pressure towards complete cultural assimilation (De la Fuente, 1958c).

Since 1970 Indianist policy has been the subject of further debate. The INI is now committed to a programme of development which will aid Mexican Indian communities to resist the pressure towards assimilation which arises from the national culture. Assimilation of 'autochthonous' cultures is thus explicitly rejected. (See INI, 1980.)

It is consistent with the history of Indian communities in Mexico that policies designed to protect them should in practice often contribute to their destruction. The opposed needs of a wider or more powerful community were taken into account even at the creation of the INI.

The INI was established by presidential decree. Simultaneously the construction of a large hydroelectric project was also decreed (Caso, 1955). The Mazatec and Chinantec Indians, along with other farmers who inhabited the area destined to become the basin of the Miguel Alemán dam, would need to be relocated. One of the first 'co-ordinating centres' (*centros coordinadores*) of the INI was to help with this relocation.[8] In other areas of Mexico, however, no such benefits to the national community were provided for, nor were such major 'readjustments' of population expected. Conditions in many Indian regions were relatively unknown and access was often difficult. Many Indian communities were distant from major market centres where a politically and economically powerful non-Indian population resided.

In practical terms the INI proposed to establish centres in different regions of the republic which would co-ordinate and administer the diverse programmes for change.[9] The co-ordinating centres of the INI are intended to work through programmes of education in health, agricultural techniques, language and literacy. Indigenous people are trained as *promotores*, that is, as agents of the INI programmes. *Promotores* represent the INI and administer specific programmes at the level of the smallest local groups. Their activities are supervised by personnel of the co-ordinating centres. In addition to educational programmes, medical clinics have been established and capital investment in roads, buildings and machinery has been provided by the INI.[10]

The study *The Economics of a Mexican Market System* pointed to the dominant market in a market system as a focal point from which regions containing diverse and often mutually antagonistic Indian communities could be reached. Thus, the decision was taken to locate the co-ordinating centres which were to administer the INI programme in major market towns rather than in territories where Indian population predominated.

Aguirre Beltrán worked with the INI until 1977. His writing constitutes the most comprehensive account of the premises and philosophy underlying the early work of the INI. In his view the decision to locate the co-ordinating centres in major market towns was a correct one. He also considers that it followed directly from the work of Malinowski and De la Fuente. He argues that the major social problems facing Indian communities in Mexico inevitably concerned the non-Indian merchants, businessmen and politicians who resided in the market centres. This population, residing in centres which Aguirre Beltrán calls *centros dominicales* (i.e. centres of domination), could not have been dealt with by the INI if the institute's centres had been located in the Indian areas. Moreover, further research carried out by the INI indicated that endemic conflicts between and within Indian communities were sufficiently strong for the INI to need to be located on 'neutral territory'. Though the choice of major market centres may now seem obvious, at the time other alternatives were attractive.[11]

The practical importance of *The Economics of a Mexican Market System* has been discussed above. However, certain aspects of the essay which are typical of Malinowski's work were equally important to students.

First of all, Malinowski insists here that it is possible to study contemporary social life independently of a wider historical analysis. He argues that the routine events, the repetitive actions of humble people, are as much history as the spectacular and unique events more often chronicled. Sociological research, he argues, can be detached from the broad conceptions of historical processes. The fieldworker is enjoined to abstract 'a norm' from the array of idiosyncratic, individual behaviour which constitutes the field of inquiry.

In the National School of Anthropology and History, at least until 1960, Ethnology was taught strictly within a historical framework. Like Archeology, the aim of ethnology was regarded as historical reconstruction. Most students at the National School had experience of fieldwork during their training. All too often we found that data collected during fieldwork were irrelevant to discussions of broad historical processes. Although Malinowski's theoretical approach was presented to us only in courses devoted to 'applied anthropology' we could see its significance for more academic research.

Malinowski, in any case, does not argue that historical theories are futile or that sociological analysis should remain detached from the study of history. He offers, instead of a historical framework, a method of research and analysis in which beliefs, actions, material objects and the constitution of social groups may be viewed in their relationships to one another. This 'functionalist' framework, he argues, can ultimately enrich the study of history.

In presenting his approach to fieldwork in *The Economics of a Mexican Market System*, Malinowski does not use the analogy of laboratory experiment in natural science for the type of fieldwork he advocates, as he did earlier in *Argonauts of the Western Pacific*. However, he constantly stresses that the formulation of problems emerges 'naturally out of observation', that generalizations which are constructed from field research are based 'not on armchair intuitions but on observed fact'. If Malinowski here is contemptuous of 'armchair intuition' it may be difficult for students reared in a post-Malinowski and post-Radcliffe-Brown tradition of anthropology to imagine the stifling effects of evolutionist and diffusionist frameworks on field work.

These effects are well described by Malinowski himself in the essay 'Culture' published in the *Encyclopedia of Social Sciences*, and cited in *The Economics of a Mexican Market System*. In effect, the presentation of a new approach to fieldwork made accessible and useful a whole world of data which, as Malinowski points out with respect to data on kinship, had earlier been often ignored or grossly misused. Macfarlane (1977), writing of historical research, makes a similar point with respect to the use of certain types of historical data in the context of historical research: the 'functionalist' or a-historical method, whatever its flaws, is illuminating precisely because it has encouraged the use of new kinds of data.

In the context of academic anthropological research *The Economics of a Mexican Market System*, fragmentary though it is, has provided a pioneering view of a market system regarded as a 'type' in studies of Meso-American markets.

Since 1941 there have been numerous anthropological studies of markets. The classification of marketing systems has been greatly refined. New models which accommodate important variations in the organization of these systems have been presented. (See, for example, Smith, 1976a, 1976b; Ortiz, 1967, for Latin America; Skinner, 1964, for China; Geertz, 1979, for Morocco; and Hill, 1966, for West Africa.) However, for market studies in Latin America, *The Economics of a Mexican Market System* has been an important reference point.

Manning Nash (1967, p. 87) describes the 'solar market system', in words which recall Malinowski's concluding description of the market system in Oaxaca:

> [A solar market system is one in which] a major market system is in daily operation. To it flow commodities produced throughout the region, goods from all over the nation, and even items from international trade. Around the major market are a series of market places which have their special days. Each of these market places tends to specialise in a given product or commodity and to carry a reduced selection of the goods available in the central market. Goods, buyers, and sellers, move around the solar system in terms of the days of the week when market activity centers in a particular market place.

This is an elegant summary of the temporal and spatial interdependence of market activities and market goods found in the Oaxaca Valley. However, it is a conception in which 'goods, buyers and sellers' circulate in analytic isolation from the activities of production and consumption. Throughout *The Economics of a Mexican Market System* Malinowski and De la Fuente also stress the importance of understanding the patterns of production and consumption which provide the basic elements of the market system. It is this concern with the overall context of the markets which provides us with a picture of social life in the Valley region, as well as with a study of market exchange.

II The contribution of Julio de la Fuente[12]

The collaboration of Julio de la Fuente was essential to the writing of this essay. Malinowski recognized the importance of De la Fuente's contribution in letters he wrote at the time, and in the preface to *The Economics of a Mexican Market System*.

Although Malinowski spoke Spanish fluently he cannot have had more than a superficial acquaintance with Mexico before 1940. At that time Julio de la Fuente's anthropology was entirely self-taught. However, he had already completed the first draft of his monograph, *Yalalag*, a study of a highland Zapotec village in Oaxaca, and he had written several short papers. The monograph is a major contribution to Mexican ethnology and the papers are still of interest.

Throughout his professional life as an anthropologist De la Fuente focused his research on what was then known as 'cultural and social change'. He was concerned with practical problems related to community development in Indian regions, and with gaining an understanding of conflicts between 'ethnic groups'. These interests were linked, in De la Fuente's work, with the INI.

Julio de la Fuente was born in a small village near the coast of Veracruz where his father worked as a civil servant. Like Malinowski, he had previously been trained in natural science. He studied chemistry at the National University in Mexico City for three years. Unlike Malinowski, however, he left university without completing his degree and took a factory job. He became a professional illustrator and journalist, and a student of marxism. During four years of the depression he lived and worked in New York City. There he learned English and shorthand. He worked at a variety of jobs ranging from dish-washing to journalism and translation.

In 1932, De la Fuente returned to his native state of Veracruz, where he was employed by the Ministry of Education to work in the League of Agrarian Committees. This league was one of a number of organizations set up in rural Mexico to organize demands for agrarian reform (see Stavenhagen, 1972). De la Fuente worked in the villages of Veracruz as a journalist, and also wrote and illustrated reading material to be used in the newly created rural schools.

In 1935 Julio de la Fuente moved, as part of a group working for the Ministry of Education, to Mexico City. There he helped to found, and became a leader in, the anti-Fascist League of Revolutionary Artists and Writers. In 1937 this group was dissolved. At the same time, De la Fuente suffered a serious eye injury. In the words of Aguirre Beltrán (1964, p. 3), the combination of events 'changed his destiny. The social agitator within him ceased to exist and the social analyst was born . . . '.

> [In the time which followed] he was able to reflect on his goals, his motivations, and on the efficacy of the actions of those political groups to which he had belonged. It became clear to him that it was urgent to know the population to which so much revolutionary preaching was directed. He concluded that the anthropological approach propounded by Gamio was the best instrument with which to acquire this knowledge. . . . Armed meagrely with his reading of Gamio's work on Teotihuacan and Redfield's work on Tepoztlán he proceeded to the field. . . . (Trans.)

Aguirre Beltrán remembers his meeting with De la Fuente in 1942. De la Fuente had finished the first draft of his monograph, *Yalalag* and was looking for advice about how to publish it. He complained at the time that during his study of Yalalag there had been no one who could teach him how to proceed with fieldwork. Gamio and Redfield certainly had little to say about fieldwork techniques.

Gamio's ethnographic data were interpreted within a historical framework. The ethnography itself was often 'slight', and the history highly 'conjectural' where it was not based on archeological data or pre-Columbian texts. The work contains no systematic description of routine social behaviour. Gamio was concerned with quantification. However, he was mainly engaged in collecting accurate demographic census data (Gamio *et al*., 1922). Redfield's work on Tepoztlán (1930) makes reference to general sociological theory which is illustrated by reference to daily life in Tepoztlán. But Redfield does not deal directly with questions of why detailed observation and description of everyday behaviour are important evidence. Nor does he mention in any detail how he has obtained the data he presents.

The excitement which Malinowski's first visit to Mexico provoked in Julio de la Fuente is illustrated by passages from a letter which De la Fuente wrote to Malinowski about the plans for his trip to Yale in 1941.

In 1938-9 the National School of Anthropology and History had been founded in Mexico. De la Fuente wrote: 'The curriculum approved for teaching there rests completely on the historicist school . . . while the other – i.e. the Functionalist approach – which exists, but is unknown here, has been ignored.'

Writing of Alfonso Caso's support for the trip to Yale, he continues:

> He [Caso] has christened it [Functionalism] the 'scientific school', and has selected me as the product which must absorb the greatest possible amount of its teaching. Given that Mexico is subject, as perhaps other places also are, to swings of fashion, the thing [the permission De la Fuente had received to leave his work in Mexico] has been accomplished and Functionalism is to be put to the test. (Trans.)

The approach of Redfield in Tepoztlán and that of Gamio in Teotihuacán differ in many respects. However, both works differ also from Malinowski's approach to the Oaxaca Valley. In Tepoztlán, Redfield (1930) focused his attention on a single 'village' community. The conception of a village community was to develop into an ideal type, which later led to Redfield's model (see Redfield and Singer, 1954) of the continuum from folk to urban culture. Gamio, in Teotihuacán, focused his attention on a territorial region which was designed to exclude contemporary urban centres. Although Gamio suggests in his work on Teotihuacán that different regions of Mexico be studied in order to provide a picture of the culturally and geographically diverse characteristics of Mexico, he also suggests that separate studies must be carried out in urban communities 'where the biological, climatic and physical environment is totally different from that of the regions' (Gamio *et al.*, 1922, vol. I, p. xi).

Malinowski, in contrast to both authors, focused his attention on a single institution which linked the urban community of Oaxaca to a series of other rural localities. The resulting picture of how the main market centre and other markets were related was precisely the feature of this research which led to its practical use.[13]

De la Fuente, in subsequent work, used various approaches to define the social universe he was considering. While supervising my own research, he once remarked that the task of defining 'society' or 'a society' is what the whole study of anthropology is about. His own highly pragmatic approach to the matter was evident in one of his earliest papers (De la Fuente, 1940), written before he met Malinowski, and presented at the first Inter-American Indianist Congress. In the paper there are brief descriptions of the sexual division of labour, inheritance patterns, the extended family, credit associations, the conflict between successive generations and an outline of political and ritual organization. These descriptions are abstract and idealized, qualified occasionally to account for cases which do not fit the idealized norm. 'The Zapotec', to whom this description applies, are not defined, however, until the last paragraph of the essay where De la Fuente commends the rural school teachers for creating a consciousness of unity among a people who 'do not form a linguistic, racial or economic unit' (1965 edition, p. 32).

De la Fuente does mention, in the course of the paper, that the Northern Oaxaca Highlands constitute a region of greater cultural uniformity when contrasted with the lowland Zapotec Isthmus of Tehuantepec. In a paper of 1944, and again in *Yalalag*, De la Fuente returns to the problem of describing the social universe of the highland region, including in it both Indian and non-Indian groups. He stressed (De la Fuente, 1944, p. 34) the significance of the local community (i.e. the basic territorial unit):

> The division of the [Oaxaca] region in Districts does not, and never has, corresponded to ethnic divisions. The important unit culturally, socially, politically and economically and possibly 'ethnically' is the local community [or pueblo]. The local community is practically totally endogamous and in the majority of cases institutions are local [i.e. based on the local community] and ethnocentric to such a degree that new institutions and innovations – the church, saints' cults and civil organizations – are converted into local institutions. (Trans.)

At the same time he records the extent to which both Indian and non-Indian populations are divided into distinct linguistic and socio-cultural groupings (De la Fuente, 1944, 1948, 1959). These are ordered hierarchically and perceived differently by members of different groups. He points out the difference in wealth between households within the Yalalag community, and the antagonism between members of successive generations, which at times reached the level of armed conflict. The strict segregation of men and women and the inegalitarian distribution of population between village sections (*barrios*) are also considered. De la Fuente's work on the Zapotec thus avoids the over-simple picture of a homogeneous community which emerges from Redfield's earlier study of Tepoztlán.

In later works, De la Fuente tried to deal with what he called in one essay (1959) 'the disappearance and passing of the Indian'. De la Fuente (1958a) had considered in detail the process by which individual members of Indian communities (and indeed entire communities) change the language and clothing styles which serve to identify them as distinct from the Latinized rural population of Mexico. Further analysis of this process is crucial to an understanding of Mexican history, for the history of Mexico has been and in part continues to be a history of the 'Latinization' of Indian communities. *The Economics of a Mexican Market System*, though it deals only tangentially with the issue, reflects its importance. (See Israel (1975) for historical background in the early seventeenth century.)

De la Fuente (1958a), in a comparative study entitled 'Cambios de indumentaria en tres áreas bi-culturales' ('Clothing Change in Three Bi-cultural Areas'), compares three Mexican areas which contain two contrasting ethnic groups, one subordinate to the other. The superordinate group is seen as a segment of the national society, and the subordinate segment of the area's population is regarded as representing an 'aboriginal culture' (*portador de una cultura aborigin*).

De la Fuente points out that changes in clothing style have occurred independently of any specific policy in the community development programme of the Indianist Institute. He compares the patterns of change in three areas where development programmes have been established, and finds that different patterns of change are associated with differences in the relationship between ethnic groups in each area. In all areas Indian clothing is a symbol of the Indian ethnic identity and of the cohesion of the Indian group *vis-à-vis* the non-Indian segment. (This fact is noted for the Oaxaca Valley region and the neighbouring highlands in *The Economics of a Mexican Market System*.)

De la Fuente (1959) suggested alterations in community development policy towards clothing style which would take into account the significance of this particular change. De la Fuente hoped to thus ameliorate the apparent 'disorganization' within families and communities which resulted from the more general processes of change.

Typical of De la Fuente's work are brief articles dealing with subjects of theoretical interest as they are related to practical problems. In a comparative description of credit institutions among the Zapotec, De la Fuente (1939) suggests these might be useful for programmes of economic development. A description of co-operative labour institutions in Indian communities includes a negative assessment of these as a basis for the organization of modern co-operatives. De la Fuente's article (1939) on colour perception in a Zapotec group must be one of the earliest considerations of the linguistic nexus of colour perception. His attention was drawn to the phenomenon by its relevance to teaching programmes in Indian areas.[14]

De la Fuente viewed his research both as a means to understand the resistance of Indian communities to changes encouraged by government, and as a basis for modifying government policies. This does not mean, as far as he was concerned, that the anthropologist acted as 'public relations officer' for government. The role of the anthropologist, as De la Fuente saw it, was both to suggest and to monitor the administration of policy. The task requires a political commitment on the part of the anthropologist to the ultimate goals of the government, and a simultaneous commitment by the anthropologist to understand the viewpoint of an Indian community. Julio de la Fuente's work was part of a dedicated endeavour to deal with this extremely difficult position.

III The essay in a wider political context

When war broke out in Europe, Malinowski was on sabbatical leave in the USA. The London School of Economics, where Malinowski held a professorship, was evacuated to Cambridge and reduced to a maintenance level. Malinowski was advised to accept a position in the USA if one were offered to him. Thus, he became a visiting professor at Yale in 1939, and accepted a permanent professorship there in 1942.

In a letter (3 June 1940) to Charles Dollard of the Carnegie Corporation, which helped to finance his research in Mexico, Malinowski wrote:

> I shall probably settle in this country [the USA] and wish to become acquainted at first hand with an ethnographic area of this continent. I am choosing Mexico because I know and speak Spanish well . . . [also] I wish to use my acquaintance, with problems of contact, culture change and the mixture of civilization gained during the years I was associated with the International African Institute of London.

Regarding his plans, Malinowski continued:

> My wife and I are planning to leave New York on June 19th arriving (by boat) in Veracruz on June 24th. From Veracruz we propose to drive first to Oaxaca to investigate possibilities in that province, returning through Puebla and Cholula to Mexico City where I have to get in touch with the anthropologists of the University. Most probably I shall wish to survey two or three ethnographic provinces before reaching a decision as to where to begin work. In this I wish to act in consultation and agreement with my Mexican colleagues.

Malinowski received a warm welcome from his Mexican colleagues despite the fact that in a lecture given in Mexico City he seems to have criticized the treatment of Indians which he observed on his trip from Veracruz.[15] Malinowski quickly chose Oaxaca as a place to work and began fieldwork on 24 July. He wrote to Dollard again on his return to Yale at the end of September 1940. He had chosen Oaxaca as the most suitable field 'partly because it was not pre-empted by other ethnographers, partly because it was the center of important archeological work directed by Alfonso Caso, but most of all because it presented a variety of historical, ethnographic and practical problems'.

The Oaxaca Valley had not been entirely ignored by other ethnographers. It was rather better described than many other parts of

Mexico. The monograph written by E.C. Parsons on the village of Mitla (Parsons, 1936) is a significant contribution to Mexican ethnography. As Malinowski points out, Parsons's data were useful to him. However, Parsons's monograph is organized around an attempt to distinguish what is 'Indian' from what is 'Spanish' in the culture of Mitla. Malinowski's choice of the Valley of Oaxaca as a place of work enabled him to contrast his approach and his definition of 'culture' with the historical (he would have written 'historicist') approach of Parsons's work.

In contrast to his negative view of Parsons's work, Malinowski expresses sympathy with the work of Redfield in Tepoztlán. Alfonso Villa Rojas, who was working with Redfield in Yucatán, actually spent a fortnight in Oaxaca with Malinowski and De la Fuente. Malinowski's research in Oaxaca could have provided the basis for a future dialogue with Alfonso Villa Rojas and Redfield, in which comparative ethnography might have played an important part.

In choosing Oaxaca as a place to work, Malinowski had chosen a region which was geographically and culturally distinct from both the Morelos valley and the Yucatán peninsula where Redfield worked. The published historical sources were equally poor for both areas. Unlike Redfield, however, Malinowski chose to focus his study on one aspect of the interrelationship of a variety of local communities and social classes in a single institution: the market. Redfield had focused his attention in Tepoztlán on multiple aspects of social life in a single local community.

In Mexico a regional focus in anthropological studies had an important precedent in the work of Manuél Gamio. In 1922 an interdisciplinary study supervised by Gamio was published. This monumental work deals with the valley of San Juan Teotihuacán, north of Mexico City. In it Gamio made a plea for a series of studies of various geographical and cultural regions of the republic. He outlined ten such regions which could be taken to represent the historical, cultural and geographical diversity of Mexico (Gamio *et al.*, 1922). Recognition of this diversity, he argued, was essential for any useful generalizations about social life in the republic.

Gamio was particularly concerned that more accurate information about rural populations be available to the government for planning purposes. In 1940 he was, in fact, head of the Department of Demography in the Ministry of Gobernacion (the rough equivalent of the

British Home Office).

The valley of Teotihuacán, where Gamio had worked, resembles the Oaxaca Valley in that it had obviously been an important centre of pre-Columbian civilization.[16] The ruins of the ceremonial centre were the focus of a major archeological portion of Gamio's study. Gamio's training under Boas, at Columbia University, had combined physical anthropology, archeology and ethnology. In the study of Teotihuacán, Gamio's approach to ethnography is imbued with an obviously ethnocentric 'evolutionist' perspective which is not surprising given the historical range of the data he was considering, and the fashions of anthropology at the time he was educated.

But if Gamio saw contemporary beliefs and customs as 'survivals' of a past civilization, he also saw 'progress' in terms of eliminating a very high (80 per cent) rate of infant mortality, controlling epidemics and diseases in the valley, and providing the inhabitants with sufficient food, work and modern education. It was Gamio's view of how the population should develop which led to his concern with collecting accurate and useful statistical data. These are the kind of 'practical problems' to which the authors refer in *The Economics of a Mexican Market System*.[17]

They also refer to the excavations directed by Dr Alfonso Caso at Monte Albán in Oaxaca. In 1932 Alfonso Caso excavated a tomb at Monte Albán which revealed spectacular treasure, including objects of precious metals and finely worked jade and turquoise. The discovery awakened a general curiosity about the Oaxaca Valley. Until the excavation at Monte Albán, few commercially valuable objects had survived in Mexican museums. Objects of precious metals and stones which did survive the conquest were to be found either in private collections or in foreign museums. The objects excavated by Caso were thus an important addition to the collection of the National Anthropology Museum, which was regarded in 1940 as an educational centre for the entire nation.

The new excavations directed by Alfonso Caso greatly increased knowledge of the ancient Mixtec and Zapotec cultures. They also awakened, among intellectuals generally, a new interest in living communities of people who spoke Mixtec and Zapotec languages. Malinowski would have been well aware of the fashionable curiosity about Oaxacan ethnography. Moreover, Dr Caso suggested Julio de la Fuente as a research assistant to Malinowski, and De la Fuente was already engaged in research in Oaxaca.

Alfonso Caso was a member of the committee which sponsored Malinowski's research. He introduced Julio de la Fuente to Malinowski and arranged financial support both for Julio de la Fuente's fieldwork and for his trip to Yale in 1941. Through the sponsoring committee Malinowski was to come into direct contact with the Indianist movement in Mexico. The four members of the sponsoring committee were colleagues who had experience of historical and/or sociological research in Mexico. They were also among the most influential exponents of pro-Indian government policy in 1940. The *indigenista* movement, as it appeared in 1940, in itself was one of the radical political campaigns which emerged in Mexico from the revolution of 1910 (Bonfíl, 1967; Aguirre Beltrán, 1957, 1967).

Mexico in 1940 was at the end of the six-year presidency of General Lázaro Cardenas. During Cardenas's administration, land reforms were intensified (Stavenhagen, 1972, p. 153, 157). Even as Malinowski and De la Fuente wrote, laws of land tenure in Oaxaca were being modified (see pp. 116-17). The petroleum industry had been nationalized in 1938. The government had encouraged the establishment of trade unions (Córdova, 1974) and the creation of rural co-operatives (see pp. 159, 161.) There had also been a dramatic expansion of educational opportunities in rural and urban areas. Moisés Sáenz, a member of the sponsoring committee, had himself been a leading organizer of the rural schools of Mexico, which were such an outstanding feature of social policy (Aguirre Beltrán, 1964, 1976).

In 1916, before Malinowski arrived on the scene to advocate the relevance of anthropology to government planning, Manuel Gamio had written:

> Anthropology in its true and widest conception should be basic knowledge for the carrying out of good government because through anthropology one knows the population which is to be governed and for whom government exists. . . . Unfortunately, in all Latin American countries the needs of the population have been and are unknown. In effect a minority made up of people belonging to the white race, and whose civilization is derived from Europe, has been concerned only with its own progress, leaving aside the majority of indigenous race and culture. . . . The obvious ignorance (even on the part of those who have wished to better the situation of the majority culturally and economically) is due to the fact that the indigenous

> population has not been studied in a sensible manner. The meagre contact between groups has occurred through commerce or through servitude. . . . The only means of knowing the indigenous peoples, their civilizations and physical conditions, consists in studying, with anthropological criteria, their colonial and pre-colonial antecedents and their contemporary characteristics. (Trans. Cited in León Portilla, 1966, pp. 244-5.)

Malinowski (1968, p. 82) had written of Africa in 1929 that 'a good deal of European planning happens as if Africans with all their needs, their own economic pursuits, their love of independence and their desire for self-expression did not exist.'

In Mexico, ignorance of the needs and desires of the rural populations, to which Gamio refers, was not the same as the arrogance implied in Malinowski's criticism of British Colonial Office planners. In 1940 the Mexican government could not ignore the needs of rural populations. It depended for survival on the support, or at least the tolerance, of armed groups drawn from these populations (Córdova, 1974).

During the civil wars which followed the revolution of 1910, as in the revolution itself, even remote regions of the republic were drawn into armed conflict. Central government in 1940 was not faced with organized armed revolt, and the local armed conflicts in much of rural Mexico might have little to do with national government policies. The schisms which divided those who fought on opposed sides in the revolution and subsequent civil wars continued to exist. This is how Julio de la Fuente (1949, p. 23) describes violence in the Zápotec community of Yalalag, Oaxaca, during the 1930s:

> The new leaders who had emerged during the revolution gave themselves the task of stimulating 'progress' or imposing it in their own way. 'Progress' in the conception of those in the region consists of changing customs, beliefs, the indigenous language (regarded as rustic or backward) for the fashions of Castillian and those of the city (the 'fine' and 'modern'). But this process was accompanied by social disorder. Political parties and acts of violence flourished. The behaviour of 'leaders' and their armed followers, those in charge of preserving order, produced more schisms in Yalalag and gained the village the general enmity of the neighbourhood. From 1923 onwards the village had a black reputation because of crimes committed there and other abuses which stopped temporarily only to

> begin again. The death of one leader and some of his relatives at the hands of his second in command was followed by the emergence of others who were leaders in turn, or potential leaders, who were also violently exterminated. These facts of politics and bloodshed have made Yalalag undesirably prominent in a region of other turbulent villages. The years between 1936 and 1939, when peace and unity were sought and progress moderated, were followed by brief lapses into progressive radicalism, and by a final return to a conservative position, no less restless or bloody. (Trans.)

De la Fuente points out here that 'progressive' and 'conservative' forces could be defined by their attitude towards Zapotec language and custom. I should like to emphasize, however, that the division between 'progressives' and 'conservatives' occurred within a community which formed a corporate group in other respects. Yalalag was typical of those Mexican local communities (villages or *pueblos*) which are almost totally endogamous, in which landholding is restricted (by village endogamy and rules of inheritance) to members of the village, and where village hierarchies of 'civil' and 'religious' offices are fused to produce a single politico-religious framework of extra-domestic group organization. Given the corporate nature of the Yalalag community, divisions within it, of language or custom, do not affect the definition of Yalalag as an 'Indian' community in the view of outsiders.

As a more general point, the situation described by De la Fuente shows that Indianist policy, conceptualized at a national level, was reinterpreted at a local level. The theory (or theories) on which policy was ostensibly based could serve to present a coherent programme, but might have little to do with the administration of that programme. This is not the place to evaluate Mexican Indianist action. However, it is important to note that relations both within Indian communities and between Indians and non-Indians were, and are, not uniform throughout the nation. 'Progress' at a local and at a national level, as De la Fuente implies, has different meanings.

Gamio (1922) argued that ignorance of the conditions of rural populations in Latin America generally derived from the cultural and racial divisions between the ruling elite and the populations to be governed. This, of course, is paralleled in the British colonial situation. However, that government exists for the benefit of the governed is not a necessary assumption for colonial governments with respect to their colonies. On this, among other grounds, colonial government may be distinguished from independent political rule.

Gamio recognized in this passage, and in his work on Teotihuacán, that ignorance of the conditions in which a country's population live is not necessarily removed by a revolution which replaces a colonial ruling elite. The new national rulers will inherit much of the ignorance of their predecessors, and may even create new areas of ignorance, though their intentions and their assumptions about the goals of government may be greatly different. (See Gamio's description of the 1910 census, referred to below.)

Why did Gamio, and other scholars in Mexico in the 1940s, consider that anthropology would provide the tools for acquiring a more accurate knowledge of 'the population for which government exists'? Mexico in 1940 was a nation in which anti-colonialist sentiment was most clearly expressed. The dissolution of Spain's American empire had yet to be overshadowed by the political independence of other European colonies. It is fashionable in some quarters to regard anthropology as tainted by its origins as a 'child of Imperialism' (Gough, 1968). But anthropology in 1940 was the only academic subject in which the history and sociology of non-European peoples were the primary focus of interest. Anthropological research, in the broad definition of the subject which Gamio gave it, had already begun to reveal a history of Mexico which was independent of Europe.

At the same time, scholars were dealing with social situations unpredicted in European-based social sciences. Gamio, when he began research in the valley of Teotihuacán, found that earlier censuses had classed the entire rural population as 'white' because the Spanish language was spoken there (Gamio *et al.*, 1922, vol. I, p. 25). The 1910 census only recorded civil marriages, though such marriages were few and far between. Neither religious nor common-law marriages were noted. Thus a population which, from a genetic point of view, was predominantly Amerindian and conservative with respect to local marriage custom, appeared in the census as 'white' and predominantly unmarried. The population in question did not reside in some remote area but was close to and easily accessible from the national capital.

Clearly, the tradition of keeping accurate demographic statistics which predated and facilitated the work of Durkheim and other European and North American sociologists, had lapsed in Mexico at the beginning of the twentieth century. Durkheim, studying suicide in France, did not have to take completely new censuses as Gamio did in Teotihuacán.

It was not simply as a new form of rural sociology, or a type of micro-political or micro-economic analysis which might improve the efficiency of government, that anthropology claimed the interest of Mexican intellectuals. It was heralded precisely because in the study of anthropology the European past and present did not need to be regarded as the source for understanding Mexico.

I have already pointed out the commitment of the Mexican government to social reform and modernization. In a country short of both educated manpower and financial resources most Mexican intellectuals were part of the government.

In Britain in the 1940s the Second World War similarly led to the employment of normally academic intellectuals by government and a general concern with practical issues.

Where in Mexico science was viewed as a source of tools which could be used to modernize and direct the future of the nation, in Britain science was regarded as a major value at stake in the war against Fascism. The war itself was seen as a battle against forces which could make scientific inquiry impossible. And scientific research was closely allied to developing a technology of warfare.[18]

In 1940, when Malinowski and De la Fuente began research, European cities were being destroyed by a new form of aerial warfare. New industrial techniques were being used in Germany for the destruction of ethnic groups, and to eliminate political opposition. A generation of intellectuals, including Malinowski and De la Fuente, saw the defence of science as part of an anti-Fascist position. The years between the wars in Europe had seen rapid progress in physics and biology. These advances led to radical improvements in engineering and medicine. The period between the two world wars was characterized by a widespread feeling that the techniques of research in the natural sciences could, and should, be extended to solve urgent social problems.

To later generations of intellectuals the war and its aftermath appear differently. The wars in Europe and Asia have revealed the extent to which scientific research provides enormously destructive, as well as beneficent, tools. Today, the benefits of science and modern technology are seen against attendant risks, and the risks are emphasized. For this reason it is difficult to reconstruct a more confident, earlier attitude towards science. Before 1940 'science', 'progress' and 'the public good' could be regarded as inextricably linked. The essay *The Economics of a Mexican Market System* should be seen in the context of this earlier attitude towards science, as well as in the context of the political situation of Mexico in 1940.

Mexico in 1940 was a unique meeting place for Americans and Europeans.[19] In 1938 the first major battle against European Fascism was lost in Spain. The Fascist victory created a major dislocation of the Spanish population and of Spanish intellectual life. Similar dislocations had occurred by 1940 throughout Europe. From the end of the Russian Revolution, European exiles had begun to arrive in Mexico. Leon Trotsky, who spent the last three years of his life in Mexico, must have been the most famous of these political refugees. After 1938, Mexico was one of the very few nations which welcomed Republican refugees from Spain. They, and other political exiles, were granted Mexican citizenship. The Spanish Republican Government in Exile lived on in Mexico as the only government of Spain officially recognized by Mexico until after the death of the Spanish dictator, Francisco Franco, in 1975.

In 1940 the Mexican intellectual community thus included and was influenced by foreigners whose political persuasions ranged from the anti-monarchist and anti-clerical views of the Spanish Government in Exile to the radical socialist views held by Trotskyites and others who supported Mexico's own radical Republican version of government.

In the field of anthropology, European refugees made an important contribution to the foundation of the National School of Anthropology and History. The first generation of teachers included, among others, the eminent Spanish prehistorian, Don Pedro Bosch Gimpera, who had been rector of the University of Barcelona; Juan Comas, the physical anthropologist; and Paul Kirchoff, a German ethnologist who had been Malinowski's pupil at the London School of Economics.

During the late 1930s and the 1940s, Mexico was able to provide a haven for foreign intellectuals without creating competition between foreigners and Mexican-born nationals. Mexican anthropologists were few in number and prepared to co-operate among themselves. Foreign intellectuals who arrived as exiles rather than as transient 'experts' also approached the Mexican intellectual scene with more modesty than is common in the latter case.

Thus, the atmosphere in which Julio de la Fuente had been working prior to Malinowski's arrival, and the atmosphere which Malinowski met in his brief encounter with Mexico, favoured their co-operation. It did not, however, dissolve their differences. One major disagreement between them is of special interest. Just as their collaboration can be seen as part of a unique situation in Mexican history, so this particular disagreement reflects their very different political orientations and personal experience.

It arose over an assessment of the degree to which the importation of foreign goods affected the market system of the Oaxaca Valley.

Malinowski wrote in the first draft of *The Economics of a Mexican Market System*: 'We cannot register a single item definitely traceable to a foreign source except some small celluloid objects.'[20]

De la Fuente commented (my translation)

> In general terms one might say something like that. We have already discussed it several times. Nevertheless, I remember English thread, foreign satins, and a good deal of other haberdashery (Sp. *merceria*) in addition to the celluloid objects. For the sake of precision I would suggest that this phrase be modified to be consistent with the tone of other such observations relating to the same topic: i.e. there are few foreign articles in the live market.

Malinowski, it seems, had been less than precise in his observations. Julio de la Fuente had noted a larger number of foreign imports, though he still agreed that the number was within the limits of 'few'. When it came to drawing conclusions from these observations, however, total disagreement emerged.

Malinowski concluded (p. 134): 'Hardly any of the foreign imports, however, affect the actual market place.'

De la Fuente commented: 'In my opinion the idea that foreign imports only affect the market slightly is incorrect and should be amended to assume precisely the contrary.'

Malinowski has referred to 'the actual market place'. It would seem that he wished to distinguish what De la Fuente calls 'the live market' (*el mercado vivo*) from the permanent stores, shops and wholesale businesses associated with the market place. In the physically limited area of the live market, both authors agree that there are few foreign goods for sale. It is their assessment of the importance of foreign imports which can be correlated with differences in their political outlooks and personal experience.

Julio de la Fuente was familiar with other market systems which resemble those of Oaxaca. He was also keenly aware, as one who had engaged in political activities in rural Mexico, of the pressure which traders who do not engage directly in market trade are able to exert on the political and economic activities of ordinary market users.

Moreover, as a Mexican, De la Fuente was deeply conscious of the colonial history of his country and of the part which the importation of foreign manufactured goods had played in that history. He was thus much less prepared than Malinowski to dismiss lightly the influence of foreign imports on market trade, or to consider separately the live market and the 'strong commercial movements' generated outside which 'are prejudicial to the poorer people' and occur 'throughout the country' (see p. 135).

Malinowski had no such compunction. He was no doubt familiar with the markets of Europe and the Mediterranean and was accustomed to finding in any given market a wider range of manufactured goods produced in distant parts. He was impressed by the relative scarcity of such products in Oaxaca. It would appear also that he wished to consider the 'live market' separately from other commercial institutions.

Our interest here is not to resolve the disagreement between the co-authors but simply to point out that the differences in both their perceptions and their analyses of the market system is consistent with their contrasting experience. As this brief item indicates, the political preconceptions of each fieldworker form part of the wider context of fieldwork.

IV The essay in the context of Malinowski's work

The Economics of a Mexican Market System is obviously a small part of Malinowski's much wider contribution to the study of anthropology. The general problems mentioned in the essay are all subjects which Malinowski treated at different times throughout his career (Firth, 1957). However, *The Economics of a Mexican Market System* is unique in that it presents Malinowski's approach, at the end of his career, to what was for him a totally new ethnographic area.

Unlike the Trobriand Islands which he describes as a culturally homogeneous region, the Oaxaca Valley is a region of extreme cultural diversity containing a set of overlapping and more complex social structures. At the outset Malinowski observes that the Oaxaca market system forms part of a national and global economy. He suggests that a complete study of the market system lies beyond the competence of an ethnographic study, and would require the co-operation of specialists in other disciplines.

In the Trobriand Islands there were no markets and no currency which Malinowski (1921, p. 50) considered to be money.[21] By contrast Oaxaca in 1940 possessed both markets and money. Malinowski and De la Fuente pay particular attention to a description of the currency, and to the different types of weights and measures in simultaneous use in the Valley markets. Malinowski is also clearly intrigued by the simultaneous occurrence in the Oaxaca markets of barter transactions and the exchange of commodities for currency. The general problem which arises in comparing the 'real income' of people with differential access to currency is noted by the authors and is still a subject of concern to economists.

Nevertheless, there were similarities between the Trobrianders and the Oaxaca market-goers which must have occurred to Malinowski. The 'daring sailors, industrious manufacturers, and keen traders' whom Malinowski christened the 'Argonauts of the Western Pacific' obviously share a compelling interest in trade with the inhabitants of the Oaxaca Valley whose 'commercial libido' impressed Malinowski.

From the outset Malinowski views the scattered market places of the Oaxaca Valley as part of a single region. The Valley is described as economically interdependent with neighbouring ecological regions: the Mixtec Highlands to the west and north, the Zapotec-Mixe Highlands to the east and south. The dispersed towns and villages of Oaxaca, like the separate islands and village communities of the Trobriand archipelago, are first located in their diversity of natural resources, and then seen as linked by a system of exchanges.

In his analysis of the Kula exchange, Malinowski begins from the observation that the ceremonial exchange of shell valuables can be viewed as a myriad of transactions between partners. Similarly, early in the market study, Malinowski looks at the exchanges between buyer and seller and comments that while such transactions are brief and finite, the resulting 'institution' is far more complex.

From the dyadic relationship between Kula partners, Malinowski moves in the Trobriand case to the analysis of relationships between and within local groups, categories of kin, groups of individuals distinguished by sex, rank and the division of labour, and to the analysis of 'magic' as an aspect of the Kula trade and Trobriand social organization.

In this work on the markets of Oaxaca, Malinowski asserts a special interest in the study of social change; a subject mentioned only briefly in the Trobriand work. Later in his career Malinowski had proposed to study social change in Africa as the result of contact between 'two cultural orders' which 'meet, inpinge upon one another' and 'produce a third cultural reality'. This approach was criticized by a number of Malinowski's students (Malinowski, 1938a) who proposed various other means of studying socio-cultural change. In Oaxaca, Malinowski used neither the approach which he had elaborated in a detailed schema (Malinowski, 1961, pp. 74-5) nor the suggestions which he presents in his introduction to the work of his students (Malinowski, 1938b). As a starting point he uses instead the concept of 'an institution' which he refers to in different ways throughout his work.

In 'The Scientific Basis of Applied Anthropology' (1938b), which Malinowski cites in *The Economics of a Mexican Market System*, the biological needs of human individuals are seen as providing the basis for 'institutions' which culturally define and serve to fill these 'organic needs'. A scheme of Culture is presented (pp. 16-17) in which 'the bodily needs' of man seem to correspond to 'Economics' which appears as the first of eight 'functional aspects' (presumably of institutions). One might conclude from this that Malinowski sees 'economic institutions' as fulfilling the 'bodily needs' of man.[22] However, he warns elsewhere that 'institutions show a pronounced amalgamation of functions and have a synthetic character . . . [they] are not correlated simply and directly to their functions; one does not receive one satisfaction in one institution . . .' (Malinowski, 1939a, p. 5; also cited in *The Economics of a Mexican Market System*).

In another definition of 'institution' Malinowski (1968, p. 50) makes no mention of physiological needs. An institution is defined as

> a group of people united for the pursuit of a simple or complex activity, always in possession of a technical outfit, organized on a definite legal or customary charter [which is] linguistically formulated in myth, legend, rule and maxim and [whose personnel are] prepared for the carrying out of its task.

Leach (1957, p. 136) suggests that in his conception of an institution 'Malinowski was pointing the road to his successors'. Here Leach also observes that Malinowski's conception of an institution 'is analogous to Weber's "corporate group" ' (verband) in that '[Malinowski's] institutions emerge as collections of individuals (personnel) who possess a common vested interest'. However, Leach considers that 'Malinowski's version tends to confuse the individual with his institutionalised role'.

In *The Economics of a Mexican Market System* Malinowski does not discuss his definition of an institution at any length.[23] However, at the end he contrasts the 'charter' of an institution with its 'function'. The 'charter' of an institution would appear to correspond to what is now called 'an actor's model' of behaviour, while 'the function' corresponds to 'the observer's model'. To specify the 'function' of an institution would appear to be the goal of research.

In his study of the Kula exchanges Malinowski (1922, p. 516) sets himself the task of 'inducing a deeper analysis of economic facts than that which considers primitive man . . . a rational being who wants nothing but to satisfy his simplest needs and does it according to the principle of least effort'.

By contrast, in *The Economics of a Mexican Market System* Malinowski asserts both initially and in his conclusions that the market is essentially a utilitarian institution. 'We soon discovered that the Indians never go [to market] to amuse themselves or for any other collateral reason. They go to market to transact business'.

> Our final conclusion is that the market is almost exclusively an economic mechanism in the conceptions and ideas of the natives themselves . . . no one ever goes to the market . . . without having as the principal motive of the visit a purchase and a sale. (p. 189)

The contrast in Malinowski's conclusions as to the function of the Kula exchange and the function of the Oaxaca market system is clearly related to differences between the two types of exchange systems. Thus, the Kula exchange is seen by the Trobrianders as distinct from and opposed to the exchange of utilitarian goods (*gimwali*), while the Oaxaca market-goer regards his market activities as utilitarian. But Malinowski in his conclusions regards the Kula as 'a type of semi-economic, semi-ceremonial activity . . . definitely relevant to a consideration of the origins of wealth and value, trade and economic relations in general' (1922, p. 515).

In the conclusions to *The Economics of a Mexican Market System* Malinowski appears to accept the actor's view of the system as exclusively utilitarian. Unless he does so, a further analysis of the market system which obviously *is* essentially tied to production, distribution and consumption of goods needed for survival, would throw into question the possibility of distinguishing institutions from one another. Here Malinowski would be forced back to his definition of institutions as fulfilling specific, physiological needs of the individual.

Given the extent to which Malinowski stressed the interrelatedness of all social phenomena, he must distinguish institutions from one another by isolating discrete physiological needs. This in turn may lead him to underestimate the complex interrelationship of the physiological and psychological processes which determine individual action.

Perhaps it is for this reason, and despite the data he presents in the course of his essay, that Malinowski seems to accept without question an actor's view of the nature of the market system.

In fact, Malinowski introduces us in an early section of the essay to an old lady selling lumps of cheese. After a bit of investigation Malin owski concludes that she has obviously not come to market to earn her living. She is provided for by other means. She has not come, he writes, 'because she needs it economically'.

Throughout the essay Malinowski also notes repeatedly the impact of regular ceremonial expenditures on market activity. Religious and patriotic festivals and saint's day feasts (*mayordomías*) are mentioned. The regular expenditures made in Oaxaca markets on such goods as flowers, votive offerings or candles are no more utilitarian than the exchange of Kula valuables. The question Malinowski asks of the Kula valuables could be just as legitimately asked of these expenditures. What purpose do they serve? Like the old lady's sale of cheese, they cannot be explained simply in terms of replenishing the larder with what is needed for survival.

Given the limited scope of the essay, it is not surprising that this question is not answered. However, given Malinowski's earlier work on the Kula exchange, it is surprising that the question is not raised.

Leach's observation that Malinowski's definition of an institution led to a confusion of 'the individual' (a complex human being) with his 'institutionalized role' is apposite here. Perhaps Malinowski, in distinguishing between the actor and the observer's model of an institution, did not also make the distinction, which Leach suggests, between individual action (inevitably idiosyncratic) and norms of behaviour which are socially constituted.

A discussion of the relationship between the needs of individuals and social needs is presently being rephrased in work on genetics and animal behaviour, using data which Malinowski could hardly have envisaged. The extent to which biological as opposed to cultural forces serve as constraints on social behaviour may be separately investigated using such data. Malinowski's view that discrete physiological needs provide a basis for distinct institutions in human societies may be obsolete. However, the idea that there are physiological mechanisms common to all animals including man, which underlie all social processes, has become more rather than less interesting.

Let us now return to the particular manner in which Malinowski uses the concept of institution in this essay. Following his own definition of an institution, he moves from the description of a typical market transaction to the description of the material endowment of the market place, the products, architecture and transport. He notes certain of the 'rules' governing market transactions, and the periodicity of these exchanges. The 'group of people united for the pursuit' of market activity is dealt with in a variety of contexts.

The terms 'villager', 'peasant' and 'Indian' are mentioned. Though Malinowski and De la Fuente state that the terms 'do not refer to any precise racial or cultural differentiation . . . but are used for the purpose of having a few synonyms available', there is more than a matter of literary style at issue. The use of these terms suggests a particular analytic view of social structures which overlap in the Valley. 'Villager', for example, is a category which can be opposed to 'townsperson', 'Indian' to 'non-Indian', and 'peasant' to 'landlord'. (See pp. 83-4.)

The category 'townsperson' is used in the essay and a subdivision is suggested on the basis of income levels which correspond to characteristic types of expenditure and consumption. Zapotec, Mixe and Mixtec 'ethnic groups' or 'tribes' are subdivisions of the category 'Indian'. The term 'peasant' is used differently. It is not analytically opposed to the category of 'landlord'. 'Landlords' hardly appear in the essay, though the authors emphasize the importance of further study of land tenure and agricultural production for a better understanding of the market system. 'Peasant' is used at times to refer (following Redfield's usage) to 'the Folk' in contrast with 'the Urban' population. More frequently, however, peasant is used with reference to the Latinized rural population in contrast with the Indian population. The term 'Latinized' is used to mean non-Indian and the reference is to cultural distinctions between the two groups. Thus the authors refer to two neighbouring and historically linked local communities: a Zapotec-speaking community which is termed 'Indian' and the Spanish-speaking community referred to as 'Latinized'. The authors point out that there is no visible racial difference between the two populations. The usage of 'Latinized' to refer to the Spanish-speaking group is unique in the literature on Mexico and Guatemala. The term commonly used for such a group in the literature is 'mestizo'. Some consideration of this term might be helpful for readers who are not familiar with the literature on Meso-America.

'Mestizo' and 'Indian' are terms which were introduced to Mexico and Guatemala with the Spanish conquest. They belonged originally to a set of legal categories established soon after the conquest by the Spanish *Ley de castas* (Law of Castes). In these laws the Spanish colonial administration attempted, in vain, to distinguish between biologically discrete groups (*castas*) whose members would hold specific rights and duties within the political system and the economic organization of the colony. In this set of *castas*, the mestizo was defined as the child of a Spanish and an Indian parent. Mexican independence ended the *Ley de castas*, but the categories mestizo and Indian persist. Mestizo thus retains, in a modified form, its original reference to biological origins.

Within the more specific framework of market transactions, the authors distinguish categories of persons who use the market differently, in terms of buying and selling. After noting that the buyer (Spanish: *comprador*) and seller (Spanish: *vendedor*) constitute a basic dyadic relationship, they observe also that most persons both buy and sell. Thus, as far as most participants in the market are concerned, the seller in one transaction will exchange his role and become a buyer in another transaction.[24]

This leads to one of the most interesting observations in the essay, that the market system is 'an always ready, always accessible and amenable bank'. It has a 'two-fold character as a source of purchasing power and convenient supply of consumer goods. [It both] represents a large-scale emporium [and] supplies a relatively large amount of ready money'.

In this context, the authors also contrast the vendor who sells his or her own produce (the *propio*) with the vendor who resells the produce of others (*revendedor*). Here the Spanish terms *regatón* and *acaparador* are mentioned.

In recent literature the term *regatón* is most often translated as middleman or market-trader. *Acaparador* seems to be translated as bulk buyer (Beals, 1975; Waterbury and Turkenik, 1976; Diskin and Cook, 1976, pp. 38, 53). However, the use of the terms has interesting historical precedents. Berg notes that before the 1930s in the Zapotec Highlands (when currency was in short supply) 'a rich man did not work and was called *propio*. He had *peons* [agricultural labourers] who did all the work for him. In reality the *propios* went to their fields, but only to supervise' (translated from Berg, 1974, p. 222). Berg (1974, pp. 224-5) notes that the *ricos* paid labourers both in food and money. I would assume from this that they were also the *propios* who sold maize in the valley markets and thus acquired the money with which to pay labourers.

The term *regatón* also appears to have a history. According to Carrazco (1978, p, 37), the Nahuatl word *tlanecuilo* was used for those who 'acquired products for resale' in the pre-conquest markets described in Sahagún. Carrazco notes that from these historical sources it is difficult to judge 'to what point [the *tlanecuilo*] were themselves artisans who brought their own products and those of their colleagues to market [or if] they were really professional merchants' [members of the group called *pochteca* in Nahuatl].

A similar problem exists in distinguishing between those referred to as *regatones* and *acaparadores* in *The Economics of a Mexican Market System*.

The terms are in fact terms of reference, never used in address. The verb *regatear* which means 'to haggle or bargain' provides the root of the noun *regatón*. The noun *acaparador* comes from the root of the verb *acaparar*: 'to acquire or keep merchandise in sufficient quantity to fix prices in the market' (Poudevida, 1969).

We have already noted Malinowski and De la Fuente's observation that most participants use the market both to buy and to sell. There is, in addition to the terms used for specialist traders mentioned above, a single reciprocal term of address which reflects this situation. The term *marchante* is used in Oaxaca markets, as in other regions of Mexico. The use of the word *marchante* is recorded in one dialogue cited in the essay. It is used there by a vendor to address a client in a typical market transaction. The term might as typically have been used by a client to a vendor. I would emphasize that the words *marchante* (male) and *marchanta* (female) are used almost exclusively in address. The fact that they are reciprocal implies some degree of equality between buyer and seller.

This is not the case with the words *regatón* and *acaparador*. These are terms of reference which I have never heard used in address. It would be as rude to address a person as *regatón* or *acaparador* as it would be unusual to refer to someone as *marchante*.

Note that *regatón* and *acaparador* are distinguished from the ordinary *marchante* (buyer/seller) by the fact that both buy for resale rather than for consumption. In addition, the *acaparador* withholds goods from the market. In Oaxaca generally, the *regatón* and *acaparador*, unlike the *marchante*, buy specific produce from more than one producer. The *regatón* normally resells – particularly foodstuffs – to the *acaparador*. It would seem appropriate in this context to translate *regatón* as haggler and *acaparador* as speculator. The opprobrium implicit in the English translation indicates why the Spanish words would not be used as a form of address. (The English translation indicates why the Spanish words would not be used in address). On a continuum of price-fixing operations the relationships among the various buyers/sellers distinguished by Malinowski and De la Fuente can be diagrammed to show the increasing influence of individuals in the setting of prices.

Individual ability
to fix prices

Acaparador buys for resale and
with older goods to manipulate price

Regatón (specialized
buyer/seller, buys for resale)

Marchante ordinary
buyer/seller & small scale
propio buys for consumption

Ability to withold
goods from the
market

Malinowski tends to see the role of bargaining, except with regard to maize, as a ceremonial procedure which has little impact on the fixing of prices. De la Fuente expresses disagreement.

Further investigation of the role of hagglers and speculators in fixing prices would have indicated, I believe, that prices of most sales were not fixed by bargaining in the transactions between ordinary (*marchante*) market users, precisely because there were particular individuals whose position in the trading or production networks gave them the ability to fix prices for a much wider range of transactions than those in which they were directly engaged.

The data presented in the essay do indicate that buying for resale took place at several different levels in the market system. Maize, for example, is bought in large quantities for resale by Malinowski's prosperous friend, Don Manuel. But poor Mixe Indians, and those individuals who engaged in barter, also bought a variety of products for resale. However, as Malinowski notes, the prices, particularly of other foodstuffs, tended to rise and fall with the price of maize. It was also maize, in particular, which was accumulated by the *acaparadores*.

Subsequent work by Alejandro Marroquín in Tlaxiaco (1957), a neighbouring Oaxaca market town in the Mixtec Highlands, should be mentioned here. The highland Mixtec market system focused on Tlaxiaco overlaps with the Oaxaca Valley system, as Malinowski notes. Marroquín's study describes the mechanism by which the prices of other goods alter with changes in the price of maize.

In the market region surrounding Tlaxiaco specialist traders (the *regatones* and *acaparadores* mentioned above, accompanied by the owners of stores, the *comerciantes*) buy up the maize crop after the harvest. Throughout the year they also buy other goods for resale. Later, when maize prices begin to rise during the regular periods of maize scarcity, maize is resold at high prices in the Tlaxiaco market. At the same time the producer-sellers of other goods (*propios*), and the resellers (*regatones* and *acaparadores*) begin a battle over the prices of these goods. The producers must charge more for their products if they are to sell them for sufficient money to buy maize.

According to Marroquín, the producer is generally beaten in the bargaining process and, though the price of his product may be increased, the increase never keeps pace with the rise in maize prices. This means that resellers (not only of foodstuffs but also of other commodities) must lower the prices of other goods if they are to be bought by consumers who have to spend most of their money on the purchase of maize.

Looking again at the essay's conclusion that the market is 'an amenable bank', we may extend the analogy to note that in the market, as in a bank, there is a significant distinction between those who hold currency or produce in quantity, and the ordinary producer/consumer (the small-scale *propio*/vendor/buyer). The market enables the ordinary producer to buy a range of goods which is wider than that which he or she produces, but it also forces the producer to sell essential foodstuffs which must be bought back again for consumption.

The observation that all market prices are crucially affected by changes in the price of maize, noted in *The Economics of a Mexican Market System*, and confirmed by the work of Marroquín, is of some interest in a historical context. Gudeman (1978) points out that Ricardo in 1815 'proposed a corn [i.e. wheat] theory of value. . . . By calculating with a single commodity, Ricardo was able to reveal some of the basic distributional relationships in the [nineteenth-century] English economy'.

Although Gudeman comments that Ricardo's work 'displays a

Mozartian elegance compared to Malinowski's rambling functionalism', Malinowski's rambles do seem to have led to the empirical observation of the phenomenon which was central to Ricardo's analysis.

Since Malinowski and Julio de la Fuente worked in the Oaxaca Valley, the Mexican government has intervened directly to control the price and distribution of maize. As far as I know the effects of government policy on the market system have not been studied by anthropologists in the Oaxaca Valley. Cancian (1972) deals with the effects of government policy on the maize-farming economy of the Chiapas region, and Warman (1977) summarizes the overall history of changing maize prices since 1940 and their effects on the farmers of Morelos. Neither author, however, is dealing with a market system specifically.

My suggestion that the *marchante-regatón-acaparador* relationships provides an outline for the social basis of price fixing in the Oaxaca market system (viewed principally in its internal aspect) is based on the data contained in *The Economics of a Mexican Market System,* i.e. data presented by Marroquín (1957), and fieldwork in Jamiltepec, Oaxaca (1957, 1958, 1960). It refers to that period (roughly 1940-60).

V Modernization in the Oaxaca Valley

The valley of Oaxaca can no longer be considered one of the more remote parts of the globe. Air transport and improved roads have made the city of Oaxaca easily accessible from Mexico City. The archeological zone of Monte Albán, which lies just outside the city of Oaxaca, is now a major tourist attraction. Products similar to those made by artisans and craftsmen in 1940 for the use of the local population can now be found in the shops of Canada, the USA and major cities of Western Europe.

Many villages of the Valley have received electricity and running water. Mule trains and ox-carts have been almost entirely replaced by petrol-driven lorries. Many of those lorries which in 1940 carried crowded passengers as well as cargoes of produce to be sold in markets have been replaced by modern buses and specialized commercial transport. Farmers from the Valley and the neighbouring highlands have emigrated in large numbers to find work in the USA and Canada, though many of these farmers tend to retain a base in Oaxaca.

The population of the municipality of Oaxaca grew from roughly 32,000 persons in 1940 to an estimated 90,000 in 1965. The market administrators of the city calculated in 1978 that the population of Oaxaca City had grown from 72,000 in 1960 to 160,000 in 1978. The spectacular growth of Oaxaca's urban population was attributed by the Market Administration to an increased movement of people into the city from the impoverished Mixtec Highlands to the north and west of the city. At the same time growth in tourism is credited with providing the city with sufficient resources to sustain this growing population (Waterbury, 1970).

In 1940 roughly 15 per cent of the total population of Mexico spoke Amerindian languages. This population was concentrated in the central and southern part of the republic. In the state of Oaxaca in 1940, speakers of Indian languages amounted to roughly half of the total population of the state (*Memorias del INI*, 1950).

Since 1940 the Indian population, defined as speakers of Amerindian languages, has decreased from 14.8 per cent to 10 per cent of the national population. Despite this decrease in proportion, the absolute numbers of the Indian population increased from 2,490,000 in 1940 to 3,030,000 in 1960 (see Gonzáles Casanova, 1970, pp. 80-3), and to 3,671,470 in 1970 (Villa Rojas, 1976, p. 122). At the same time, the rural population of Mexico has moved in steadily increasing numbers to the larger cities. The Indian sector of this population tends to remain on the land and thus forms an increasing percentage of Mexico's rural population.

In Oaxaca the Indian population is divided into numerous socially and culturally discrete local communities. The languages spoken by this population are not necessarily mutually intelligible, even where they may be classed within a single 'language group'. The Mixtec, Mixe and Zapotec peoples who appear in the pages of the essay recognize a common origin only in so far as they accept a Roman Catholic cosmology. They are not represented in the national government structure as distinct from more Latinized farming communities, excepting in so far as the INI can be said to represent them. Spanish is the lingua franca of the market in its broadest definition, and of the national government structure. The regional economy and the Roman Catholic church together with the national political organization provide the major frameworks through which these communities are related to one another and to the Mexican state. The number of 'Latinized' communities, and individuals who have 'passed' from Indian to non-Indian status, in the population of the Valley has not been assessed, but it is clear that a process of Latinization begun with the conquest has continued in Oaxaca as elsewhere in the republic (see Drucker, 1963).

The market system as it exists today is clearly continuous historically with the market system as described by Malinowski and De la Fuente. Studies carried out in 1964-9 (Diskin and Cook, 1976; Beals, 1975) indicate that the same villages described in the 1940 study retain the same market days. The same products are still exchanged by vendors and buyers. The ethnic groups described in 1940 could still be distinguished in 1978.[25]

One author (Kaplan, 1965) suggests, in a re-study of a comparable market system in Patzcuaro Michoacan (originally studied by Foster, 1948), that the market system there has increased in size, but that the overall structure of the market has not been affected.

A recent study of markets in Oaxaca City (Waterbury, 1970) indicates that there have been structural developments as well as growth in the size and number of Oaxaca City markets. One important new structure which Waterbury's study reveals is an organization of market traders. This labour union (*sindicato*) of traders deals with an expanded municipal organization and a more bureaucratic government political party than existed in Oaxaca in 1940.[26]

Since 1940 the government has created centres throughout rural Mexico at which staple foodstuffs (particularly maize) are bought from producers. Government prices for buying and selling these foods are fixed throughout the republic (Hewitt de Alcantara, 1976). This intervention in the distribution and pricing of staple foods must have crucially affected the Oaxaca marketing system. The creation of a specialized government agency for buying coffee from producers must have affected the marketing of this commodity too. The sale of other agricultural products in the markets has similarly been influenced, if not by government intervention, then by increased demand for foodstuffs in Mexico generally, and by improved transport facilities. A wide range of fruit and vegetables can now be exported from the Valley. The national inflation must also have local repercussions (see Warman, 1977, p. 231).

There has been an increase in the distribution of foodstuffs, clothing and household goods through modern shopping facilities. (Beals, 1975, mentions this development, but does not discuss its impact, or lack of impact, on what he calls the traditional market system.)

One further change in the market system of Oaxaca began in 1978. The dominant market of the system described in this essay was located in the Benito Juarez market place, at the centre of Oaxaca City. In an interview with the administrator of the market (15 August 1978) I was told that a major portion of this market was to be moved within a week to a specially constructed site at the periphery of the city. In 1978 the site had already been standing empty for several years. However, more than 500 private stalls had by then been sold by the municipal government to would-be vendors. The market administrator claimed that it was essential to move the main market from the city centre (1) to protect tourism, (2) to allow for a free circulation of motor traffic and (3) to improve hygiene. A much smaller market was to remain in the city centre. By November 1978 the move had begun.[27]

The market administrator observed that the central market in Oaxaca had increased enormously in size over the years. He attributed this to the increasing impoverishment of the countryside. The impoverished farmer who comes to the city, in his words, 'gets hold of a wooden box and some oranges and starts a business'. Such a vendor, in other words, enters a network of middlemen.

In addition, I would suggest that very small-scale selling, such as the sale of oranges, by the poorest vendors may be seen as a form of begging. Successful begging must take place in circumstances where the beggar is able to approach the more affluent. The market administrator pointed out that relocation of the market at the city's periphery is one way of protecting tourists in the city centre from importunate street vendors. He did not add, but it is also true, that tourists would be spared the sight of the poverty and illness which are exhibited in the market. Relocation of the market will have the effect of making poverty less visible.

The change in location of a major market place in Oaxaca also affects agricultural producers, artisans and middlemen. Kaplan (1965) considers that in Mexican markets the networks of middlemen increase in size as the urban population increases. He also suggests that this is perhaps characteristic of the way in which major market centres serve rural communities of agricultural or artisan workers in which production can no longer provide subsistence. What effect will the movement of Oaxaca City market have on these networks of traders?

In many other major cities (London, Paris, New York) market places have been moved from central city locations to more peripheral ones. This change must be consistent with features of urban development, which are hardly random. Traffic flow, hygiene and the protection of tourism are no more insignificant considerations in these cities than in Oaxaca. Urban development itself has become an issue which directly affects the citizens of industrialized nations where the majority of the population live in cities. It is equally important in nations where enormous urban centres develop without the same degree of industrialization.

VI A note on subsequent research

Research in the Oaxaca Valley since 1940 has widened our perspective and increased our knowledge of the market system described by Malinowski and De la Fuente. An anthropological bibliography of Oaxaca lists 1,002 items published between 1974 and 1979 which deal with topics of anthropological and archeological interest in Oaxaca (La Luz Topete, 1980).

Brian Hamnett's historical work (1971) is an important contribution to the economic history of Oaxaca. In an introduction to the study of Oaxaca markets some of his conclusions should be noted.

Hamnett shows that by the eighteenth century not only the city and valley of Oaxaca but the hinterlands near the Pacific coast (municipality of Jicayan) and the Zapotec Highlands (municipality Villa Alta) were part of a trading system which linked metropolitan Spain with the American colonies. Cochineal, a precious dye-stuff, was produced in Oaxaca.[28] The export of cochineal was an important source of revenue to the Spanish crown as well as a source of profit to Peninsular traders. In 1786, for example, cochineal of Oaxaca was the fourth most valuable trade item imported into Spain from all the American ports in the New World (see Hamnett, 1971, Appendix 5, p. 175).

In Oaxaca, production and trade in cochineal and cotton were:

> central activities of the indigenous population upon whose labours the Spanish element depended for their prosperity and political supremacy. . . . Spanish Peninsular merchants and the Royal administrators . . . considered Oaxaca to be next in importance to the silver-mining regions of Guanajuato and Zacatecas. (Hamnett, 1971, pp. 1-2)

Production and trade in cochineal and cotton were imposed, often forcibly, by administrators and traders. The activities of traders and administrators were often illegal. A major part of Hamnett's study

(1971) deals with the contradiction between Spanish law and accepted practice with regard to this commerce. A constant revision of Spanish law resulted from the need to protect the indigenous producers from extinction at the hands of competing representatives of the crown and private commerce.

At its peak the cochineal trade appears to have bypassed the market system. But Hamnett (p. 124) writes that in a period of decline 'commerce was reduced to small purchases of the dye in the Friday and Saturday markets'. In the Mixtec and Zapotec Highlands which border on the Oaxaca Valley, the cochineal-producing areas were dependent on the Valley to provide them with maize. Wage labour was common in these highland regions at least from the eighteenth century. Until the demise of the cochineal trade in the mid-nineteenth century, maize prices were directly linked to the rise and fall in the price of cochineal, and thus to the economic crises of Europe as well as to the fortunes of local maize production. Thus the cochineal and cotton trade must have shaped the Valley market system to some degree.

Exactly how the export of commodities from the Oaxaca Valley and neighbouring regions affects, and has affected, the social and economic organization of the Valley markets is a subject still to be explored. However, any assessment of the evolution of markets in the Oaxaca Valley must incorporate the results of Hamnett's research.

Historical research on the archeological Mixtec and Zapotec cultures has proceeded rapidly since the 1940s. For a summary of historical research on the Mixtec region see R. Spores (1967). For a summary which includes archeological, historical and contemporary ethnography of the Zápotec see Whitecotton (1977).

The most recent studies of Oaxaca Valley markets are those of Waterbury (1970) and Beals (1975) and the collection of essays edited by Diskin and Cook (Mexican edition, 1975; US edition, 1976). The work of Beals, Diskin and Cook has been critically reviewed in the context of other recent work on Latin American markets by Carol Smith (1976a).

A research project directed by R.L. Beals from 1965 to 1969 has been the source of many of the recent publications dealing with Oaxaca. Although one of the avowed first steps of the 1965-9 project was to replicate the Malinowski/De la Fuente study (Beals, 1976, p. 30), no systematic comparison of the results with the earlier work has yet appeared. Certain differences between Beals's approach and *The Economics of a Mexican Market System* should be noted.

Unlike Malinowski and De la Fuente, Beals conceptually divides the 'traditional' from the 'modern' marketing system (1976, p. 29). While introducing this new classification of marketing institutions, Beals rejects the simple model used by Malinowski and De la Fuente for describing the Valley markets. In *The Economics of a Mexican Market System* the weekly cycle is seen as one of the major bases for the integration of neighbouring markets with one another and with the central Oaxaca City market. A three-tiered system of markets is described in which secondary markets occur with greater frequency than tertiary markets, and the primacy of the Oaxaca market is reflected in that (a) Oaxaca alone (in 1940) operated as a daily market, and (b) no other market in the system overlapped with the Oaxaca City market on a Saturday.

Beals does not compare the periodicity of markets in the 1960s with that shown by Malinowski and De la Fuente for the same localities in 1940. He also fails to compare the periodicity of these markets with respect to one another. Instead Beals lists forty-five markets which he considers dependent on the Oaxaca City market. Each of these is shown to occur on a 'primary market day'. The primary market day is defined as the particular day of the week on which the market in a particular locality is largest. Does this imply that all forty-five localities now have daily markets? Beals nowhere mentions whether or not the markets he lists occur on more than one day. Diskin (1976, pp. 50-1), dealing only with the Valley markets mentioned by Malinowski and De la Fuente, also writes of 'major plazas' which occur once a week. However, the periodicity of markets is crucial to the earlier model of the system and a study of changes in the periodicity of the Oaxaca Valley markets between 1940 and 1960 would be of great interest. Skinner's (1964) hypothesis that marketing intensifies in response to population growth has been briefly discussed by Polly Hill with reference to West African markets (1966), and is relevant to the Oaxaca material.

Beals (1976, p. 35) justifies his disregard of the model used by Malinowski and De la Fuente because 'when details are examined this order [presumably of primary, secondary and tertiary markets] is often violated'. The details he refers to, however, have nothing to do with market periodicity. They refer to the commodities exchanged in different markets. Thus, Beals writes (p. 35): 'Tlacolula is the primary market-place for parts of the Sierra . . . Ocotlán is the primary market-place for cattle for the entire valley region.'

Malinowski and De la Fuente had already noted that the interlinking markets seen from Oaxaca City would appear differently if viewed from another point in the system. *The Economics of a Mexican Market System* uses both market periodicity and the complementary distribution of special products from more or less specialized markets as criteria for judging that the Valley markets form a unified system. The authors also suggest that further research is needed in order to indicate where, at the boundaries of the Valley market system, the influence of market centres of the scale of Oaxaca City displaces the influence of Oaxaca.

Although Beals considers a wider geographical area than the one dealt with by Malinowski and De la Fuente, he does not approach the question implicitly raised by the earlier study, of how the primary market centres (that is, the cities like Oaxaca, Mexico, Puebla and Jalapa) are related to one another or separated by distinctive, dependent market systems. This kind of question has been considered at length for China in the influential papers of G.W. Skinner (1964).

On the other hand, the Oaxaca research project directed by Beals has provided information in depth on numerous markets in the Oaxaca Valley and on specialized production for the Valley market system. The wider geographical range of later studies has given us some idea of the market cycles which operate in the Zápotec Highlands (Berg, 1974), those centred on Nochixtlán in the Mixteca Alta (Warner, 1976) and those of the Isthmus of Tehuantepec (Chiñas, 1976). The work of Higgins (1974) describes budgeting in a poor section of Oaxaca City and is particularly interesting as it reveals the place in the domestic economy of cooked food prepared for market sale. Independent of the Beals Project, Nahmad's study of the Mixe (1965) provides a new outline of the Mixe marketing system. Iszaevich's study (1973) of a valley farming community is important. among other reasons, because it describes how a community, centrally located with respect to the geography of the Valley market system, participates only peripherally in that system.

These examples serve to show that work in the Oaxaca Valley has in many aspects developed and gone beyond the questions raised in *The Economics of a Mexican Market System*. New questions have also been raised by work outside Oaxaca. Bonfil's study (1971a) of Lent fairs in the neighbouring state of Morelos indicates that an important market cycle, based on the annual religious observance of Easter, operates in that area. The simultaneous operation of an annual cycle of fairs and a weekly market cycle is also described by Bonfil

(1973, pp. 85-9) for the town of Cholula in Puebla. Diskin (1976) mentions briefly, as do Malinowski and De la Fuente, that annual fairs outside the Valley have long been associated with the Valley market system. The question of how annual fairs associated with religious pilgrimage are related to secular markets operating on a weekly cycle would bear further investigation.[29]

Malinowski and De la Fuente concluded in 1940 that in the Oaxaca Valley 'the typical average peasant produces sufficient maize to cover his annual needs'. This appears to be true no longer. Beals (1975, p. 57) writes of Oaxaca that 'both the state and the [Valley] region are maize deficit areas'. He calculates that not more than one quarter of the Valley villages produce a maize surplus. De la Fuente and Malinowski emphasized the crucial importance of maize marketing to the organization of the market system. It is unfortunate that Beals does not comment on this recent data.

In the nearby state of Morelos, Arturo Warman's work (1977) has shown how maize farmers were increasingly affected by the expanding capitalist economy of Mexico between 1940 and 1960. He argues that national government programmes designed to influence the local production and national distribution and storage of maize and other staple food crops are motivated by the need (at a national level) to keep food prices low while other commodities are allowed to increase in price. In this situation the maize farmer has to increase production constantly in order to meet the rising costs of other essential goods. Simultaneously the overall population increase in Mexico has led to greater pressure on food supplies in rural as well as in urban areas.

The unequal effects of inflation in the national economy have had devastating results for the maize producers of Morelos. Warman concludes (p. 238) that, contrary to accepted economic theory, maize production in Morelos increases when maize prices are low and may fall when prices are raised.

> The price of maize has many aspects for the peasant. Maize is not only a source of income, it also represents the principal expenditure for consumption. The multiple relationship (of cost and income) has many implications and is altered not only by the relationship between the changing prices of maize and those of other food products, but also by the possibility open to the peasant of autonomously producing his maize and conserving it. For a landless peasant high maize prices are a blow, not an advantage. For

peasants cannot keep maize to consume it, but must sell it in order to buy other essentials; to those who sell maize when the price is low and buy it when the price rises, the rising price of maize is no clear advantage. It may be a decisive factor which increases their indebtedness. (Trans.)

Although Morelos and Oaxaca differ both in ecology and history, Warman's conclusions could be checked against data which must be available for Oaxaca.

Cancian (1972, chapter VII), working in Chiapas, which borders Oaxaca to the south, has described the impact of government purchases of maize, and the opening of new land to cultivation, on the economy of Indian maize farmers. For a general study of changes in Mexican agriculture since 1940 see Hewitt de Alcantara (1976).

The literature on the Oaxaca Valley and its markets is extensive. Not all the relevant material has been mentioned, though much recent work is cited in notes to this present edition of *The Economics of a Mexican Market System*. There have also been important theoretical advances in the study of market systems. Their consideration is beyond the scope of this introduction. I hope, however, that the republication of *The Economics of a Mexican Market System* will contribute to the analysis of the large body of new information which is now available. *The Economics of a Mexican Market System* is, without doubt, an important part of the historical background to research in Oaxaca and it has a permanent place in the development of anthropology in Mexico.

Notes

1 Malinowski spent some time between 1900 and 1908 in Spain, the Canary Islands and in the Mediterranean basin. Later he lived in Tenerife for a year (1920-1) where he wrote *Argonauts of the Western Pacific*. His first wife, the author Elsie Masson, helped with the preparation of that manuscript. She died in 1935 and in 1940 Malinowski married Valetta Swann.

2 It is difficult to assess the contribution made by Valetta Swann since the drawings and diaries she made were not available for consultation.

3 Malinowski also wrote that he did not intend to incorporate into the publication, *The Economics of a Mexican Market System*, the new data gathered in subsequent fieldwork. He wrote, however, that some changes in Chapter 4 might be necessary. De la Fuente, in his commentary, was also very critical of Chapter 4. The full text of Malinowski's note reads:

> This is the preliminary draft of the memoir. It will remain substantially

in its present form and will only receive stylistic corrections and the re-wording of certain pages from the point of view of later presentation. This refers notably to section 4.

The manuscript will also be illustrated by some 24-30 photographs of which enlargements are being made in Mexico. About six maps and plans will further supplement the concrete documentation of the memoir.

It is not proposed to re-draft any parts of this memoir which present the joint work of the group mentioned in the preface, in the light of further researches which will be carried out by Professor B. Malinowski with a new group. Probably when some radical corrections might appear advisable, they will be included in an Appendix.

The memoir is primarily intended as an essay in fieldwork, and the presentation of two phases of research may have a special value, both theoretical and practical.

Although both authors were unhappy with the text of the original Chapter 4, this has not been altered. However, the placement of the texts of the original Chapters 2 and 4 have been changed.

In this edition, Chapter 1 consists of the original Chapter 1 with the addition of all but the first three pages of the old second chapter. Chapter 2 of this edition consists of the old fourth chapter, preceded by the first three pages of the old second chapter. For this reason the present edition has one chapter less than the original. Chapters 1 and 2 now contain all of the original Chapter 4. The old Chapter 5 is now Chapter 4 and all subsequent chapters are numbered accordingly.

4 On Malinowski's return to Oaxaca in 1941 he and his second wife were accompanied by a research student from the USA, Lew Wallace. Mr Wallace was subsequently killed in an accident.

5 In 1954 Professor Cámara Babachano led a group of students to observe the Tlaxiaco market studied by Marroquín. In 1957, Alejandro Marroquín took a group of students to the Sunday market at Xochimilco, just outside of Mexico City.

6 De la Fuente's official title was Jefe de la Comision Técnica Consultiva (Head of the Technical Consulting Committee).

7 This and all other translations from the Spanish are by the editor, S.D.B., and will be marked (Trans.).

8 In 'Hydraulic Development and Ethnocide' (Barabas and Bartolomé, 1974) the authors accuse the Mexican government of ethnocide on the basis of the disastrous results which the relocation had among the Mazatec and Chinantec communities. The same issue of the journal (*Critique of Anthropology*, vol. I, no. 1) contains a further discussion of this accusation (K.Y. and F.E., 1974). Aguirre Beltrán (1976) has responded with a defence of national government policy in *Obra Polémica*.

9 See Alfonso Caso (1955), *Que es el INI?* ; also Caso (1950, pp. 9-11) which cites the text of the law creating the INI.

10 See Aguirre Beltrán (1976) and others for a summary of the history, phil-

osophy and practical results of INI policy and a positive evaluation of this policy. See also *De Eso Que Llaman Antropología Mexicana* (Warman *et al.*, 1970) for a deeply critical commentary and generally negative evaluation of Mexican 'pro-Indian' policy. See Aguirre Beltrán (1976) for a response to some of the specific points raised in the 1970 work.

11 The densely populated Indian region outside San Cristobal de las Casas in Chiapas was considered as a possible location for the first INI co-ordinating centre. It seemed an attractive site because the centre was easily accessible to the local population. However, after research, the central market town of Las Casa was chosen instead. The market centre of Tlaxiaco was chosen as the site of the co-ordinating centre in the Mixtec Highlands; the archeological site of the capital of a pre-Columbian kingdom had been proposed first.

12 Material in the following section has been drawn from biographical notes written by Aguirre Beltrán in the introduction to the collected work of Julio de la Fuente (De la Fuente, 1964, 1965) and a conversation with Aguirre Beltrán in 1958. I have also drawn on my personal acquaintance with Julio de la Fuente.

13 Skinner (1964, pp. 36-99) shows that in post-revolutionary China, policies formulated by central government for the organization of communes were crucially affected by the manner in which local market units were integrated with 'central places'.

14 In addition to the papers and monograph mentioned here, De la Fuente wrote more than fifty essays of varying lengths. See De la Fuente, 1965, for a bibliography of his work.

15 The lecture did not please at least one representative of the press, however, and a Mexico City newspaper made unpleasant remarks about Malinowski. To judge from Malinowski's correspondence, the matter was of no further consequence.

16 The ceremonial centre of Teotihuacán (like the Monte Albán zone of Oaxaca) had been abandoned before the Spanish conquest.

17 Malinowski met Gamio briefly when he visited Mexico in 1926 on his first visit to North America. In 1939 Malinowski again visited Mexico, driving with Valetta Swann from Arizona. On that occasion he remained in Mexico for about a month, travelling from the northern border as far south as the valley of Morelos.

18 Malinowski himself, writing in 1936 ('Culture as a Determinant of Human Behavior', p. 170; Malinowski, 1963), expressed this view:

> Just now when we are faced with the danger of a complete breakdown of the scientific approach and of faith in science, combined with a corroding pessimism as to the value of reason in dealing with human affairs, the power of reason must be affirmed and its functions clearly defined.

Joseph Needham, in the Schiff lecture given at Cornell University in 1940 (subsequently published as an RPA war pamphlet), was equally anxious.

He began his lecture with a quotation from W.H. Auden:

> . . . Out of Europe comes a voice
> Compelling all to make their choice,
> A theologian who denies
> What more than 20 centuries
> Of Europe have assumed to be
> The basis of Civility.

Then he continued, envisaging the possibility of a new Dark Age:

> In this new Dark Age, superstition will triumph over reason, science will be retained only in so far as it is necessary for a narrow technology, and this technology will be applied not for the common good of humanity but for the domination of power-seeking groups by force of terrible armaments.

The lecture then documents, with ample references and statistics, the degree to which scientific endeavour had drawn to a halt in Germany during the decade 1930-40; Needham concluded: 'should the nazis be victorious, science in Europe may disappear for several generations, and all social progress with it'.

19 'Americans' is here taken to mean the inhabitants of both North and South America; 'Europeans' is meant to include the British.

20 This was modified after De la Fuente's comments to read as on p. 134.

21 See Malinowski (1921, 1922). Also see Codére (1968) for a reconsideration of the classification of 'shell valuables' in terms of a new model of the development of 'money'.

22 See also Malinowski, 1939b, reprinted in 1962, pp. 223-44. Note the table 'Synoptic Survey of Biological and Derived Needs and their Satisfaction in Culture', p. 226.

23 Malinowski, in this context, cites the 1939 article 'The Group and the Individual in Functional Analysis', then recently published in the *American Journal of Sociology*.

24 Geertz (1963, p. 33) makes the same observation of the *pasar* (bazaar) in Modjo Kuto, Indonesia. 'In fact there is little if any differentiation between the buying role and the selling role as long as one remains within the *pasar*; the trader is either or both indifferently.'

25 Taylor (1972) indicates that by 1576 a number of the Valley settlements which now contain markets were already trading centres or had developed some degree of craft specialization.

26 The dominant Mexican political party, called PRI (Partido Revolucionario Institucional), can be regarded as an institution of government rather than as a political party analogous to those in countries governed by constitutional democracies. See Gonzáles Casanova, 1970.

27 Newspaper coverage of the first stages indicates that some problems did attend the move. A verse published in *El Imparcial* (1 December 1978)

accused 'agitators' and 'extremists' of causing scandals designed to 'make everyone into communists', and threatened reprisals. The same paper (27 November) had already published a story headed 'Agitation among stall-holders' ('Agitadores mueven a los locatarios'). Other reports of problems confronting the vendors of particular goods also appeared. *Carteles del Sur* (25 November) mentioned butchers; *Panorama Oaxaqueña* (1 December) mentioned vendors of earthenware. *El Imparcial* (13 December) reported, however, that the roughly 350 vendors of Christmas ornaments were happily settled in the new market.

28 Cochineal is a dye-stuff first discovered by Europeans in Mexico. It consists of the bodies of the females of a species of insect, *Coccus cacti*. The insect lives on the cochineal fig (*Opuntia cochinillifera*) and two other species of cactus. A pound of cochineal contains about 70,000 insects. Some 293,250 pounds of cochineal were exported from the port of Veracruz in 1799 (Hamnett, 1971, p. 175). The insects were brushed gently off the leaves on which they lived and dried in the sun or in special ovens. The dye produces crimson and scarlet colours.

29 My own fieldwork in the region of Jamiltepec suggests that on the Pacific coast of Oaxaca annual market fairs held on the occasion of religious pilgrimages, and special markets for the seasonal sale of tropical produce, were more important trading institutions than a weekly cycle of markets.

The economics of a Mexican market system

An essay in contemporary ethnographic and social change in a Mexican valley

by Bronislaw Malinowski
and Julio de la Fuente

Prefatory note and acknowledgments

The research on which this preliminary account of the market places in Oaxaca Valley is based was done by a small group consisting of my wife, myself and Señor Julio de la Fuente. We received assistance and support from several institutions in Mexico and the USA. The Carnegie Corporation of New York gave me a grant of $1,000 for 1940, to be followed by another in 1941. The Mexican Ministry of Education financed the trip of Señor De la Fuente, as well as his stay in Oaxaca. The Institute of Human Relations of Yale University made possible the journey of Señor De la Fuente to New Haven and his sojourn at Yale University between January and May 1941. I would like to express here our indebtedness to Dr Mark May, Director of the Institute, Professor G.P. Murdock, Chairman of the Anthropology Department, and Dr John Dollard, member of this department, not merely for general assistance, but also for the interest and co-operation in the work.

In Mexico we received most generous and helpful support from several of the outstanding scholars of the republic, as well as from the federal authorities. A small committee was organized to sponsor our research, to assist us directly and indirectly in the execution, and to give guidance to the fieldwork. The experience and local knowledge of the committee members proved invaluable. The committee consisted of Dr Alfonso Caso, Director of the Instituto Nacional de Antropología e Historia, Dr Manuél Gamio, Chief of the Demographic Department of the Secretaria de Governacion [roughly equivalent to the British Home Office], Professor Chavez Orozco, Chief of the Department of Indigenous Affairs, and Professor Moises Saenz, Director of the Inter-American Indianist Institute. The committee issued recommendations to the state authorities at Oaxaca, and above all, they put us in touch with Don Martin Bazan, a former scientific associate of Dr Gamio and now a representative of the National Institute of Anthropology at Oaxaca. Señor Bazan gave us substantial scientific and practical assistance.

To the good offices of the sponsoring committee I owe the assignment of Señor De la Fuente as my research assistant in the field. His help proved very substantial in many respects. He did most of the detailed work in sketching the plans, preparing the maps and collecting concrete data. He made a number of special observations on problems which might otherwise have escaped my attention. He also remained in the district from 15 September, when my wife and I left Oaxaca, till the middle of November, and returned for a few days again in December. He was thus able to observe the crowded markets and the religious context of the market place during the important season of All Souls, and again during the celebrations of the patron saint of Oaxaca, La Virgen de la Soledad.

Señor De la Fuente was well prepared for his co-operation in functional fieldwork through the practical interest he had previously taken in Indian affairs and through his genuine zeal for Indian welfare. His previous experiences in this district, especially in the Sierra Juarez, gave us comparative data. His knowledge of the general principles of Zapotec culture enabled us to work more rapidly. He was very quickly able to assimilate some of the theoretical principles of social anthropology and culture. In this, his previous association with Dr Alfonso Caso proved of great benefit.

My wife contributed to the work by drawing a number of plans and keeping a detailed diary during one of the most interesting phases of our fieldwork: the fiesta of the Virgen de la Asunción and the *mayordomía* presided over by our best informant, Don Manuél Andrés Jarquín, in the village of Abasolo. Some of her independent observations on the market place are incorporated in the text, notably those on barter in the villages of Atzompa and in Ocotlán.

I am naturally responsible for the general direction of the work, as well as for the theoretical digressions and interpretations. I would like to state here, however, that most of the general problems were discussed by our group conjointly and the questions to be solved by further observations were formulated co-operatively with my wife and Señor De la Fuente in the course of our work. In this also I would like to acknowledge the quick and effective response which I always received from Señor De la Fuente. Wherever the results are due mainly or exclusively to one of us, this is clearly indicated in the text. The whole memoir, as dictated by myself in Señor De la Fuente's presence, has been carefully read and revised by him, and his valuable corrections are incorporated.

I would like to say, finally, that in no other fieldwork, whether in New Guinea, Melanesia, Bantu Africa or among other tribes of North

America, have I found the actual ethnographic techniques more pleasant, easier and more fruitful than among the Zapotecs of the Valley. A number of informants whom I had the good fortune personally to discover contributed more to our success than all the methods and tricks of an old fieldworker. Here I would like to mention especially our best informant, Don Manuél Andrés Jarquín. We met Manuél Jarquín on an occasional excursion to Tlacochahuaya. My wife and I were told that a fiesta was being prepared in the village of Abasolo. There we met the *mayordomo* of the fiesta, who was none other than Manuél. It took him five minutes to place us as 'historians who look out for antiquities in custom'. He started by explaining to us the essential features of the *mayordomía*, of its economic and social relevance. From that moment on he was our constant companion and visited many markets and villages with us. He requested to be taken with his wife and daughter to the ruins of Monte Albán, which he had never seen before. Some of his archeological hypotheses were reported later on to Dr Alfonso Caso, who was impressed by their intelligence and constructiveness, as we were ourselves. In looking at details of sculpture and mural painting, Manuél observed twice as quickly as any of the trained and professional ethnographers and archeologists present. He is the type of informant a lucky anthropologist meets once in a lifetime.

We are also grateful to Don Antonio Sumano of S. Juan Chilateca, Don Raymundo Crespo of Coyotopec and Don Tomás Martín of Zaachila. The information obtained from some of our friends in Oaxaca itself was of great orienting value. In addition to the scholarly advice received from Don Martín Bazán already mentioned, I would like to express my indebtedness to Professor Enrique Unda, to Don Jose Zorilla, Mr Fritz Holm, and Señor Solana y Gutierrez, a young Spanish historian and scholar whose knowledge of the past was of great value to us. Last, and not least, I wish to mention the assistance given to my wife and myself by Father Edward Rickards, through whom we were able to approach the Catholic clergy of the region and gain the confidence of those Indian members in many communities who often look with suspicion at outsiders trying to collect information.

B.M.

Institute of Human Relations,
Yale University,
New Haven, Connecticut

May 1941

1 The actual problem of fieldwork in Mexico today

Fieldwork in Mexico is at the present moment (1940-41) in an important and decisive phase of development. Many projects are being started and some are well under way. Several theoretical points of view, not entirely perhaps in agreement with each other as regards method or ultimate goal, jostle each other in the field.

Yet there is one fundamental premise on which all fieldworkers ought to agree. There is one criterion by which they can be judged. Anthropology in Mexico, of all places, can and must become a vital force in the framing and in the implementing of national, social and economic policies. The Indians are the decisive and determining factor in the life of the republic. On their development in education and prosperity, in national cohesion and in their talent for enterprise and their ability to control matters private and public, the future of the country as a whole depends.

Therefore, knowledge of the Indian as he is now, as he lives, works, calculates and aspires to better things, is necessary. That this implies a study of traditional values derived from bygone ages is indisputable. Yet all vital historical influences are to be found today, alive and active. They can be studied through fieldwork. Their existence and their survival are the proof of their relevance and vitality.

We have, then, to understand the present-day Indian, his abilities, his promise and potentialities, as well as his physiological, mental and material handicaps. Knowledge of the past as it still lives, embodied in Indian custom, ideology and organization, and also as it can be reconstructed from records and monuments, is important. Knowledge of the present is indispensable. Interest in prediction, in planning, and the translation of intentions into reforms is essential. Modern anthropology is equipped for this type of work, with the goals here indicated. It has been initiated in the Mexican field by the pioneering work of Dr Manuél Gamio and his associates in the now classical work on S. Juan Teotihuacán. It has been continued in the researches of

Dr Robert Redfield and Dr Alfonso Villa Rojas by methods and with a theoretical approach with which we are fully in sympathy.

The type of research of which the present essay is an example embraces interests in daily life, in ordinary concerns and in the standard of living. It combines the description of such vital phases of native existence with a clear analysis in terms of economics, sociology and educational processes. No selection is made on the basis of distinctions between ancient and modern, or between the new forces of cultural change and the survival of old traditions. In what we regard as the true scientific spirit, we studied the full cultural reality which we had before our eyes, selecting only with criteria of vitality, relevancy and generality of principle, rather than on the basis of mere antiquarian charm, picturesqueness or any other sensational indices. In all this we had the work of Gamio, Redfield and Villa to help us as regards the specific theoretical and practical problems of Mexico.

We are also indebted to other predecessors in the field. Dr Elsie Clews Parsons's book, *Mitla, Town of Souls* (1936), is a storehouse of information. It is invaluable in suggesting local problems and instructing us on many of the customs, ideas and institutions prevalent among the Zapotec Indians. It is invariably a standby in matters of detail, although in method and outlook it is almost diametrically opposed to our own point of view. The contributions of Oscar Schmeider in *The Settlements of the Tzapotec and Mije Indians of the State of Oaxaca, Mexico* (1930), and above all the little book written in a popular style but containing some sound information gathered with scientific method by Messrs Steininger and Van de Velde, *Three Dollars a Year* (1935), were profitably used in our work.

The work of W.C. Bennet and R. Zingg on *The Tarahumara* (1935), and the older fieldwork of K. Lumholtz, could also be mentioned here in the line of important precedents.

Genuine and active interest in Indian welfare is a historical tradition of Mexican policy. But, in order to help and to guide the indigenous part of the population, it is necessary to know this population, to understand its social structure, ideas and economic techniques. Also, it is as well to be in touch with the indigenous point of view and in sympathy with it. All planning and directing, especially in matters affecting humanity, must be based on knowledge. We would not devise roads or bridges and start factories without preliminary study on the part of scientific, competent engineers. We do not organize practical measures in preventive or protective medicine or hygiene without a scientific diagnosis, some laboratory work, and the translation of practical requirements into scientific principles which can then be applied.

The same obtains in our own subject matter. Anthropological and sociological fieldwork must be avowedly and definitely inspired by the consciousness that real science has to submit to the acid test of applicability and practical value. Facts, because they are vital, because they constitute practical problems, are not, therefore, less theoretically relevant or scientifically important. On the contrary, the magnitude of a problem in terms of its real, practical pervasiveness, in terms of how far it affects large masses of human beings, is the index of its interest to a student of man. This was the guiding principle of our research. It appears to us, therefore, advisable to publish even a preliminary account of the work so far done. This will allow us to demonstrate once more the character and the feasibility of the approach, and perhaps also to stimulate some of our fellow-workers to discuss cognate problems and to include them in their fieldwork.

In order to eliminate rather than to provoke misunderstandings, we wish to state quite clearly that our functional approach combines historical interest with scientific and practical orientation. The functional method is in no way opposed to any legitimate historical approach. It attempts to widen and deepen the historical point of view, rather than to discount it. It proposes, above all, to chronicle the contemporary events of Mexican history. It considers that the day-to-day occurrences in the life of the humble and half-educated Indian are as important to the historian as the large-scale world events in which the republic participates as a whole. It assumes that the chronicle of today will become an important historical document of tomorrow. It aims, therefore, at making historical research in the field essentially scientific, in the sense in which economics and sociology, jurisprudence and the study of government can be scientific.

To give an unpretentious yet clear definition of the term, we regard any research primarily based on experience and observation and controlled by general principles as falling within this category. We are interested in testing, on the facts of our observation, some general principles of economics, sociology and political science, as well as psychology. We have not neglected history in the sense of written records, archeological evidence, the analysis of stories and legends, and memories of old people. We are, however, clearly conscious that history is happening before our own eyes and that the history of today must not be consistently sacrificed to the reconstruction of past events from incomplete sources by means of sometimes vague hypotheses. The study of the present in order to obtain the fullest insight into the past, as well as signposts for the future, is our definition of a correct historical method. Thus, we claim that there is no difference as regards respect for history between the functional approach and any other legitimate interest.

In organizing our fieldwork, which is being planned over a period of consecutive visits to the region, we looked for a subject matter to start with. We wanted to find one in which the facts would be accessible, public, non-political, non-esoteric, and yet significant for the study both of traditional modes of life and of problems connected with cultural change and the development of Indian and mestizo culture. The natural choice was the system of markets in the Valley.

The market places of Mexico are the happy hunting-ground of the tourist interested in the varied and picturesque medley of people, objects and customs. They are equally interesting to the anthropologist. They constitute the main economic mechanism of distribution. Observation of the market discloses the manner in which people dispose of their products and acquire their necessities. The market place epitomizes, in short, the economic organization of every district and locality. From every home, from every village and tribal area, we have a concourse to the market place on market day. Members of many social groups bring agricultural produce, the handiwork of their workshops, the product of a factory, a yoke of oxen, an ass or a horse. In a market place one can study the people, the material objects, and also the values and customs displayed, as it were, in an ephemeral, dramatic museum of the day. Religious practices and beliefs can be studied in the adjacent church which is frequently visited on a market day. Old customs and traditional ways are sometimes revealed by a pre-Columbian article, such as a *metate* (grinding-stone), or old types of earthenware or of dress. Usages which do not belong to a developed, monetary, economic system, such as barter, can still be observed. But the market place is also occasionally invaded by the most recent importations from abroad. In educational inscriptions and in the activities of the health services, it becomes the locus and the exponent of progress. At the same time, one can study trade routes dating from pre-Columbian days, or purchase newspapers and articles which have come by train from Mexico City.

In the market place you meet the artisans of the district, you become aware of the industries, local or foreign, which feed the district, and above all you meet the people from the surrounding villages or from distant tribes who come primarily as householders and agricultural producers. Meeting such people in the market leads you directly to homes and to municipalities, and also to the study of agriculture and cattle-raising, and to the technology of workshops and factories. In the market itself, you study directly the main mechanism of distribution, but you learn a great deal about other forms of exchange and collateral transactions. The market, finally, is the place where large groups of consumers purchase practically everything for the satisfaction of their economic needs, and most consumers of the district acquire part, at least, of their supplies. Starting from the market, you are inevitably led to problems of domestic and municipal consumption. The market, in short, is a place where the economic pulse of the region is most easily taken and from which the streams of incoming and outgoing economic life blood can be followed. Having chosen the region of Oaxaca, made archeologically famous through the recent researches of Dr Alfonso Caso, we attempted ethnographically to supplement his work by starting on the market system of Oaxaca Valley.

In the market systems of Mexico, the Zapotec Indians have a well-deserved reputation for commercial talent and economic avarice. They can hold their own against the mestizos, and apparently anywhere in the republic the educated Zapotecs make easy headway in commerce. We also found that wherever a few Zapotecs come together for a saint's day or fiesta, or for a village bullfight, a small market springs up. Some of our native friends would tell with delight and unmistakable passionate interest how, on a small quantity of toys and earthenware taken by rail to Puebla and Mexico, they had made some 5 or 6 pesos net income.[1] If we wanted to coin a neologism in the combined slang of psychoanalysis and advertising, we might speak of the 'commercial libido' of the Zapotecs. Nor are their other partners in the Valley markets very far behind. These remarks are not intended to prove that people in our region are the only good merchants in the republic. Similar observations should be made in other areas, and then a relevant comparison can be made.

The markets of the Valley bear a clear testimony to the commercial abilities of their inhabitants. Up to the present day they show great vitality, which is also attested by the historical records which we have of this district. Except for the capital, many of the towns are just empty shells of large stone buildings, open spaces and wide streets which become filled and alive only on a market day. On such a day the town harbours a temporary population four or five times as large as the normal one. It becomes the stage of a crowded, brisk and extensive performance in trade and commerce. All communication becomes intensified on such a day. The local trains which function, somnolent and empty, twice or thrice a week, run on the market day full to overflowing with people and merchandise. The bus services, multiplied by four or five in number, bring to the market centre people from neighbouring villages and the other towns, as well as the capital. The roads and paths are crowded with people on foot, riding donkeys and horses, or driving in ox-carts. The courtyards and porticoes of the inns and hostelries (*mesones*) fill up with people, merchandise, asses and horses.

Some market places apparently have slightly declined; some have even disappeared. But others are being formed, and in some places, such as Zaachila and Ocotlán, we find a clear increase in activities.

On a market day, in the crowded movement of the place, the observer receives a strong impression of the huge and concentrated vitality and intensity. The market is not noisy or strident. The proceedings are orderly and the crowd quiet. Unlike some other areas in the republic, in Oaxaca markets are not filled with loud calls. No advertising litanies are chanted, nor have the loud-speaker and other contemporary noise-makers yet appeared. Only some of the patent medicine vendors and those who carry round local or Mexican newspapers occasionally call out somewhat unimpressively. One of our friends who has previously worked in the states of Veracruz, Jalisco and Guerrero complained of this: 'The places are dead here. I can not sell my wares. I like shouting and calling people to my stall [*puesto*].'

The rhythm of movement in the market is slow and intense, purposeful and orderly. People walk, looking for the needed articles. They stop, examine the *puesto*, and if attracted, begin to bargain. An unwritten law generally prevents other vendors from intruding and starting competitive bargaining or trying to distract the buyer. Only when the bargaining comes to an end or an impasse are other offers made or articles dangled before the buyer. Sometimes, in a quiet voice, a vendor calls out '*Marchante*! [Buyer!] Look here, come, I have what you want!' Usually the vendor simply sits and waits.

The typical scene in a market section consists of two rows of vendors, one on each side of the path, with groups standing near them. A stream of people move in either direction, at times tied into knots and unable to proceed. The soft, meek, good-natured manner of the local Indians excludes pushing, quarrelling and other disturbances.

The ethnographer becomes easily lost at first, and fieldwork in a market place is by no means easy. The difficulty consists in the chaos of the general picture, combined with the appalling simplicity of each concrete transaction. The chaos makes it difficult to see the wood for the trees. The triteness and finality of each individual act short-circuits any full development of problems, and in a way paralyses observation.

Examples, all taken from actual experience, will illustrate the point. The ethnographer sits down on a kerbstone beside a woman who sells small lumps of cheese. Like most of the poor vendors, she is friendly and talkative, and after accepting a couple of cigarettes and a few centavos she gives information which proves to be correct on further checking. She came to the market with 3 pesos' worth of stock-in-trade. She sells her pieces at 3, 5 or 10 centavos. Her net gain averages 75 centavos or maybe a peso during the day. Poor peasants or Indians from remote districts buy cheese to eat with their tortillas. The story is short, simple and apparently ends all inquiries.

The ethnographer moves to a more sophisticated selling site, where a professional vendor sells *rebozos* (shawls). An Indian family are crowded near his booth. They bargain, and finally buy a shawl for the eldest daughter. The transaction has been observed from start to finish. The price asked is 5 pesos, the counter-offer 3. The sale goes at 4. Similar transactions are being observed in the adjoining booth. We know that the price of an article sold at 3 pesos in Ocotlán or Ejutla is about 2 or 2.25 pesos if bought from the producer in Oaxaca, so the profit can be calculated. Once more, the story is short, simple and may seem devoid of consequences.

We may move to the Indians who barter their fruit and vegetables. An impressive uniformity obtains here, and once more, after having registered six or seven transactions, we move on. We stop at a site for selling medicinal herbs, which arouse our ethnographic and antiquarian interest. Yet here also one sale follows another, at times rapidly, at times very slowly. The notebook is filled with figures and names of articles, and the work seems to be finished.

In the cattle market we can spend hours without witnessing as much as one transaction. When it comes, we note the price, which is registered officially by a municipal supervisor, and our work is over. In the maize market, where invariably trade is brisker, measure after measure is sold. We distinguish between very small quantities displayed by some vendors and the large site obviously manipulated by a *regatón* (re-vendor), and here the story ends.

The task would seem simple. We might rewrite our notes; make a full inventory of the various dealings; give vivid impressions of sight, movement and even smell; show the medley of goods and types, the hither and thither of the people, and illustrate it with a few photographs.

A very good example of such excellent but 'first approach' observations of a market scene are to be found in Dr Parsons's book. There we also find excellent data on commercial journeys in the district, which we have utilized and acknowledge here with gratitude. Yet Dr Parsons, who apparently is convinced that the fieldworker's task is to 'collect facts', has not tried functionally to relate her observations, nor yet to follow up all the implications of economic and sociological relevance which they contain.

After the data registered thus are looked at carefully, we see that we are just at the beginning of our task. Some real problems begin to emerge. First the question arises, how can we tame and harness the complexity of details, first impressions and other raw data of early observation? To make them manageable, significant and, above all, related to one another we must reduce the chaotic picture into documents which can be handled. We apply here the old principle of 'documentation by concrete evidence' in the form of plans, diagrams and numerical computations.[2]

In *Argonauts of the Western Pacific* (1922) by B. Malinowski, especially Chapter 1, sections 5 and 8, the principles of method followed in this study were first formulated. The method of concrete documentation has been even more fully developed in the same writer's *Coral Gardens and Their Magic* (2 vols, 1935), where the numerous plans, maps, diagrams, tables of evidence and quantitative computations illustrate the method.

After the chaotic complexity of the market place is reduced to manageable documents, we can start the real theoretical task of digesting the evidence. Facts have to be related, implications drawn, and the ethnographer has to see where and how far his market data allow him to peer behind the scenes of what is happening then and there. The details given in our examples, at first sight simple and nonconsequential, obtain significance and lead to new problems. Take our cheese vendor. She sells her pieces of cheese at 5 centavos each. In order to calculate the profit, it is not enough to take her word. We have to inquire where she obtains the cheese and how much she pays for it.

The question further emerges, What is her role in the market? Is there any real need for a reseller? Why does the producer not appear personally? Again, it is somewhat difficult to understand how a woman, however, old and unassuming, can live on the 75 centavos or 1 peso which she earns during the only market day of the week. We are thus led to inquire into her social position, and into any income which she might enjoy besides her market earnings. In this case, as in many others, we found that many people who actually live with their families and are provided with their subsistence add to their livelihood by occasional visits to the market.

When we look more carefully at the clientele of this woman, the poorer peasants or Indians, we discover by totalling their gains on a market day that they also are marginal cases. They live at the threshold of bare subsistence. To understand the role of such persons in the market, we also have to inquire what they produce, and why they attend the market. They come, at times, considerable distances. What is their standard of living at home? The less impecunious professional merchants also present problems which emerge from an analysis of their dealings. Do they also have to make a livelihood from the couple of pesos earned during a day? We meet some of them all over the district, attending practically every market. This throws some light on the nature of their business. We have, however, to pry into the accountancy of their commerce, as well as into their own personal budgets, as these are related to their standard of living. Thus, the more fully the first-approach evidence is scrutinized, the more directly it leads to problems of an economic and sociological nature; that is, to questions of profit and standard of living, to detailed inquiries including those into the costs of transportation, types of provision, production and consumption.

Another observation which the ethnographer soon makes is that the market spills over its stricter and narrower physical limits. After their market dealings are finished, the natives go to the adjacent grocery or textile shops. They may sit down in groups under some portico and eat in the open food, some of which they had brought, some purchased. Some might go into the church, pray, wail, rub their faces, necks and heads with sprigs of flowers from the altar, sanctified by contact with divinity.

This introduces two important sidelines of theoretical inquiry. In the first place, we realize that the market is primarily an economic mechanism. The question thus emerges how far most of the participants attended purely or mainly with economic motives. This question leads us to two lines of inquiry. We have to define the concept of *economic*, not in terms of philosophy or of a new system, but directly with reference to our problem, to our area and to such facts as can be actually observed. We have taken the most concrete and simple definition. The economic aspect of any transaction is that it links this transaction with the processes of production, exchange and consumptions. In so far as a complex act contributes towards the maintenance of an individual or a group, it has an economic side.

In the second place, the spilling over from the market to the other surrounding institutions forces the ethnographer to contextualize his observations and to relate them to all those factors which influence commercial dealings in the first place. The study of transport facilities and transport costs, the inquiry into the organization and functions of the *mesones*, and the subsidiary and, at the same time, important role played by the shops – all these are subjects without which the study and description of the market place is incomplete. Incidentally, we have drawn up plans and taken photographs of all these collateral factors and activities.[3]

Relating two other types of commercial establishments with the market raises the problem of why the majority of dealings take place in the market. Detailed observations of the behaviour of Indians in a shop compared with on the market site have given us interesting indications. From direct conversations with some participants casually met in the market, but especially with some of our best informants, we were provided with even better data. As sound 'behaviourists' in the ethnographic sense, we realize that speech is also a system of behaviour, and when it is related to collateral action and well checked by further observations, it can provide conclusions which a dogmatic behaviourist might miss. We obtained a flood of light on many questions of native outlook and behaviour when, after a good deal of direct experience, we discussed our conclusions with some men and women who, though Zapotec peasants and people of a humble station in life, could give us clear, reliable and intelligent comments on their own activities and those of others. Our friend Manuel of Abasolo told us – often with detail and with a sound sense of humour – about some of his own exploits, including tricks and even minor frauds. He once acted as agent for a large buyer of maize. He has attended most of the markets, often lost money, and equally often has been able to drive hard and successful bargains. He and several others, whose confidence and, I might almost say, friendship we gained, provided us with details of events which were as illuminating as they were trustworthy – trustworthy since they were afterwards checked and found to be correct.

In this manner the inchoate mass of impressions, disparate data and statements was gradually sorted out, documented and translated into problems of economics, social control, native ideology and the tastes, preferences and values of the inhabitants of the Valley and the surrounding mountain ranges. We were gradually able to differentiate social groups of producers, consumers and merchants. We achieved a classification of articles with reference to primary production, native manufactures, traditional craft and imports. It became possible to concentrate more fully on such articles as maize, which determined the price level of the market, and other important consumers' goods, such as vegetables, meat, bread and earthenware. The concrete data will be found in the following sections.

In the background loomed the question of the integral function of the market place. At first many an easy and superficial suggestion occurred to us or was suggested by some of our more 'intellectual' informants from the educated class. 'The market is a survival.' 'The natives like the market.' 'On the market day it is cheaper to buy.' Facts showed the futility of some of these answers, and investigation disclosed the emptiness of others. We soon discovered that the Indians or peasants never go to amuse themselves or for any other collateral reason. They go to the market to transact business. In comparing the behaviour of a simple villager in a shop and in the market place we soon found, through the study of detail and through the interpretations of natives, that in the market villagers enjoy facilities which they greatly appreciate and which bring the transaction within the range of their traditional habits, not only as regards the immediate act, but also with reference to their role as producer, buyer and consumer. We gradually came to the conclusions, for which evidence will be found in the following pages, that the market is indispensable as a combined mechanism for the convenient acquisition of purchasing power and as an extensive emporium which caters, through the great variety of goods exhibited, and the ease of choice, to the necessities of the native. The function of the market is closely related to the hand-to-mouth existence of the poorest Indians. It is also related to the short-term budget of the majority of the inhabitants of the area, townsmen, villagers and mountain Indians alike. The regular flow of limited income from the sale of the producers' commodities and the small range of consumers' requirements combine to make the market in the Valley a well-adjusted mechanism for the satisfaction of most economic needs of the participants. As further and related functions, we found that the market is also the main mechanism for establishing price levels in the staple goods, above all maize, but also cattle, vegetables and meat. The market is still the best way for the large-scale exporter to acquire the commodities he wishes to pool, and through this he and his numerous agents and independent middlemen gain the greater part of their income.

2 General aspects of trade in the Valley, and a visit to the market place of Oaxaca

The market system consists primarily of the big market place in Oaxaca, the capital, and of the related dominant markets at Ocotlán, Tlacolula, Etla, Zimatlán, Zaachila and Ejutla. Its unity is determined by a number of physical and cultural factors. Looking at a map of Mexico, we see that the state of Oaxaca adjoins to the north the region which was under Aztec domination when Hernán Cortés arrived. To the south of the Valley, and connected by natural trade routes, lies the Mexican isthmus, the bottleneck of all communication, trade and cultural influences between Central and North America. Our district, therefore, is one of the principal links between two vast and historically, as well as archeologically and ethnographically, important cultural areas. The Aztecs, in order to control some of the trade routes to the isthmus and beyond, maintained a garrison on the very spot where the capital of Oaxaca is now.

Oaxaca is the centre of a natural basin consisting of several valleys at an altitude of 1,500 metres, surrounded by several mountain chains. The basin is, in the first place, more fertile than the adjacent mountains, and it must always have been, as it is now, easier to traverse and supply with good means of communication. It is, also, the natural meeting ground and outlet for the inhabitants of the surrounding mountain ranges. The elevation, climate, rainfall and winds are fairly uniform in the Valley. Some of its parts are more fertile, especially those which have a better supply of water, or else are naturally saturated.

Culturally and historically, the Valley has thus been the centre of political control, communications and trade routes, and it is the seat of pre-Columbian cultures. The recent discoveries of Dr Caso, as well as previous archeological work, have laid bare remnants of old civilizations, mainly Zapotec or Mixtec. The whole area is indeed dotted with mounds and barrows, testifying to the architectural activities of the prehistoric inhabitants. Ethnographically we have at least three main

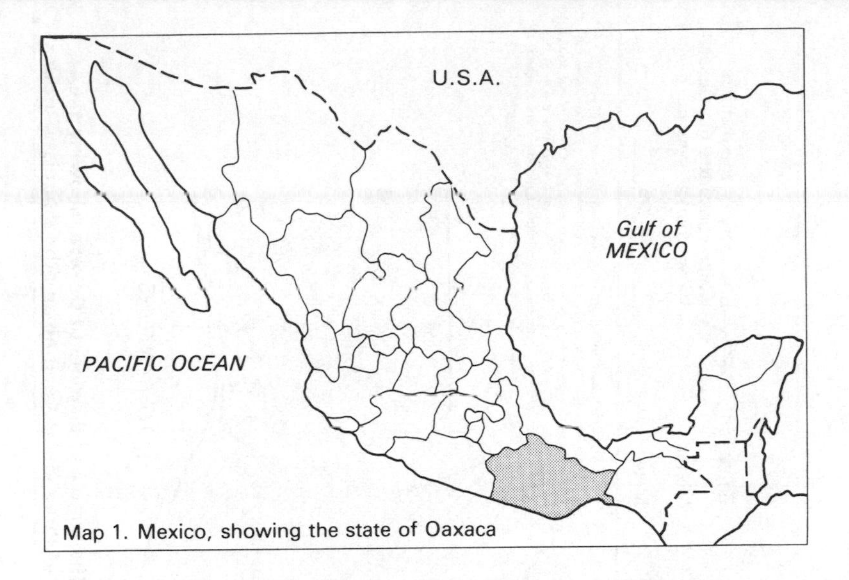

Map 1. Mexico, showing the state of Oaxaca

stocks to consider, since we meet representatives of them in many a market place. Those are the Zapotecs, the Mixtecs, and the Mixes. As regards the new population, especially urban, we meet the mestizos, that is the real Mexicans, who almost invariably boast of Indian as well as Spanish blood. In addition, immigrant Spaniards of the first or second generation play an important economic role in this area, as do a very few foreigners, such as Syrians, Greeks and Italians, and one or two Germans and French, mostly engaged in business on a larger scale. Most of the British and American entrepreneurs withdrew from the scene during the revolutionary years and the following economic reforms.

Historically, we do not need to go beyond the well-attested fact that the Valley was the centre of political units formed by Zapotecs, who were at war with Mixtec kingdoms [see Paddock, 1966; Whitecotton, 1977]. Supremacy moved between the two groups. The most important capitals were probably Teotitlán del Valle and Zaachila, which at present are reduced to second-rate or even third-rate importance. They are still fairly populous villages with their own industries and commerce. The village of Mitla, at the south-east of our basin of valleys, was the centre of the mortuary and religious cult of the district, a fact still attested by imposing ruins of temples and tombs to be found in the area. At the time of the conquest and following the Aztec

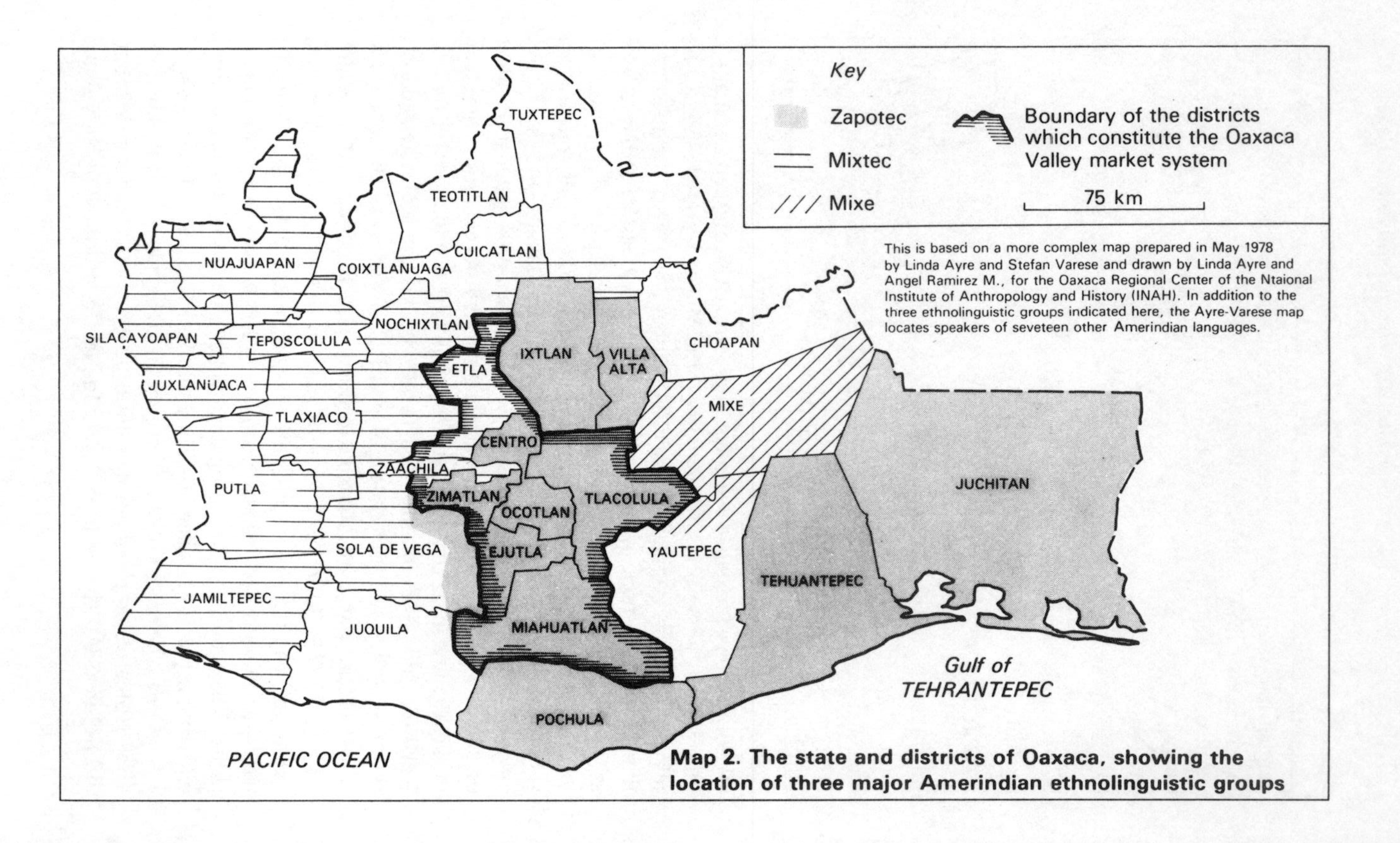

Map 2. The state and districts of Oaxaca, showing the location of three major Amerindian ethnolinguistic groups

invaders, the Spaniards occupied Oaxaca (1522). Oaxaca became the capital of the province, the seat of a bishopric, and it soon gained commercial importance. After independence it became the capital of a state, and for a very short period became a sovereign political unit. The charm of the landscape, the fertility of the soil and the dominant position of the area are documented by the fact that Hernán Cortés, the Conquistador of Mexico, chose the title Marqués of the Valley of Oaxaca, and acquired large estates in this region [Chance, 1978].

We have now to take a direct look at what actually happens in one of our markets. In Oaxaca the business of the market is to be found in the immediate neighbourhood of the *zócalo*, or central place round which are crowded the cathedral and the government building, the museum and the local colleges. From the inevitable *zócalo*, we travel one block south down a busy street with shops, in which Indians, as well as townsmen, crowd on a busy day. If it be a Saturday, the street fills early; people stand and look at shop windows or discuss prices, elegantly dressed Spaniards mixing with Mixe Indians in rags and tatters. Occasionally the old Mexican *huipilli* [Nahuatl: a woman's blouse] can be seen worn by a woman from the Sierra or a characteristic dress from the Isthmus appears on a lady from Tehuantepec. The main market itself is lodged in a large building of concrete and mortar. It consists of four wings, all alike, with tin roofs, surrounding a central uncovered patio with a fountain. The adjacent streets already constitute an open market.

As we approach we see and hear a singer or a group of singers surrounded by a crowd of people. This is one of the regular appurtenances, the typical recreations which function at every market place. The songs are partly devoted to amorous recitals, but also to politics, satire, patriotism and religion. The singers expect a donation, or they sell their songs printed on thin paper.

Leaving the group and walking along the street to the north, we see a stall with pineapples sold by a man from Ejutla. Passing through a display of ready-made clothing for men, in which trousers and coats are placed in bundles on a mat directly on the pavement, we approach a long row of some twenty to forty vegetable vendors. They all come from the same village, Tlacochahuaya, which is located in the centre of an exceptionally fertile and well-irrigated agricultural district. The village specializes in horticulture, and we would see on this spot people with fresh vegetables according to the season: tomatoes or chillies, spinach or cauliflowers. From the same village there are always, and in every market, half a dozen or more women selling spices. Mexican cooking is always highly seasoned. Besides the traditional chilli and pepper, such herbs as caraway seeds, rosemary, parsley and some twenty others, of which we have collected the Spanish and Zapotec names although not yet the botanical descriptions, are carefully dried in the village and sold in small quantities directly to the consumer.

[J.D.L.F. notes that the spinach and cauliflower come from Oaxaca rather than Tlacochahuaya.]

Walking along the street, the tourist, as well as the anthropologist, would probably be tempted by a wide open portal leading through a massive doorway into an imposing courtyard surrounded by two storeys of arched colonnades. This is the Casa Fuerte, once an imposing colonial building, now one of the important attractive sites of the city and the principal hostelry of Oaxaca. The doorway is usually crowded with people coming and going, driving their horses and burros. There are three of four vendors of water, local *pulque* [maguey beer] and sweetmeats.

In the doorway also, on a comfortable seat, the landlady of the place sits and collects fees. For every ass 5 centavos are taken, and the same sum is paid for a night spent on a mat under the arcades, while a higher fee is charged for the rent of a room. The courtyard is filled with beasts of burden, predominantly donkeys. In the background a few barbers are busy in the open air under one of the arcades. One of the corners is adapted as a place of storage for merchandise. We obtain a better view from the second floor, where we can survey the courtyard and the surrounding arcades. Some sixty to two hundred animals may be standing, left for the day, while people lie, sit or walk under the arcades. The rooms upstairs are used for lodgings, mostly without bedsteads, for the people sleep on reed mats or mattresses on the floor. Near the entrance we would see two or three people selling fodder, usually alfalfa, two or three handfuls for 5 centavos.

Leaving the hostelry and walking west, we see the north front of the new market place with open shops. A rough survey would disclose that unrefined brown sugar in chunks is sold from tables put on the street. As we walked along, we would see the ices, vegetables and again brown sugar displayed in the street. Behind, in the open shops of the market building, fourteen butchers' establishments retail the meat for the town. The tourist or ethnographer who would like first to take stock of all that happens and retain impressions, might then enter the building through the middle gateway in the north front. Passing a few small tables where bread, chillies and fresh water are retailed, we would enter a gallery where we see permanent stalls for the first time. Here professional merchants sell ready-made clothes, materials, grips and valises, and also an important garment used by the Mexican woman, the head-shawl or *rebozo*.

Going directly towards the central open space, we would leave on the right hand fixed stalls with hardware merchants, bottle vendors, sellers of chillies, and beyond those the two galleries filled with eating places. On the left we would see in the distance the main bakers' stalls and the assortment of fresh water sellers, mercers and some sellers of fruit. The part through which we pass is filled with textiles, mostly made locally, and there are one or two sellers of earthenware. Around the central fountain and large basin of water a picturesque medley of small sites, where mostly Indians sell their apples, peaches, and peanuts and chillies, gives a crowded and agitated impression. On one side locally made soap is displayed in boxes and on tables. Round the fountain also there is usually a crowd of people, who come from various parts of the market to refresh their flowers, wash some articles or fill vessels. Going further south, we pass through an astonishingly large display of flowers, vegetables and dairy products, once more leaving to the right a large section filled with more substantial vegetable stalls and, as we proceed further, leather products and ropes, net bags and other articles made of *ixtle*, a fibre made from the maguey plant (*Agave americana*).

To the left are dairy products and vegetables, and immediately beyond them is an imposing permanent display of large Mexican hats made locally of wool. Thus, we enter the southern side, where poorer vegetables, inferior meats, and tortillas are sold in the open by the producers. Once out in the street, we would perceive on our right on any market day a display of quicklime, sweet potatoes and groundnuts. Were we to proceed to our left, that is, go east and turn, walking along the street which runs east of the market, the first section we would see would be filled with vendors of the same type of fruit we have already seen in the street running south of the market. Diminutive apples, peaches bruised and broken, bananas, walnuts and groundnuts, according to season, are brought here, usually by the poorest Indians, often from long distances. These goods are sold at prices ranging from 1 to 10 centavos, according to quantity and quality. This street, but not this street alone, is flanked by groceries and *cantinas*, or Mexican taverns, which in this region mostly deal in *mezcal*, alcohol distilled from the maguey. On a detailed computation we counted as many as two hundred odd vendors of fruit, nuts and vegetables in one morning. Comparing this with the large number of vegetable vendors from Tlacochahuaya or with the fourteen permanent butchers' shops, or with some twenty-five permanent stalls within the market, the figure gives an idea of the small scale and poverty of this class of vendor. On a market day we would find that the corresponding street to the west of the market is almost completely filled with earthenware.

The tourist who craves for an old setting and picturesque detail in the market will probably not linger in the ugly new building with its iron railings and pillars, tin roof and concrete, but will cross the street and enter the smaller market of San Juan de Dios. This nestles behind the old church of the same name, and consists of a large, uncovered area surrounded by four open galleries extended along attractive pink walls. Part of the area is occupied by five or six permanent little huts, which can be closed for the night and in which professional merchants sell earthenware. Besides this we have, in the open space between the pillars, two main markets, one composed of the products of rush reed and bamboo: mats, plaited baskets, and heavier, larger baskets made of wickerwork. Here, also, on the east side, are the permanent sites for the sale of maize which extend on market day to the street which runs south of the enclosures. This street serves also as market place for sugar-cane in season, and further to the west it is filled with large heaps of fodder as well as with the ox-carts which bring them.

The long corridor which leads into the enclosure behind the church of San Juan de Dios may make the strongest impression on the visitor. Picturesqueness is often associated with a certain lack of cleanliness, as well as with strong smells. Both sides of this corridor are filled with meat stalls, kitchens, and braziers on which the steak which you buy for 5 or 10 centavos can be immediately roasted. Within the enclosed space of the long, sombre, vaulted corridor, smoke, pungent smells, flies and human odours concentrate and accentuate the Rembrandtesque atmosphere of the place.

The picture of the market is not yet finished, even if we only deal with superficial impressions and general stock-taking. The competent guide who would like to show us all that is alive, active and relevant on a market day would lead us along the street where maize is sold, through the heaps of fodder and accumulations of unharnessed ox-carts, and once more through a large doorway into an open space, which is the market for asses and pigs. The testing of the animals requires a study in itself, as do the processes of bargaining and final sale. At a table in the doorway to this place, there sits the *registrador* who registers the sales and, of course, collects a fee. He is not the only tax collector present, as the natives will tell you with some acrimony during practically every conversation. The mestizo who carries on more regular business will also refer to him with due political comment. Cattle are sold in a different courtyard one block to the north of the market described here. The proceedings there are less dramatic. You see a group of oxen standing and ruminating and a group of people walking and looking. Here, too, the inevitable *registrador* sits in the doorway.

We have so far given a general survey: a rough inventory which indicates the various factors present for a study of the market place. But the competent guide and informant who leads intelligent tourists or assists the ethnographer at the beginning of his fieldwork would not stop here. He would point out that at the south-eastern corner of the market place is the administrative office of the deputy of the Market Administration (Administración de Mercados). The main business transacted there is taxation. For each place in the market, for every transaction carried out in one of the hostelries, for all the goods brought into the town, something has to be paid. Most of the difficulties and disputes in the market place centre on this. Apart from this, the maintenance of order is handled according to customary and traditional rules by the people themselves.[1] Indeed, during the time of our joint fieldwork, and also during the much longer period which one of us (J. D. L. F.) spent in this region and in adjacent parts, hardly any serious disputes were observed. Not only law and custom, but even the manners of the market place, are remarkably well ordered.[2]

Were we to look for all the places, activities and interests which affect the behaviour of those who come to participate in the market, we would have to visit and observe several more factors. First of all, we would find that many people attend churches early in the morning and occasionally come in to pray, to adore the saints, to rub themselves with the health-giving flowers from the altar during the day. The most important place from this point of view is the church of the patron saint of Oaxaca, La Virgen de la Soledad. There early in the morning the local inhabitants, but above all the Indians from the surrounding ranges, make offerings in money and candles to the patron saint, so as to be successful in business. Obviously, if a feast day in any of the local churches coincides with market day, the attendance is greater, but there is a regular type of religious devotion connected with the success of a market place.

We have already met singers, and there are one or two soothsayers who prophesy using canaries. The activities of patent-medicine vendors belong to an intermediate category – partly economic, partly medicinal. They may even be counted as entertainment. Here we might mention one of the oldest and most traditional types of commodities sold in the market: the medicinal herbs for which, in Oaxaca, there are some six or eight selling sites distributed over the market. When there has been a feast in one of the suburbs, a merry-go-round, swings and so on remain for several days, and are patronized by children and adults.

The main diversion, however, consists in meeting friends, talking to them and drifting into one of the bars. The Indians from the surrounding ranges here celebrate their successful business deals, and can be seen moving on definitely alcoholic trajectories. However, crude, excessive and aggressive drunkenness is not characteristic of market day. Some respect for the powers of the police is probably a factor in the situation.

The student of the market system would draw in two more important factors. So far we have dealt with the main market in the centre. The capital boasts three more markets, each directly adjacent to and often named after one of the famous churches of Oaxaca. We have the market of La Merced, that of El Carmen and that of La Soledad, the latter usually, however, named El Marquesado. Each of them is organized and arranged very much on the same pattern as the main market, only on a smaller scale and with the distinct predominance of foodstuffs over textiles, hardware and earthenware. Each of these smaller markets normally supplies the adjacent suburbs. Whether or not the local population attend the 'suburban' markets or the central Oaxaca market is a matter of convenience and location, rather than of differentiation of role.

Another important type of competition with the large market is to be found in the permanent shops. As we walk along the streets surrounding the market, which constitute the commercial district of the town, we find some shops where objects which are not to be found in the market at all are sold. Here we can enter the liquor stores – no liquor is sold in the open market place; the pharmacists' shops; shops selling musical instruments; and, of course, shops which sell predominantly modern manufactured articles imported from abroad. There are others, such as grocers', hardware stores and textile shops where certain types of more expensive, more refined or more specialized articles can be found, not to be obtained in the market. Thus, even the poorest and humblest Indian has to go to a shop if his village needs a modern lamp or maybe a guitar, or if he, by any chance, wants to acquire the luxury of a pair of shoes. Ordinarily, however, only the more progressive peasants from the Valley, those who speak Spanish and who prefer quality to cheapness, would buy their groceries and textiles, or their bread, at one of the shops. Why they prefer the market to the shops is interesting as an economic, social and psychological question. Below we shall have a few words to say about it.

Our walk across and around the market took place on the full market day, that is, Saturday. In the following chapter we will deal with the daily sequence, the weekly rotation and the annual cycle of the market. It is possible here to indicate rapidly some other variations. In most markets we find principally the eating places, a number of vegetable and fruit vendors, and the butchers' shops opening very early. By noon the whole market is in full swing, including the sale of cattle and beasts of burden, and of goods in the surrounding shops. In the afternoon, when the main market gradually subsides, the careful observer might notice an additional phenomenon: there are pedlars who carry some of the remainder of their wares from house to house across the city. This house-to-house commerce is characteristic of every day and of every place in our region, even including small villages where vendors and pedlars from neighbouring places often hawk vegetables, fruit, eggs and other articles, purchased at a large centre.

A description of an ordinary day in the city of Oaxaca would show that the market invariably functions, but in a much reduced form. The streets are now practically empty, with the exception of a few permanent stalls and the southern street facing the church of San Juan de Dios, which fills out with three or four earthenware displays. Again, we might walk through the town during one of the village fairs, a religious fiesta or a national celebration. On such a date, whatever the day of the week, the market takes on a similar appearance to a Saturday market. There are one or two principal festivities. On each such occasion, the market assumes special characteristics. Thus, one of the most important celebrations is the combined feast of All Saints and All Souls.[3] About a fortnight before, a large market is held on a Saturday. This is the 'market of the outsiders' (*plaza de los de fuera*). On this date people come from near and far to acquire textiles for festive apparel, gifts for family and friends, but above all with the necessary items of food. Of course, the middlemen will also buy the necessary articles to retail them later on in their own local markets. There are a number of special items of food produced for that occasion. Many of those will be ritually offered to the spirits of the departed in the church and the cemeteries, to be afterwards consumed within the family. [See photo 22.]

The 'bread of the departed' (*pan de muertos*) is prepared in a special shape symbolically representing the human being. Sweets are also shaped in special forms, and pieces of chocolate are specially produced for the occasion. At this time, also, enormous quantities of fruit will be sold and consumed, and a large crop of flowers appears on the market, to be offered in church and on the domestic altar. The observer finds the prevalence of flowers throughout the market places of the region somewhat mysterious, until he has learned that all of them will be used to adorn the altars in the church and the domestic altar which appears in every Mexican house, however poor and run-down.

The market on this day is near to the churchyard and presbytery. Masses for the dead are supplied by the church, but votive offerings to God and the saints have all to be supplied from the market. Candles have to be bought, incense and flowers purchased, and at the same time, many toys, sweets and chocolates are sold, which the purchaser will afterwards place on the graves of children or adults. The ritual offering of cooked food on the graves and on the domestic altars stimulates also the purchase of fowl, including turkey, and better quality meat, as well as the condiments which are necessary in the preparation. All such food is naturally offered to the spirits, but eaten by the living. [See photo 22.]

Another important feast which determines the economic aspect of marketing is that of the patron saint, La Virgen de la Soledad. While the previously described celebrations associated with saint and spirit are, on the whole, sober if not sombre, now the town attracts merry-go-rounds, swings, chairs hung on chains rotating round a pole (*voladoras*), as well as games of chance. This time the main market is held, not in the principal place, but around the church, in the streets, park and churchyard. As in all the fiesta markets, large and small, four elements predominate: food, recreation, sacred objects and refreshments. This feast occurs soon after the pilgrimage to the Pacific coast shrine of La Virgen de Juquila, so sweets made of coconut, small fresh coconuts, bananas, preserved and fresh, and other tropical or semi-tropical fruits are characteristic of the festivity.

During the period of Christmas celebrations the traditional Feast of the Radish (*fiesta del rábano*) takes place. The largest radishes obtainable are cut in the shape of the human face and decorated, or dressed in masks, and displayed and carried round in procession. There is also a lively market in which ample provision has to be made for the sumptuous Christmas Eve vegetarian meal, which contains fish but no meat, that has to be provided for rich and poor.

De la Fuente: *The luxurious salad is for the upper class alone. It is possible that poorer people may eat dried fish, but I was occasionally told that on Christmas Eve there was no special diet. Some people eat fresh greens with vinegar and sugar, and there is a kind of special fast (*vigilia*) among the poorer people.*

In Oaxaca itelf, a special type of sweet pancake (*bunuelo*) is prepared, and the plate on which these are offered has to be broken afterwards. The destruction of earthenware vessels and other domestic goods is characteristic of the day preceding New Year's celebration.

De la Fuente: *Breaking the* bunuelo *plates begins at the celebration for the Virgin of Solitude (La Soledad) and continues till New Year. The breakage of inexpensive earthenware which occurs at the New Year is not generalized throughout the Valley and seems to occur on the last day of the old year rather than on the first day of the new year.*

These brief indications must suffice for a rapid inventory and characterization of the market system in the capital, as related to the social, religious and ritual life of the community.

3 The Valley markets in their cultural and economic interdependence

We have seen that the Valley is a definite geographical and economic unit. So is the market system of the Valley. Were we to start our work at any point within the natural basin of our district, our inquiries would lead us invariably to the capital as the centre of the related market places. We would find that a considerable quantity of merchandise comes from there, and some of the local produce purchased by the middleman is, in turn, transported to the capital. From everywhere the lines of communication, the mechanisms of distribution or of pooling, converge on the town of Oaxaca. This is due both to the physical configuration of the district and to its cultural re-shaping by man. As a political centre, the see of a bishopric, the place where banks, wholesale companies and various educational institutions and administrative agencies are situated, Oaxaca is the focal point of the region. This region embraces not merely the valleys, but the surrounding slopes and mountain ranges from which the Indians and mestizos, as producers and as consumers, descend to carry on their commerce.

At the same time the system of markets is segmented. The main centre is related to other market places, such as Ocotlán, Tlacolula, Etla and others, and through them it is related to other districts. Each surrounding district, again, has its centre, the groups of villages which immediately surround the centre, and also its adjacent hinterland. All these factors characterize and determine the nature of the specific market place. The differentiation between the districts as regards production, natural resources and the consumers' needs integrates the system. In short, the fact that at one place you can buy certain articles at a good price, while in the same place you are prepared to purchase others at a higher price stimulates the flow of goods and of merchants, and establishes the interdependence of the component parts.

It hardly needs to be stressed that we do not present here the market system of the Valley as a self-contained unit with fixed limits.

Were we, starting from Oaxaca, to move through Ocotlán, through Ejutla, and then proceed to Miahuatlán, we would obviously find that this place is commercially related with regions further south. From here, as everywhere else, we might make a circuit of the world if we wanted to follow up each connecting thread of the last link studied. Indeed, it will be made clear that the capital itself is directly related to other large centres in the republic, and through them to the wide world. The extent of these relationships and their limitations, as well as the economic barriers to any great influence by the outside world on our system, will be clearly indicated. The facts presented in this memoir, however, will show that the system is a natural unit very much dependent on its component parts and in a limited manner dependent on world markets. The weekly variations in the price of maize at Ocotlán, and even at the smaller market place at San Pedro Apóstol, have their repercussions on every market in our system. They affect, in very exceptional circumstances, the other markets of the republic. In turn, what happens in a market place in Puebla, Jalapa or Mexico is hardly felt at all in the selling and buying of our area. The exact limits of our system have not been fully established in our investigation so far. It will be necessary to carry further specific investigations to the north of Etla and to the south of Ejutla in order to define where the influence of the capital and its surrounding districts begins to fade into insignifance.

The centre of our system, Oaxaca, supplies its own inhabitants, numbering about 30,000.[1] For this purpose there is not only the weekly large market on Saturdays, but daily markets in the main establishment and in three additional ones. The surrounding villages also depend primarily on these markets. As regards the hinterland, Oaxaca is important to all the adjacent regions. We meet here the Indians from the northern Sierra Juarez, from the mountains of the Mixe, from the extensive ethnographic areas of the Mixtecas, and from the western ranges inhabited by a few Zapotec villages, but mostly by Mixtec.[2]

Incidentally, the terminology adopted here, in which 'villagers', 'peasants' and 'Indians' are frequently mentioned, does not pretend to refer to any precise racial or cultural differentiation. The term 'villagers' is used in opposition to townspeople. It covers any inhabitant from a rural district. The term 'Indian' might be applied to a number of villages in the Valley, where the vernacular is spoken and some of the cultural characteristics of the Zapotec group obtain. For purposes of having a few synonyms available we are also making the following distinctions which refer to the occupational character of the inhabitants: 'villager' means an inhabitant of any peasant community; 'peasant' means a native from the Valley engaged in the typical agricultural pursuits or the traditional craft of his community; 'Indian' means a member of the more definitely tribal, traditional communities from the adjacent mountain ranges.

Oaxaca is the main link in the connections by railway, by telephone and telegraph, and even by air, with the outer world. In Oaxaca the old historic and prehistoric routes leading to the Isthmus, to Puebla via Huajuapan, and to the southern and western districts of Pochutla and Juquila converge. In many ways Oaxaca thus controls the whole market system with its hinterlands, approaches and more distant sources of supply. It does not, however, monopolize the system. Ocotlán has primary control over its immediate neighbourhood, important because of its productivity in maize, vegetables and as a centre for cattle. Through the commercial enterprise of some of its residents, many of the long-distance commercial journeys are undertaken from this centre.

Ocotlán is the gateway to the southern districts, and links the other markets of our system directly with Ejutla, and through it with Miahuatlán and the region of Pochutla. To the district of Ocotlán cattle are first brought from the south and south-west. Cattle can be better grazed there in preparation for sale. Ocotlán, on the whole, enjoys the reputation of being the cheapest market in cattle, maize and many vegetable products.

Tlacolula is the focal point of the long valley running south-east from Oaxaca as far as Mitla, and connecting the the valley of Totolapa. The Tlacolula valley is more liable to drought, except at one or two points round Tlacolula where agriculture flourishes and feeds the surrounding district. Tlacolula is also the place where the Mixes enter the Valley, and where many of the products from the Sierra Juarez are brought to the market.

Etla has a very fertile but limited neighbourhood, in which maize and, to a large extent, wheat are grown. It is renowned for its bread and for its cheese industry. Its hinterland consists of the northern parts of the Sierra Juarez and also of the large Mixtec region. Mixtecs attend this market quite as often as that of Oxaca. The exact relationship between Etla and the northern part of the Valley constitutes one of the problems yet to be tackled in our prospective fieldwork.

The two neighbouring places of Zaachila and Zimatlán lie in a very fertile, naturally drained district renowned for sugar-cane, beans, many vegetables and flowers. The district is also well supplied with walnuts, which grow on the lower slopes of the nearby mountains. The Indians who attend these markets from the adjacent highlands belong to a small group of Zapotec villages (see Steininger and Van de Velde, 1935) as well as many Mixtec communities.

Ejutla, at the southern margin of the region, lies in a relatively dry and agriculturally not very productive region. There is some mining in the district, which hardly affects the local markets, except in so far as it is a source of income for native labour. A good deal of castor-oil plant is grown, and there are several presses in the town. Here, incidentally, we have one of the articles in which the regional market has been directly affected by world events. Castor oil is the best lubricant for the most delicate internal combustion engines. The World War, with its great consumption of castor oil as a result of the extensive use of military aircraft, has sent the price of castor oil soaring. Thus the natives of the peaceful valley are able to sell a single measure (*almud*) of their ricinus seeds at almost treble the former price (43 centavos instead of 15), while at the same time those who burn their little lamps in front of the holy image have to pay more. On the whole, the ruthless aerial warfare of the Nazis has benefited the natives of Ejutla and of its district.

De la Fuente: *The same is also said to be true of alfalfa. As far as castor oil is concerned I think the increased use of the oil for soap-making both in Mexico and in Oaxaca accounts for the rise in price. The price rise began five years ago. The Cultural Mission in several places taught how to extract oil from the seed with rudimentary methods, such as one finds in Roalo.*[3]

Having thus given a brief characterization of each centre, district and hinterland, and shown how the differentiation leads to interdependence, and through this to unity in the territorial sense, we can pass now to the time element. The market days in our district follow a weekly routine. Although two market days may overlap (see Table 1) the overlapping markets are some distance apart. Thus a weekly cycle of rotation establishes, once more, a definite interdependence. Prices which obtain on a certain day in an important centre can and do influence those of the following market days, especially the price of maize, vegetables and fruit. Again, many a merchant or commercial agent makes it his business to attend several of the weekly markets. He has, obviously, to choose on Wednesday between Etla and Zimatlán,

Table 1 Daily sequence of markets in the Oaxaca Valley

Weekday	Village where market is held
Monday	Miahuatlán
Tuesday	Atzompa, Totolapan
Wednesay	Etla, Teotitlán del Valle, Zimatlán
Thursday	Ejutla, Zaachila
Friday	Miahuatlán, Ocotlán
Saturday	Oaxaca
Sunday	Cacaoatepec, Cuilapan, Ejutla, Etla, Oaxaca, Ocotlán, San Antonino, San Pablo Huixtepec, San Pedro Apóstol, Tlacochahuaya, Tlacolula, Zaachila, Zimatlán

Diagram 3.1

The density of weekly markets in the Oaxaca valley and their spatial orientation from Oaxaca City (see Map 3 for more precise location of the markets).

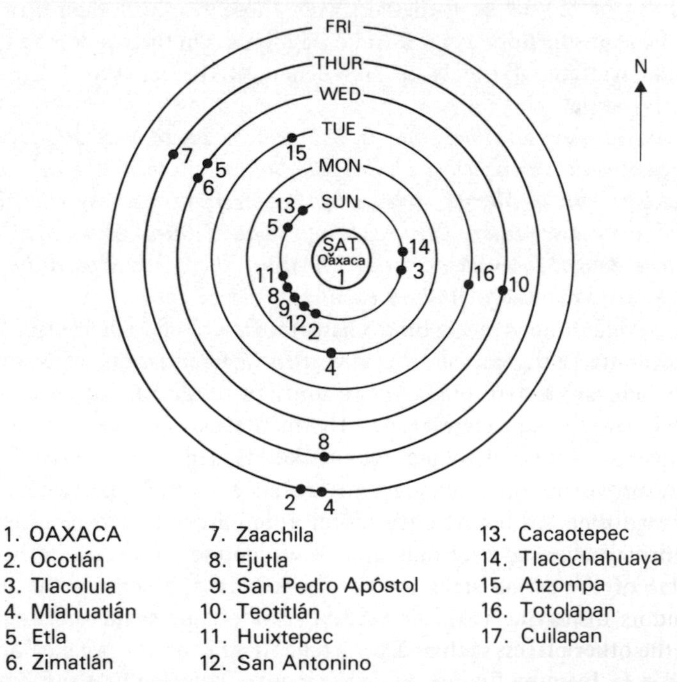

and on Thursday he can go either to Zaachila or to Ejutla. Few merchants make a complete weekly cycle for on Monday and Tuesday there are no markets of importance in the whole district. (See Table 2, p. 105, for a classification of markets.) A villager in any neighbourhood, at least once a week and usually more than once (for he usually lives between two market towns), has the opportunity of providing himself with money by selling, and with goods by buying. Here again it is easy to see how the weekly cycle integrates the system. As we shall see, for a number of articles the speculative middleman or large-scale buyer follows the movement of prices even at some of the smaller markets. He is certainly aware of price fluctuations and fluctuations in the supply of the principal goods. He calculates his operations on that basis.

Table 1 shows the markets of various centres listed according to day of the week.

Were you to observe the course of events in any market town from the afternoon before the main market day till the morning following the main event, you would see a typical sequence. Thus, for instance, on Thursday afternoon in Ocotlán a gradual influx of people begins to take place. As regards merchandise, you would observe that commodities necessary for the maintenance of the people and of their beasts of burden are brought first: large carts with fodder, supplies of food to be cooked or sold raw, and fruits to be sold for immediate consumption. There is also an influx of people from the mountains and outlying southern regions of the plain, where the distances are too great for them to make the journey early on Friday. They arrive before dusk on Thursday to avoid the risks of a night journey. They usually make their sales and purchases very early on Friday morning, and set out immediately for home in order to arrive before nightfall.

Another early arrival is the *regatón* from Oaxaca, who comes to purchase from the primary producers quickly and cheaply and to resell in the same market or to carry goods away. Some merchants who store their wares during the week and display them on Friday may arrive on the Thursday afternoon, so as to be on the spot to arrange their site and transfer their goods from the store rooms. On Thursday evening we would find some of the hostelries partly filled, some of the eating stalls in the market active, and a number of fruit vendors displaying their wares. The same picture would obtain in any of the other places, such as Tlacolula, Etla or Zaachila.

De la Fuente: *I think the* regatones *generally arrive on the market day itself and very rarely before that; especially those from Oaxaca.* Regatones *only arrive early for Oaxaca Market. The arrival of* regatones *is often seasonal and related to particular markets.*

In Oaxaca we find a similar phenomenon, only on a larger scale. There, many producers come on Friday afternoon or evening with the express purpose of selling rapidly to middlemen. They soon return home, perhaps after having made some purchases the next morning. Also in Oaxaca the contingent of middlemen, large buyers, and exporters is very substantial. These people scour the hostelries and attempt to purchase all the raw palm leaf, large quantities of maize, of perishable vegetables, of eggs or of charcoal in order to pool the produce and manipulate it on a large scale.

At times the Indians bring small quantities of gold, which have to be sold *sub rosa*, and this is done in a secluded corner of a hostelry on a Friday afternoon or evening.

The main market of the next day, whether in Oaxaca or elsewhere, follows a definite routine. The sale of non-perishable types of merchandise, such as textiles, dresses, shawls, leather goods and hemp products, begins somewhat later than the rest and remains active in Oaxaca till the market gradually dissolves in the afternoon or evening. The daily rhythm of the market affects primarily perishable goods, cereals, above all maize, vegetables, flowers, fruit and, of course, cooked food for immediate consumption. The sale of cattle, horses, donkeys, pigs and fowl starts early and disperses soon after midday.

The most characteristic variation of the day would have to be described in terms of the actual feeding and provisioning of men and animals. The first booths to open are the *fondas*: the local stalls of cooked foods. In connection with them, and independently, there is also a swarm of tortilla vendors, whose first batches appear in the morning. The people who have arrived have to be fed. The poorest may have brought some provisions with them and will buy only a few tortillas, the Mexican's daily bread, for the price of approximately 1 centavo each. The wealthier will consume a meal at one of the tables, which may cost from 20 to 50 centavos. Coffee or chocolate, a bowl of soup or of *atole*, the thin maize porridge, is usually eaten in the morning.

An increase in the activities of the local eating places occurs at about midday, when a more substantial meal, including a bowl of meat with chilli sauce, black beans, or else a bowl of strongly seasoned soup will be eaten, always accompanied by some tortillas. Here, as elsewhere in Mexico, tortilla rolled up with many combinations of chopped meat, chilli, cheese and condiments are a culinary delicacy.

In Oaxaca itself, at about five o'clock, when the rest of the market is practically dead, women (from surrounding villages or from the locality itself) bring their tortillas to sell.

[De la Fuente seems to doubt this. He writes: *Women do not walk out at night; in smaller villages they may be jailed as 'prostitutes'.*]

People come at times from some distance to display their barbecue meat, and the market kitchens start once more on a brisk trade. In Oaxaca there is an interesting shift of location. The market kitchens, which in the morning occupied the north-west quarter of the market, cease to function in the afternoon. The south-east wing, on the other hand, where in the morning there were no restaurants and only hats and a few other articles were sold, opens up as the evening supplier of cooked food. The people who have concessions for the morning and those who work in the evening are different. This part of the market and this part alone remains open to the public and active till fairly late in the night: on slack days till about nine o'clock, on well-attended occasions till ten or eleven.

Not all people, however, are wealthy enough to eat in what to us would appear extremely rudimentary and absurdly cheap restaurants of the market. In Oaxaca the streets surrounding the market building – in other towns the now empty square itself – are littered with small groups who sit on mats, on the kerb or on benches, and eat their own provisions. Meanwhile, the bars are full, and music from radios, from professional performers, and occasionally also from amateurs who strum the guitar and sing, reaches us from many a spot. Many people remain overnight. The poorest sleep in the street under open arcades. Those who can spend as much as 5 or 10 centavos go to a hostelry [where they sleep outside under arches. Ed.]. For 20 centavos one can have the luxury of sleeping in a room on the floor. There are even a few 'hotels' in the market towns. These charge 50 centavos or 1 peso for room and bed.

De la Fuente: *Elsewhere, people sleep on benches, in galleries and archways, or in the proximity of the church as happens at Tlacolula during the fair. Alfonso Villa once found mountain people (*montañeses*), when they brought apples, sleeping next to their fruit. In Ocotlán they sleep beneath the trees. Lack of money, lack of lodgings, anxiety about their merchandise and the desire to be ready for early mass in the morning are all considerations determining the fact that in certain seasons the Indians sleep in the open air.*

On the day following the market, there may be a busy morning. This certainly is the case in the capital, where on Sunday morning a considerable amount of commerce takes place, falling off sharply towards noon. In Ocotlán there is probably a slight increase in activities on Saturday morning. In Tlacolula Monday is a dead day, however.

The markets are subject to a yearly cycle as regards intensity and specialization. The climate itself affects them directly. October to about May or June is the dry season. In June the rains begin, and last until the end of September. This obviously affects communications. Man, beast, ox-cart and motor car are often unable to move, especially on the marshy grounds of Zaachila and Zimatlán. The only permanent roads[4] run between Oaxaca and Ocotlán, and from Oaxaca to Tlacolula and Mitla. The segment between Oxaca and Etla is permanent, but inferior in quality, and at times cannot be used by bus. The railway runs from Mexico City and Puebla to Oaxaca and through Etla as far as Tlacolula on one of its lines, and also through Zaachila to Zimatlán. It also unites Oaxaca with Ocotlán, running parallel to the permanent road. In the wet season driving cattle from place to place is more difficult, and at this time the peasants are hard at work on their fields.

The markets of our system are only partially under permanent roofs. A violent afternoon shower disorganizes activities immediately. On a day of steady rain commerce is much impaired. Thus, by and large, the rainy season is the slack season. During the dry period all the roads are open, the traditional arteries of commerce function regularly, and the markets are larger on appointed days and last late into the afternoon.

De la Fuente: *I have argued that the slack market season is precisely the season which follows the harvests despite the fact that the periods of greatest and most lavish expenditure [Spanish:* derroche*] fall at the festivals of All Souls, New Year and Easter Week (1 and 2 November, 31 December and 1 January, and March-April).*

*One must consider, however, that the recently harvested maize crop ensures that certain expenses due to maize shortage will not occur. The first agricultural work and the new rains coincide. Maize consumption increases with the increase in labour. This occurs at the end and at the beginning of the year. The expenditure of money from the harvest in the purchase of cattle, and in the payment of hired labour (*peones*), also occurs just before or during the rains. This, it seems to me, would lead to a larger volume of transactions and larger markets* *despite the disorganization which is brought about by the rains. The disorganization caused by rain is not complete, and the intensity with which people buy provisions increases. In the rainy seasons, at the period of smaller harvests like vegetables, which play an important part in the diet, it is possible that the sale of* abarrotes *[dried and tinned goods] decreases. This sale increases in what I would consider the slack season, the beginning and the end of the year.*

*In the coffee-producing region of Veracruz the coffee-bean harvest determines the increasing seasonal movement in the market. The period immediately preceding this harvest and sale is 'slack' (*de guayaba*), but the mestizo economy of the region seems considerably different from the economy of the Oaxacan Indians, which seems to pick up again after the harvest, in part due to the fact that the drying process necessary before maize can be sold is longer than that needed for coffee.*

Having made these observations in order to draw attention to such an important aspect of the system, I would only add, in the first place, that we have seen very muddy market places, like those of Tlacolula, Zimatlán, Zaachila and Etla, and even Oaxaca, with flourishing markets. In contrast the drier December markets are lazy. In the second place, the corollary of disorganization of the market caused by the rainy season seems insufficient explanation of the slack periods. There could be, and are, other factors which lead to slowness.

We have, nevertheless, made it clear that there are different market rhythms: continuous, continuous and strong, and those which I would call 'spasmodic' – these last, I think, occur at the beginning and end of the year.

However, in general I think the length of time markets last depends on the need for them, rather than on the wetness or dryness of the season. In fact, the markets are not interrupted except on occasions of greatest hardship, as during revolution. Even then they are not totally disrupted.

The dry season is the time when the main October harvest of maize begins, and when the principal cultural influences, especially religious ones, intensify the marketing. The festivals of All Souls, Christmas and New Year, Holy Week and Easter all intensify the market. Some of the main festivals in Tlacolula, in Oaxaca itself, and in Etla fall in these periods. All festivities are times of eating and over-eating, for the wearing of new apparel, for the distribution of gifts to friends and toys to children. More specifically, during carnival, at New Year and at Easter, as well as at All Souls and All Saints, many commodities have to be bought to celebrate the occasion. The custom of replacing clothing and even kitchen utensils at New Year still prevails.

There is perhaps one specific item of merchandise which affects the market more profoundly than all the rest, and does so seasonally. This is maize. In Chapter 9 we shall briefly discuss the influence of maize on the general standard of living and on the price level of the market.

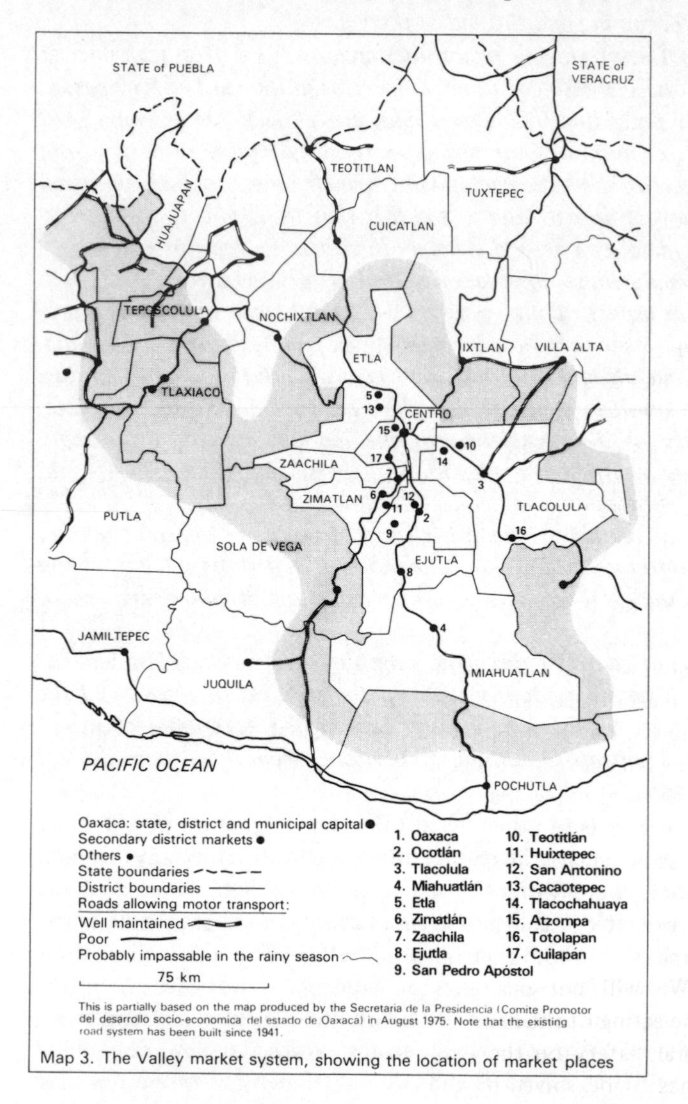

This is partially based on the map produced by the Secretaria de la Presidencia (Comite Promotor del desarrollo socio-economica del estado de Oaxaca) in August 1975. Note that the existing road system has been built since 1941.

Map 3. The Valley market system, showing the location of market places

4 A brief survey of the surrounding district and townships

We return here to a brief survey of the district surrounding the city of Oaxaca. The market day of Ocotlán is Friday. If we were to join some villagers who attend Ocotlán market, even from near Oaxaca, or if we were to take one of the crowded buses which carry merchants, middlemen and ordinary persons from the capital, we would have to take the permanent road joining the two towns: a distance of some 40 kilometres. On the way, we would pass the village of Coyotepec. In Coyotepec an ancient earthenware industry still flourishes, using pre-Columbian techniques and reproducing some of the forms found by Dr Caso and his associates at archeological sites in Monte Albán. Following the road, we come to a low range of bare hills, where the road ascends. Behind us is a good view of the plain covered with green maize fields, watered by the river Atoyac. There we can see, dotted on the plain, dark groves indicating the positions of the townships of Zaachila and Zimatlán, the ancient monastery of Cuilapan and many other villages.

The hill we are traversing, Cerro del Montecón, is interesting because it has the reputation – well deserved – of being a suitable place in which to ambush travellers. Only a year or two ago, a large herd of cattle driven from Ocotlán to Oaxaca was captured, the drivers beaten and sent home. Later on some of the stolen animals were found in a neighbouring village – two in the house of the municipal president, one with the local judge, and three with the head of the Social Defence League, an organization for the maintenance of safety in the villages. Near that same village, local robbers engaged in a mutual vendetta. Several people were wounded, a woman killed. The killer then was run down, executed, his heart taken out and eaten with tortillas. (This was perhaps the most sensational discovery we made during our research. We will not analyse legal aspects of the case, or inquire whether the eating of the heart was a 'survival' of some old sacrifice.)

In general, safety on the roads in the whole district is a problem that still has to be solved by the authorities and the inhabitants. The region between Tlacolula and Ocotlán – and it was in this region that the incidents mentioned here occurred – is regarded as one of the most enterprising in robbery, murder and vendettas. Some of the roads leading from our basin to the northern mountains are 'guarded' by members of the local Social Defence League. This means that the brave local defenders, like medieval robber barons, hold up the travellers or merchants and exact a small tribute. We did not record any murders in this region. But this is not proof that there were none. On such points the villagers are understandably somewhat reticent. Again, on the traditional routes from the Valley to the Isthmus and also to the southern districts, one has to take steps to ensure safety. People band together for a journey. If any extra money results from the transaction at the other end, it is not carried back but is sent by mail. Our best data on this point refer to the overland journeys to Tehuantepec, of which we shall presently give a fuller description.

The facts about robbers, the tribute levied and general safety have not been given here merely because they are 'ethnographic news' and add colour and zest to the narrative. The differential safety of communications is an economic factor in calculation, and in behaviour. It affects a number of economic mechanisms. Thus, the difference in the price of cattle between Ocotlán and Tlacolula is unquestionably due to the fact that a peasant from the latter region will not willingly walk across the dividing range of hills with money in his pocket, or drive his yoke of oxen back single-handed by the shortest route. At best he might go to Oaxaca by bus or train, and from there to Ocotlán by the same safe means. But all this adds up to a waste of time and expenditure of money.

Again, he could drive the cattle back along the main roads, but he might remember the capture of the large herd of Don Taurino Barriga, the cattle magnate, who, even with several herdsmen, was unable to protect his property. Nor is it completely safe to travel by omnibus. During our stay last summer, two or three cases of shooting occurred. These were due to rivalry between two competing commercial enterprises. The villagers, however, are thus taught to distrust even this means of communication, since a successful shooting might also lead to successful looting.

De la Fuente: *We had discussed briefly, without arriving at any satisfactory conclusion, the difference between the price of cattle in this region [Tlacolula] and others. Aside from the factors noted here, it seems to me that all merchandise is more expensive in Tlacolula than in Ocotlán – this due in part to the insufficient production [in Tlacolula], the earlier building of roads [to Ocotlán], etc. I have no precise correction to make of this part of the paragraph, but it does seem defective and inconsistent to me.*

The journeys made by groups of merchants are 'traditional' and certain ceremonies are performed at particular hamlets where the travellers stop to rest. The Indian muleteers of the last century and early in this century did the same. Moreover, there is a history of insecurity associated with such travels. The Mexican conquest of Mitla was said to be due to the killing of Mexican merchant-spies[1] *which was later avenged. I do not mean to connect the events, but to show that there are antecedents for the groups of travelling merchants.*

Proceeding on the journey to Ocotlán, as we cross the low range, we obtain the first glimpse of the Valley to the south, again dotted with hills and covered with fields of maize, beans and sugar-cane, while the darker groves indicate human settlements. In the distance, there emerge the white cupolas, towers and walls of the parish church of Ocotlán. The plain which we now traverse is well populated and mostly agricultural, although we pass on our left one or two villages in which pre-Columbian handlooms are still used in a home industry to produce coloured belts. As we approach Ocotlán, the road becomes crowded with ox-carts, people on foot, donkeys, riders and a few small herds of cattle, goats or pigs.

Ocotlán, like every small Mexican town, consists of square, small houses painted in all the colours of the rainbow and dominated by the church. As we pass along a street, we may see through open doors the interior of a workshop or a large courtyard with women washing or cooking. We may be struck by the shop of a carpenter who specializes in white, blue and black coffins. The white and blue ones are small. They are for the children, with whose death the black of mourning is not associated. The coffins for adults are black or the natural colour of the wood.

We proceed along the straight street and enter the main market place from the north. On our right, people come busily in and out of arcades crammed with stalls. At the back the entrances to the main shops of the central square stand open. The only house with two floors belongs to the commercial magnate of Ocotlán, Sr Delfino Díaz. On the left is the central square. Here again, we find wares distributed in a definite order. The whole north side is filled with displays of earthenware. Each vendor displays his goods on the ground so that everyone can see his pots, basins, bowls, jars and plates. Proceeding now along the east side, where our road runs, we find in certain seasons large quantities of sugar-cane or sweet potatoes. If we were to cross the market to the west side, we would find produce of *ixtle*, quicklime and a small group of people selling the pre-Columbian grinding-stone and handmill.

In the middle of the square stands the inevitable bandstand. South of it we find, on the eastern side, chilli vendors, in the middle sellers of fruit and vegetables, and further east a large group of ragged Indians selling their own little apples, peaches and firewood. The statue of the national and regional hero, Benito Juarez, dominates the southern part of the market, and the Indian president looks benevolently on the surroundings.

[Malinowski had written, 'The statue of Juarez . . . looks benevolently on the beans, onions and garlic sold around him.' De la Fuente commented, 'I have already said that this paragraph might raise the hackles of some patriots – moreover, I don't think there are any onions.' Ed.]

All the market south of the bandstand is dominated by the vegetable market. Economically and socially there are clear divisions between a group selling onions, garlic and fresh vegetables from the adjacent village of San Antonino; a number of people from outside who are middlemen in fruit and vegetables, but above all in chillies; and the numerous small Indian vendors clustered in the south-east corner, who sell rather different fruits – the produce of their mountains, especially apples and peaches of poorer quality sold at lower prices.

On the south side the market is fringed by several booths of candles and 'miracles' (*milagros*), that is, scapularies, crosses and votive offerings. These face you if you stand on the steps of the municipal government building (*municipio*), which occupies the southern side of the square on your right, that is, in the extreme eastern corner. On your left, you would see half a dozen or more booths with ready-made clothes and cotton-wear. [See photos 11 and 19.]

The market place of Ocotlán is divided into two main parts, with a number of additional courtyards or open spaces for cattle, charcoal, pigs and turkeys, and also for the daily storage of unharnessed ox-carts. The main market is completely open. Directly adjacent to it, on the south-western side, there are four newly built, covered galleries, with four corner shops, surrounding an open patio. The southern gallery is taken up exclusively with butchers' stalls. A row of tables runs the whole length of the gallery. The vendors stand on the inner side of the gallery; the buyers pass along the outside. The northern gallery is for the sale of head-shawls. The eastern gallery specializes in textiles, while the western, somewhat empty, has a few kitchen utensils. Sometimes the sale of fowl goes on there also. The patio fountain is surrounded by flowers, vegetables (among which the onions of San Antonino predominate), stalls with refreshments, and, on the north side, several bread stalls.

The part of the market which is perhaps the most important, that of maize, centres on the street which runs along the western side of the new market. Here, in two files divided by the mid-street gutter, the producers and the middlemen face one another. The latter use a number of store rooms on the other side of the street. There they can lock up maize for the night. A very wide street running on the south side of the new market sometimes fills up on busy days with vendors of maize and beans. There are some ten or twelve permanent sites for vendors of ironwork, a craft well developed in Ocotlán. The street flanking the new market on the north has two rows of stalls, the western end mostly occupied by eggs, the middle by refreshments and the eastern end by spice sold by a regular group of vendors from Tlacochahuaya.

A walk through the neighbourhood of the market would reveal to us a large display of fodder in the streets surrounding the municipal building and the church; many hostelries, simpler and cruder than those of the capital, but equally busy; the inevitable bars, active mostly late in the afternoon and the evening; and, of course, the livestock market. Cattle are sold in an open space five minutes' walking distance from the centre. Other animals are sold in the street. The church would be empty during most of the day, but apparently there is an influx of faithful in the morning.

The municipal building, which faces the market, is active during the whole day. The president receives complaints and watches the fiscal transactions of the tax collector. The sanitary inspectors sally forth to supervise the display [of propaganda to do with health and hygiene] and occasionally to vaccinate some of the Indians whom it is easier to catch in the markets than in their homes. The legal offices are open for the registration of deaths and births.

De la Fuente: *These offices are open every day but Sunday. However, marriages and deaths are normally registered in the localities (*pueblos*) where they occur. I understand that each month the district* *authorities are notified of demographic changes registered in the district's outlying offices.*

A closer survey of Ocotlán would reveal to us that it is an entirely urban settlement. Few people in Ocotlán speak the indigenous languages, and even fewer engage in agricultural work. They are essentially a Latinized community consisting of a few officials and a considerable number of shopkeepers, artisans and middlemen. However, if we were to proceed only a few hundred yards along the road which runs west from the new market, we would enter the adjacent suburb or, administratively speaking, independent village and municipality of San Antonino. Though inferior in status, it is very much more productive and important in agriculture and commerce.

De la Fuente: *According to the 1930 population census the total population of Ocotlán is 4,567. The population of San Antonino is 2,861. The populations of these two municipalities are differently distributed. In the municipality of Ocotlán, 334 persons live outside the* villa *(town), in five different localities. The 284 persons included in the municipality of San Antonino who live outside of the* villa *live in a single settlement.*

The most striking ethnographic fact is that whereas Ocotlán belongs to the Latin type of culture and to a certain extent to the twentieth century, San Antonino is still thoroughly Zapotec, carries on some of the old Indian traditions, and in spite of its strong economic advancement retains a number of traditional customs of the region. Thus, San Antonino is probably the strongest agent in the historically founded traditional system of voyages to the Isthmus. The relationship between these two places is an interesting problem for the functionalist, the historian and the student of diffusion.

De la Fuente: *There are many other settlements from which such traditional journeys have been undertaken. These journeys proceed to the south and south-west from a number of Zapotec settlements in the region. However, there may have been an increase in such journeys due to a loss of land which coincided with an extension of the native population towards the south where they are now established. That is, the natives of Ocotlán may have moved into the town and its immediate neighbourhood as a result of cultural and biological assimilation of indigenous and foreign population which occurred outside. Meanwhile, the people of San Antonino may have moved, as cultivators and merchants, outwards from the urban centre which became too small to contain the population.*

[De la Fuente is considering here the possibility that trading journeys south and south-west from contemporary Zapotec settlements might be associated historically with more general movements of Zapotec and Latinized populations. He suggests that the Zapotec people might have moved in that direction due to the increasing encroachment of non-Indians on the land resources of Zapotec municipalities. The trade journeys might have been one way in which the population of San Antonino compensated for the loss of land to Latinized peoples in their municipality. He suggests that the development of commerce in the centre of San Antonino would have been accompanied by a movement of San Antonino people southwards where new cultivation was established. In the neighbouring municipality of Ocotlán, to the south, De la Fuente seems to suggest that the urban centre might have been completely occupied by a Latinized population which previously would have been located at the fringes of the Zapotec settlement. Ed.]

The district of Ocotlán is characterized by the existence of highly productive agricultural settlements, such as Chilateca, San Pedro Apóstol and Santiago, as well as San Antonino itself. To the east there is a famous shrine of La Virgen de la Asuncion at San Miguel. Santa Catarina, nearby, is renowned for the excellent quality of the local liquor (*mezcal*) produced there.

We can only briefly complement this description of one market place on a market day with some glimpses of the other townships. On a Sunday we would naturally visit Tlacolula. The market there is characterized by the fact that the two sites on which it is held are separated by the church with its large parish buildings and wide courtyard. The church is, in many ways, a magnificent building, and it contains, in a side chapel, the miraculous figure of Our Lord of Tlacolula. The faithful, commercially minded but also aware of supernatural blessings, have to pass through the churchyard to go from the *mercería*, hat stalls and salt-fish sites of the northern portion of the market to purchase their maize, vegetables or baskets in the southern portion. They may linger under the large banyan tree, dating probably from the time when this was the site of a pagan sacred temple. They may purchase one of the holy objects which are retailed within the churchyard at three or four *puestos*; or they may enter the chapel, rub themselves with holy flowers from the altar, pray, weep and offer a coin. Here the church, the churchyard, devotion and business are directly and visibly integrated.

North of the churchyard is the smaller part of the market. It has been recently embellished with four wide and tall open galleries, running diagonally across the square, with fountain and basin in the middle. The projected roofing of all these galleries was halted when the newly erected roof of one gallery was lifted by a strong wind. Now only one gallery, for vendors of straw hats and Mexican blankets, is shaded. In this part of the market locally produced salt can be purchased, as well as dried fish and other products brought from the Isthmus. Here also, in the south-eastern corner, you would find a group of Mixe Indians selling their chillies. Near the church entrance, there is a jerry-built wooden structure where some nine or ten tables are usually to be found, at which local merchants and one or two other people sell an assortment of goods which go by the name of *mercerias*: ribbons, lace, toys, hand-mirrors, combs and an assortment of pins and needles.

The bigger part of the market to the south is a medley of open galleries and open spaces. As we leave the churchyard, we find on our left to the east side of the market the maize exchange. Towards the centre meat is sold, while the whole western side is mostly taken up with fruit and vegetables. All along the western border run booths with the characteristic *rebozos*. Moving south, we pass through galleries of earthenware. Round the large fountain in the centre, again flowers, fruit and vegetables. To the south-west, wickerwork and mats. Outside the market to the east, a large place is reserved for the ox-carts, and south of the market fodder is sold.

De la Fuente: *On special days when fairs are celebrated, the ox-carts move to the south-east.*

Here, as in other places, a walk through the town would show the hostelries, bars and shops, the market for cattle and other animals. Tlacolula market is attended by neighbouring villagers, some of them able to boast of excellent soil and producing a quantity of maize as well as vegetable produce. The products of the main harvests of the Valley, however, depend on rain, and usually the price of maize in Tlacolula is higher than in Ocotlán or even in Oaxaca. Tlacolula is the main market for several Indian groups from the north, the inhabitants of Sierra Juarez and especially the Mixes. Some of them have to pass through the town of Mitla, where they may carry out certain preliminary transactions, but for their main sales and purchases they wait to come to Tlacolula [see Parsons, 1936].

There are a number of markets which depend on a large market like that of Tlacolula. Thus, at a considerable distance, but partly connected by an excellent permanent road – one of the abortive parts of the projected Pan-American highway – lies the town of Totolapan.[2] Here the market really consists of the aftermath of the Sunday commerce in Tlacolula. The commercial inhabitants of Totolapan go in an omnibus to Tlacolula on Saturday, buy goods at the Sunday market, sell their own local produce, mostly bananas and oranges, as well as incense, and then return on Monday. On Tuesday, apparently, there is a special market day in Totolapan, and the inhabitants live on their purchases during the rest of the week. Several other markets play a subsidiary role, and many of the small local shops replenish their stocks not only from wholesale dealers, but also at the larger markets.

Another market dependent on that of Tlacolula is Tlacochahuaya market. At dawn on Sunday, which is market day in Tlacolula, the large roof of Tlacochahuaya market covers a square which is still empty, for the local inhabitants are moving towards the large colonial buildings of the church which overlook the market from a broad terrace. Others go to the main well to fetch water. Groups of people pass along the main street on their way to Tlacolula. At about half past five in the morning, one or two of these stop under the covered market, open their bread baskets, and immediately a number of women from the locality, as if attracted by magic, swarm towards them, and a brisk sale ensues. Bread usually comes from Santo Domingo. Sometimes the whole supply is exhausted here, and the women are spared another two hours' walk to Tlacolula. Those who arrive later and cannot sell their bread have to go on. In addition, meat may be sold, or sweets or fruit. The market is small, ephemeral and in one way dependent on that of Tlacolula. People returning from Tlacolula market place in the afternoon may sometimes stop in Tlacochahuaya under the roof and attempt to sell a few things which they purchased in Tlacolula for resale, or else were not able to sell.

We can only very rapidly survey the main characteristics of some of the remaining markets. Etla, dominated by a large yellow church, has a sloping market place surrounded by new galleries, in which again we have a fixed distribution of selling sites. On the whole, we can generalize in stating that ready-made clothes, textiles, hats, haberdashery, cane sugar, meat and other goods readily affected by rain are usually placed under a roof. Vegetables, fruit, maize, earthenware and fodder remain in the open, or their vendors erect a temporary shelter as best they can. Etla is a very small town of normally no more than a thousand inhabitants. On market day the influx consists very largely of people from Oaxaca, from the Sierra to the north and, of course, from the surrounding villages. There is also attendance from the Mixtec region.

De la Fuente: *Etla is one of several points of entry from the Valley of Oaxaca to the Mixtec regions.*

An entirely different picture as regards scenery, setting and activities in the market is seen in the overgrown village of Zaachila (population in 1930, 4,567). Here we have far fewer of the solid stone buildings, which in a place like Ocotlán, Tlacolula or Etla give the visitor an impression of a much larger town than the number of inhabitants indicates. In Zaachila, most of the village consists of large, open, square gardens, each enclosed by a tall reed fence, overshadowed by large trees and divided by partitions, one section containing the house and the people, another being a kitchen garden, a third reserved for the beasts.

De la Fuente: *The area in which the people reside is* ponse [in Zápotec] English: house – [Spanish: *casa*] *and the Spanish term* solar *comprises the kitchen garden and the area in which animals are kept.*

Only round the main square of the town, which here, as in most other centres except Oaxaca, doubles as the market place, do we find a few houses built of stone or painted adobe. On Thursday the concourse here is considerable. Indeed, this market seems to be developing in strength and importance. Zaachila is a centre for a fertile region extending between this town and Zimatlán to the south. Black beans, vegetables, nuts and sugar-cane are the main contributions from here. The market is attended by Indians from the Sierra, by peasants from the surrounding villages and at times by middlemen from Oaxaca, while the local inhabitants also supply a good contingent.

Zaachila has an interesting minor daily market in maize, to which we will briefly have to return.

On a Wednesday we would naturally visit Zimatlán. This, again, is a small place with one or two imposing stone buildings, and we estimate that it is one of the recessive markets, gradually yielding in importance to that of Zaachila. Here the usual type of produce is sold in the market, and in addition the sale of maize is perhaps greater here than in Zaachila, because the drier districts to the south bring their quota. Both in Zaachila and Zimatlán, even to a greater extent than in Ocotlán and Tlacolula, we can observe an interesting type of transaction: a new type of barter. The Indians, as a rule, exchange the bulk of their produce – fruit, firewood, at times some quicklime – not for money but directly for maize or crops, lemons, oranges, pumpkins and those vegetables which grow more readily in the plains than in the high mountains. Barter here, as elsewhere in the region, is carried on with reference to money as a standard of value; that is, each article is assessed in terms of centavos, on which numerical basis the bargaining is done, but money is not used in the exchange. All articles change hands directly.

We have been able to observe one small market where practically all the transactions are carried out in forms of this type of barter. Remarkably enough, this takes place in the village of Atzompa only about eight kilometres from the capital of Oaxaca. Atzompa is perhaps the most important centre of earthenware production in the region. Atzompa products reach the whole region and are even exported to Mexico City. Atzompa still carries on its traditional craft of pottery-making using techniques shown by Dr Alfonso Caso to be pre-Columbian. Despite the widespread distribution of Atzompa ware, local exchanges occur in the form of barter. On a Tuesday the small square, flanked by an old church and a new school and overshadowed by two or three ancient banyan trees, is filled with some twelve to twenty-five selling sites. From the regions of Etla, Cuilapan and even Zaachila a number of women bring bread, cheese, cooked meat, sweetmeats and fruit. Local people, almost exclusively women, sally forth with their earthenware. Buyers are predominantly local people. Bargaining, in most cases, seems inevitable. A large green glazed jar is offered at 25 centavos. The counter-proposal may be 10. Finally, the price of 15 is reached. The price of bread, sweetmeats or meat, as a rule, is known to both sides, and the bargaining refers to the variable price of the village product rather than to variations in value of the food supplied.

De la Fuente: *However, lively bargaining over the price of maize sold from houses has been noted in Atzompa and there, as elsewhere, the price of most products, both local and foreign, may be the subject of bargaining in a non-barter transaction. Products rarely, if ever, subject to bargaining are: tortillas,* chicharrón *[fried pork skin], sweets and ice-cream, though small pieces of bread may be exchanged for larger ones. . . .*

We have made a brief survey of the bargaining technique in Atzompa, as well as an assessment of the economic aspect of village industry. But this subject will require a much fuller subsequent investigation.

The village lives almost exclusively on its pottery craft, and its population, which we estimate at about 1,500, supplies the whole region with a product in many ways indispensable. The jars, casseroles and cooking pots of Atzompa are used in every household of our region. Among other reasons, the preference is attributed to the fact that less firewood or charcoal is consumed in cooking with Atzompa ware, owing to the thinness of the pottery. It is also said to be more durable.

De le Fuente: *The production of ceramics (*alfarería*) is one of the most extensive manufacturing crafts in the republic. Atzompa ware is found in relatively small quantities in the local markets compared with Oaxaca ware. Atzompa ware is extremely costly to transport by train. However, its sale is increasing and is of a seasonal nature, coinciding with the festivals of Holy Week and All Souls and, above all, with 12 May. That is the date on which people from Oaxaca customarily make their pilgrimage to the shrine of the Virgin of Guadalupe in Mexico City. At that time in the* villa *of Guadalupe (the section of the federal district in which the shrine is located) and elsewhere in Mexico City, one finds pottery from Oaxaca and Atzompa. 'That date is Oaxaca's day.' 'Es la fecha en que le toca a Oaxaca'.* [In other words, the state of Oaxaca takes its turn. Ed.]

All this implies complicated organization, on which we have obtained some very interesting data. But our glimpses into the production, distribution and use of ceramics are not yet sufficient for publication.

We visited the market of Ejutla only once. Ejutla is a beautiful and imposing town with some old buildings and a large church overlooking the market place, which again is in two parts, divided by a gallery where the local kitchen stalls function from morning to night and meat is sold. A crowded part near the church is filled with clothing, textiles, shawls and vegetables, which occupy a considerable part of it. The wider, completely open space to the north, overlooked by one or two typical old houses, is a market for earthenware, maize, beans fodder and animals. At one end, in the galleries, is the characteristic display of Mexican hats made of wool or straw. Ejutla is famous for its tanneries. It is also one of the points at which tropical products from the south – pineapples, coconuts and bananas – enter the region.

It will be remembered that, apart from the ordinary weekly markets, in each of the places mentioned we would find display and commerce intensified on the days of special religious observance. Thus, at All Saints, at Christmas and during Holy Week the markets are considerably busier. A few national days of festivity are also important. The Day of Independence on 16 September, the celebration of the hill near Oaxaca (connected with memories of Benito Juarez)[3] are no less important than the religious festivals which intensify market activity.

This brief survey will have disclosed that, while the market of Oaxaca has regional – in some ways even national and international – importance, those of Ocotlán, Tlacolula, Etla, Ejutla, Zaachila and Zimatlán might be described as of a secondary character. We might also classify a few markets as dependent or contingent, such as those at Totolapan and Tlacochahuaya. To these we might further add half a dozen or more seen and recorded but not yet fully studied.

Table 2 Categories of Oaxaca Valley markets

	Principal market		Main regional markets	Secondary district markets	Important minor markets	Minor markets	Special markets
Monday		DAILY MARKET OF OAXACA		Miahuatlán			
Tuesday						Totolapan	Atzompa (barter)
Wednesday				Etla Zimatlán	Teotitlán		
Thursday				Zaachila Ejutla			
Friday			Ocotlán	Miahuatlán			
Saturday	Oaxaca						
Sunday			Tlacolula	San Pedro Apóstol	Huixtepec San Antonino* Ocotlán Ejutla Etla	Cacaotepec Tlacochahuaya	

* De la Fuente: *I felt that San Antonino should not be included in 4, but that Zaachila should be placed in 4, though its Sunday market is larger than Ocotlán's.*

[The market place of Atzompa, characterized by barter, has been listed in a special category by the authors. Ed.]

The daily market of San Antonino is of a slightly different type. Here the inhabitants are provisioned every day with foodstuffs, but no other merchandise appears except perhaps a few pieces of earthenware, which indeed are found in most small markets. The market of Atzompa, with its surviving barter system, stands apart. We were not able to match it anywhere in the region, nor has Julio de la Fuente, who has studied the region of the Sierra Juarez for over a year, seen a similar phenomenon.

In Table 2 different categories of markets are defined by size, volume of transactions and relative importance within the system. Oaxaca is undoubtedly the principal market. It is in daily operation, and on Saturday no other market in the system operates. Ocotlán and Tlacolula are the two main regional markets. The distinction between these two and the six listed in Category 3 is indicated by the fact that the latter overlap. It can be seen from Category 4 that on Sunday there are 'important minor markets' not only in some places which have no market on other days, but also in the market towns which have a special market day.

We have not listed a phenomenon we observed in several villlages – two or three selling sites, usually for bread, fruit and sweets, which crop up in the morning in front of the church on the main square of the village.

5 Problems and methods in the analysis of market transactions

The general survey of each market place, as described in previous pages, was followed up by frequent visits to each locality and to every weekly market. Here a description will be given of the manner in which the first general impressions and the inventory of facts and events were gradually transformed into a more analytical and theoretical work. It is necessary to say a few words about the methods of fieldwork adopted, the emergence of problems, the drawing up of general rules and the gradual construction of a theoretical definition of the market system as an institution.

Some general principles could be discovered merely by repetitive observation, that is, by frequent visits to the same place. Thus, for instance, several visits to the market of Ocotlán or of Tlacolula would disclose even to a superficial observer that not only the same produce would be found in the same place on every occasion, but also that people from one village get together to form a row of vendors or to occupy a group of selling sites, and that ethnic groups, such as the Mixes or the *Serranos* [Highlanders – Ed.], are always to be found together. Each group is always on the same spot,[1] selling their wares in the same manner. The size of the selling site and the wealth of the vendor are correlated factors. The professional merchant from Oaxaca is able to construct a wooden booth or an elaborate tent, or else to hire a compartment in the permanent market structure. The middleman in earthenware may display his wares on mats on the earth, but his stock-in-trade will be varied and voluminous, and he can afford to pay more for the larger space occupied. The poorer Indians, on the other hand, will be found huddled together selling their wares out of a bag or a basket or on a frayed mat, each occupying a very small space and disposing of a small quantity and limited range of articles. Thus, one can see that the fixity of configuration, the type of selling site, the class of transaction and the economic background of the vendor are all intimately related.

Such conclusions were embodied in the plans[2] which we drew up on each visit to a market place (especially J.D.L.F.). By comparing the various plans and collating them with each other and with the observations made, we were able to formulate some problems and to establish the type of direct observation which would help to solve questions which arose. It was clear that the categories of transaction had to be defined in terms, first and foremost, of the economic function of each transaction. This was also related to social class (of the participants in the transaction) as well as to other types of production, and to the categories of consumer to whom certain goods are primarily useful. In this we soon found that it was impossible to observe, discuss or analyse the market without including the context of collateral business: that is, the surrounding shops, and the role played by wholesale agents who sell and also buy in the market in order to pool or corner the produce. What happens within the framework of the market has to be related to the mechanisms occurring behind the scenes.

First, perhaps, one or two concrete instances of how we discovered certain principles and were led, by one occurrence or another, to follow up theoretical points. On one occasion we met a woman with a large quantity of eggs classified by size and quality into baskets. An attempt to inquire about the prices or to buy disclosed that she was not a vendor, but a purchaser. In this she was actually aided and abetted by the local municipal official, whose main business is to collect taxes. This gentleman, incidentally, proved very helpful to us when we were obtaining some fuller insights into the main imports of that locality, the prices current, the industrial production and even the wages in the local, smaller factories. It became clear, however, that he was assisting in the buying up of eggs and probably also of some other produce for one of the large purchasers. This observation, related to inquiries made at Oaxaca and elsewhere, allowed us to ascertain that a person of wealth and power had developed an extensive organization for purchasing the produce already mentioned, principally maize and eggs, and that in this organization his control over other local tax collectors was extremely useful. Obviously, the collector, on whose decision the amount paid for a selling site depends, can 'advise' the local sellers to retail part of their wares to the buying agent of the *acaparador*, i.e. the bulk purchaser of specific produce.[3]

Again, a discussion of the manner in which some modern manufactured products are obtained leads outside the market. A vendor of shawls may be the producer himself.

De la Fuente: *There may be producers who sell* rebozos *in the market, but I did not meet any. I think the system for selling is different. There is sale of* rebozos *(a) on commission* [de entrega] *and (b) by lots* [a destajo], *i.e. to a retailer. Somewhat different also are the methods of the small-scale producers of sandale [huaraches] who both deliver to home and sell in the market.*

The reboceros *[sellers of shawls] usually sell more local produce than* rebozos *from Mexico, Tenancingo (Puebla) or San Luis, etc., . . . this partly because the local products are cheap and in demand, and because of the system of selling which predominates. The greatest differences exist between those who sell in the plaza and at fairs and those who sell in the stores. In other words, the* reboceros *seem a homogeneous lot (i.e. they are essentially resellers of products bought* from *the producers or from other resellers).*

Examining a store of ready-made clothes, we would find that they are mostly the output of a well-developed local industry. Many women in Oaxaca, and also a number of tailors, import textiles from other parts of the republic, work with them in their homes, and sell them to middlemen, who then retail them on the market. Indeed, detailed inquiry in the homes of the producers would reveal an even more complicated system. The wife of one of our friends who is the owner of a hostelry, a cousin of one of our best informants, as well as several other persons we observed, all make a small profit by organizing tailoring and dressmaking. They have sufficient capital, knowledge of where to buy and how to organize, and, of course, technical knowledge and ability. They mobilize a dozen, or perhaps two dozen, poorer workers. They give the material and all the paraphernalia to women, who do the work, and receive payment for making a dozen or so articles each, which allows each of them to earn some 50 centavos to 1 peso per day.

De la Fuente: *I have already objected slightly to considering 'our informant's cousin' as the organizer of a dressmaking workshop. We do know that such workshops exist, but the cousin is a piece-worker.*

Making friends with one of the vendors of 'notions' (*merceriás*) – that is, ribbons, mirrors and other articles for the enhancement of feminine beauty – we would probably find, if his booth is fairly large and his stock substantial, that he is economically a hybrid figure. He probably imports articles directly from Mexico City or Puebla, corresponding by post with the wholesale houses there and acting at times as agent for a commission. On the market day and in his booth, he sells larger quantities to shopkeepers and to minor retailers in more distant places, but he also carries on a brisk retail trade directly with the consumer. In another part of the market we would find a very small selling site with exactly the same articles retailed by a man who has just replenished his stock from his more powerful colleague. He, of course, has a small quantity of each type of product, but his booth, usually placed at a conspicuous corner, with his wares displayed on a small table, seems to have sufficient selling attraction to make his business possible. One interesting question here is: why do smaller businesses survive in competition with more powerful, direct buyers?

In all this, obviously, our study will lead to the consumer. Clothes, ornaments, mirrors and combs are obviously used by the peasants and Indians who buy them in the market. We find here a seasonal variation. Every large festival, every date on the calendar which implies a festive appearance or a change of clothing, affects the market. First, there is a steady replacement of goods due to normal wear and tear. Second, goods are distributed on specific occasions. According to our present preliminary assessment, more goods seem to be distributed due to the organization of specific occasions than are distributed in a steady and routine fashion. The feast of a local saint and the institution of the *mayordomía* are of major importance in this context. The *mayordomía* involves an organized expenditure on a large scale financed primarily by one person. It always implies relatively large purchases of clothes, ornaments, and cooking as well as eating utensils. Marriages, which are seasonal and occur primarily between Christmas and Holy Week, baptisms and burials, birthdays and personal saints' days are also minor festive occasions, which mobilize a family or group of kindred to make expenditures. The direct influence on the local market of several large festivities in the neighbourhood is conspicuous. The peasants or Indians not only have to purchase large quantities of the objects thus mentioned, and also of better quality food, but they also have to provide themselves with money. Consequently, they have to bring to the market crops, beasts and, above all, considerable quantities of maize.

One type of transaction connected with both import and export which occurs behind the scenes of the market is the sale of toys. One of the permanent toy vendors, Jesus Soto, has a large display of children's toys: miniature roundabouts, swings, trumpets, diminutive guitars and, of course, dolls and figurines. He also sells some objects of domestic use, stirring sticks for cocoa and *atole*, wooden spoons and tin goods. He trades regularly with toy makers in the state of Michoacán, from where he hails, and others in Mexico, Puebla and the state of Guanajuato. At times he acts as a wholesale importer. He and his wife each have a selling site, she permanently in Oaxaca, he travelling around to the regular market places and also to fiesta markets. When he is on an expedition he will sleep in the tent, guarding his stock-in-trade, spending perhaps 50 centavos a day on his food, and making on a good day some 5 pesos, on a less fortunate one ending up almost out of pocket.

De la Fuente: *He does not buy local products for resale, but he does buy articles from his colleagues in the market: for example, lacquered goods from the state of Guerrero.*

We know that the sale of earthenware products in the market is part of a much larger system. In that system we have to study the extensive exports from this region, and also to relate marketing to the techniques of production, the mechanisms of distribution and the quality of the ware. This latter cannot be defined by any set of adjectives or by technological inferences. It has to be studied from the consumer's point of view.

One must observe the performance of each category and each article of use under the strain of firing and possible breakage. They must be studied with reference to the standard of living of the user i.e. of his purchasing power and the specific uses to which each object is put.

Three main local sources of supply dominate every market: the goods from Atzompa, the gradually growing production of Oaxaca, and the old traditional craft of Coyotepec, which lately has begun to adapt to new uses and new designs. (One or two brief accounts have already been published. Dr Rubin de la Borbolla has studied the processes in Coyotepec.)

As regards the economics of production, Atzompa and Coyotepec are villages in which the industry is entirely domestic.[4] The supply of clay comes from communally and privately owned neighbouring quarries, and is free except for transportation and a nominal payment of about 10 centavos for 200 kilograms. The labour comes from the domestic supply, men, women and children. Occasionally helpers are hired. Expenditure in cash for materials and hired work becomes necessary for the fine grinding of the raw clay, the transport and hewing of the wood, at times for transport of the clay, and also for the purchase of chemical substances used in the glazing. A producer who wishes to be independent in all minor monetary expenses might need a capital of about 50 pesos, in order to purchase an ass or two, to employ an assistant and to invest regularly in a quantity of materials. Our study of earthenware production, local export and incidental expenses has yet to be completed.

Production in Oaxaca is in some ways more complex, in others more standardized and easier to follow. There are a few large-scale producers who each own a workshop establishment: a large house with patios and corridors in which the work is done and the wares are stored, displayed and sold. They control a dozen or so regular workmen and they are able to organize the export of their goods to the outside world, as well as distribution in the local shops and markets. There are also smaller producers who specialize in one or two of the local varieties. We were able to study a poor woman whose work consists of moulding, baking and painting little dolls, which gives her a net income of 50 to 60 centavos a day. She lives with her six or seven children and is the caretaker of one of the local vegetable gardens. This provides her with a house – also her workshop – and an income of 5 pesos a month.

As regards technology, the processes in Oaxaca imply the use of the potter's wheel, practically unknown in Atzompa and Coyotepec, as well as some fine glazing. The economics are obviously more complex, and we shall only mention here that the clay is obtained locally, the hired labourer receives about a peso a day, and the producer has to buy a fairly wide range of materials for glazing and finishing.

In Coyotepec the techniques are most archaic, the clay is communal property, and production is exclusively by domestic labour.

As regards the quality and use of the objects, the production of Oaxaca furnishes a very wide range, including entirely modern articles for export to the USA and other parts of Mexico, as well as for the use of wealthy and sophisticated local families. At the same time Oaxaca provides the bulk of bowls, plates and flower vases used by the peasants and Indians. The ware of Atzompa is the mainstay of the kitchen, in so far as it is the best for casseroles, basins, cooking pots and pitchers. Coyotepec maintains itself mostly by the production of *cántaros*, enormous jars used for storing water and for transporting water and liquor. Coyotepec also supplies some of the large basins which compete with Atzompa ware. Wherever there is competition, it is determined by the cheapness of Coyotepec products and the better quality of those from Atzompa. In all three centres – Oaxaca, Atzompa and Coyotepec – a number of small toys are made, which sell at 3 to 5 centavos per piece. These toys drift towards the more distant Mexican and the foreign markets.

As we walk through the markets, we see here and there, besides the three types of earthenware already described, which dominate the whole region, a small amount produced locally. In Ocotlán, a red ware decorated with white designs supplies a decorative touch of colour, as well as a range of cheap but inferior cooking utensils, toys, incense burners and plates. These articles are not seen in any other market, except perhaps at Zimatlán and the smaller places in the immediate neighbourhood. There is a village near Ejutla where the large flat dish (*comál*) is made for the cooking of tortillas. This article is also made, and of much better quality, in Atzompa and three or four other villages. A small village near Tlacolula produces red earthenware of inferior quality, mostly the flat dish for cooking tortillas and shallow pots.

Foreign porcelain, made usually by German-run factories in Mexico, is brought into the district. It appears regularly in small quantities in the markets of Oaxaca, Ocotlán, Etla and Tlacolula, as well as in shops near the market places.

From all these details some general principles emerge. Above all, we are aware that in order to discuss the transaction of the market, that is, the exchange, we have to know something about the economics of production and also the needs of the consumer. This becomes obvious when we study the other side of the market, so to speak: the primary products supplied by the district and largely consumed within it. The observations on maize reveal the distinction, on economic and sociological grounds, between the primary producer (the *propio*) and the re-vendor (the *regatón*). If we investigated all the financial transactions of a *regatón* we would probably find that he is the agent of a large buyer, while at the same time he may have a personal sideline of selling and buying. To the complexities of the maize market we shall have to return presently. For the moment, we want to indicate here that the mechanism of haggling in the market is but a symptom of wider organized realities ranging from the subsistence needs of a poor Indian to the speculative activities of a large-scale importer. Between these we have a whole series of middlemen, the ebb and flow of daily markets in some small localities, and the role of a professional buyer and seller who purchases at a large market in the morning in order to resell in the afternoon and during the ensuing week.

In a careful study of the maize exchange, we would also have to observe annual variations. If we were to spend a couple of hours among the oxen, the peasants and the cattle dealers who roam the squares or the markets where the beasts of burden are sold, we would be led to a study of extensive importation from other districts, to problems of grazing and feeding, to seasonal variations in the use and hence in the need for oxen, and also to the enterprises of butchers and meat vendors. There are specialists who make their living, and a good one at that, by making large purchases in the southern districts of the state, in the state of Guerrero, and in the region of the Mixteca. Locally, there are two or three cattle magnates – notably Don Taurino Barriga of Tlacolula, who purchases at every market a number of beasts and resells them in another district, always following the level of prices. There are smaller middlemen ready to buy from a peasant when he needs money and to resell on a market day at a relatively small profit. The peasant himself knows that in the season when he does not need the oxen he will obtain only a low price for them.[5] When he wishes to buy again for ploughing, the transport of crops and harvesting, he will have to pay much more. This, obviously, allows some middlemen to earn their living. The peasant, on the other hand, depends partly on his opportunities for grazing, which are affected by climate, and at a certain moment he may have to sell all he can in order to raise money for a *mayordomía* or some other expensive festival.

Only a brief analysis can be given of some other important articles. The antiquarian would be charmed to discover salt in Tlacolula produced by traditional techniques and retailed locally at a small price. The majority of the district, however, is provided with salt from salt works in the Isthmus of Tehuantepec, or from the state of Campeche. Salt comes by railway and is sold by large importers, shopkeepers and retailers. However, many of the natives who buy their salt in the market still believe that it has been imported on beasts of burden, brought along old trade routes which used to supply the need some twenty years ago.

De la Fuente: *I think relatively few natives believe this, and those who do are Indians from one particular district. A woman in Ocotlán who spoke of 'sal del Marquesado' [salt from the Marquesado] was referring indirectly to the Marqués salt work in the Isthmus. Note also that the natives buy two types of salt: crystalline salt and a greyer variety. The first type comes, I believe, from Campeche, and one type is preferred to the other.*

The white sugar, used more and more now by the wealthier peasants, is imported from Mexico City. It has to compete with the local brown sugar, *pironcillo*, a semi-refined, crystallized substance which can be used in coffee and local sweetmeats, but is not pleasant in chocolate or other sweetened beverages.

1 Bronislaw Malinowski (in white hat). To his left is Alfonso Villa Rojas; to his right, Don Manuel (these last two identified by Professor R. Waterbury)

2 Julio de la Fuente at the periphery of a market

3 Procession en route to market. Note the highland valley vegetation. Ox-carts have largely been replaced by motorized transport. Many roads in the Oaxaca Valley have been well paved and most people no longer travel long distances on foot

4 Ox-carts passed over cobbled streets to enter the market area. Stores like Casa Arce, pictured above, sold haberdashery *(merceria)* and other goods in the region of the market, but outside the market place

5 Pack mules stabled in the main hostelry of Oaxaca City. This hostelry no longer exists. Pack mules are now used only rarely to move products from the highlands to the valley

6 Zapotec woman (photo by Bodil Christensen, 1933). Note the woven wool used as a skirt, and the typical use of the *rebozo* as a covering for head and shoulders. The wool may have been locally woven but the *rebozo* is likely to have come from outside the Oaxaca Valley

7 Zapotec man (photo by Bodil Christensen, 1933). Note the same type of woven wool here carried over the shoulder to be used as an overcoat. The peaked hat is probably of felt and may have been locally made. The design is Spanish, though now used in Mexico exclusively by Indians. The skirt and trousers of heavy white cotton are also of Spanish design but now used only by Indians in the Oaxaca region. Note the leather sandals *(huaraches)*

8 An old woman wearing a *huipil.* This loose-fitting one-piece garment was usually made of cotton spun and woven using indigenous pre-Colombian techniques

9 Contrasted clothing styles. The woman is wearing a long-sleeved ruffled blouse which is probably a Mije Indian style of clothing. She uses a *rebozo* only as a head-covering. She thus has both hands free to carry her shopping basket and to restrain the small boy. Note the elegant, urban, European style of clothing worn by the child

10 Woman selling cooked food. Note three types of clothing: the one-piece dress worn mostly by urban women; the blouse and skirt worn by peasant women in rural areas; and the apron worn by servants in the city

11 Clothing. Above the couple shopping, to the right are kerchiefs favoured by peasant men *(paliacates)* and scarves used by the women; to the left are one-piece dresses. To the left of the couple is a haberdashery stall *(mercería)*, which includes cosmetics and jewellery as well as thread, lace, buttons, etc.

12 *Rebozos.* These were sold in a covered arcade of the Oaxaca City market. The *rebozo* has been an indispensable article of peasant women's clothing throughout Mexico. It is used not only to cover the head and shoulders, but also to carry children, and to carry and cover objects which range in size from baskets of market produce to small coins

13 Salted meat sold by length in a covered section of the Oaxaca City market. The special hygienic uniform worn by the woman dispensing meat was undoubtedly introduced as part of the government programme of health education

14 Cooked food and cheese. Note the cheese sold here in small wedges. In the foreground a basket contains tamales of a type characteristic in Oaxaca. The maize dumpling is wrapped in banana leaves and probably steamed in an earth oven

15 A client examines an earthenware pot

16 *Ixtle* fibre products

17 Brooms

18 Firewood

19 Votive offerings: candles, scapularies, papers, including printed prayers. The baskets may contain medicinal herbs, which were often sold with votive offerings

20 Iron machetes, knives and hoe blades. The knives and machetes come from the region of Oaxaca which borders the Pacific known as Costa Chica

21 Oxen for sale in the livestock market

22 Sugar skulls, sugar coffins and toy skeletons sold in the Oaxaca City market for the Day of the Dead *(El dia de los muertos)* (photo by Maria de los Angeles Romero, 1976)

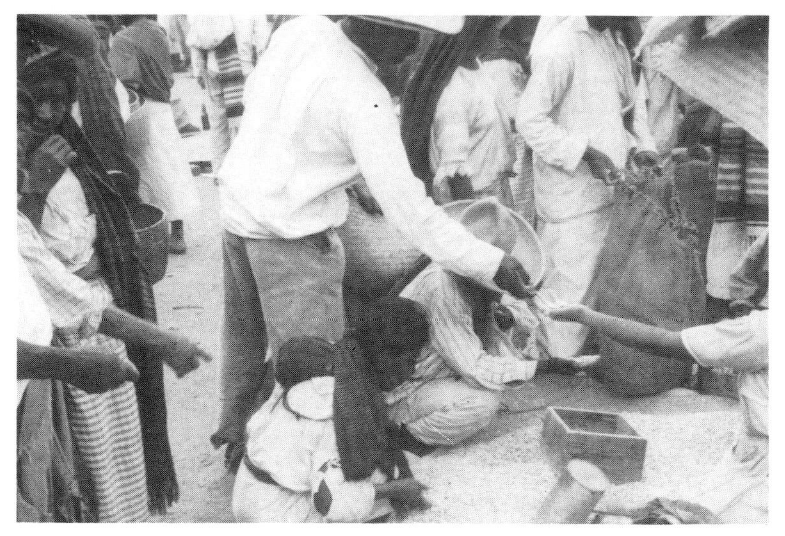

23 Maize. Dry maize kernels were sold in the special maize market of Oaxaca City or in a special section of the smaller markets. The wooden box and tin were used as measures

24 Lime. Chunks of limestone *(cal)* were used to soften the maize kernels which were soaked overnight in water containing dissolved lime

25 The *metate* was then used to grind the softened kernels into a maize dough (*masa*) used to prepare the maize-bread (tortilla), which is patted into a thick pancake

26 *Metates* with grinding pins on sale

27 A decorated *metate* for a bride is prepared for a dance in the wedding ritual. The *metate* was tied to the dancer's back. Most ingredients used in cooking were ground by women on the metate. It was thus a fitting symbol of wifely duties

28 The sale of earthenware griddles. The griddle (*comal*) was used to cook the tortilla, which was placed on the dry earthenware surface and turned once in the cooking process

29 The sale of tortillas. Note two women in the centre. One is counting out the tortillas. On her left the client holds a bucket prepared with a cloth to receive the purchase

30 The *almud* used to measure maize. To the left of the sack which contains maize is a tin measure, topped by a calabash scoop

31 Scales used to measure chile

32 A barter transaction (see pp. 146–7)

33 A *regatona* sorting eggs

34 In September 1978 a large portion of the Benito Juarez market moved from the centre of Oaxaca to a permanent site at the periphery of the city. The clothing section was photographed on 2 September 1978 by Manuel Esparza. The banner reads: 'Merchants of the 4th block of J. P. Garcia Street, General clothing', and directs the merchants to their new location

35 The section selling woven baskets in the new market (photo by M. Esparza, 2 September 1978). Note the wide street between the stalls, the zinc roof and the brick pillars

36 The section selling woven baskets in the Benito Juarez market, 1941. Note the wooden stall roofs and the clustered distribution of the individual stalls which contrasts with the single long row of stalls in the new market

6 Economic background of the market place

In the course of fieldwork, it was our habit to interrupt our observations for a day or two to compare our notes and to make a theoretical digest. This allowed us at the same time to formulate general principles and to frame problems, as well as methods of observation which would lead towards their solution. From all the facts surveyed, we have found that the study of the market as a phase in the economic processes of the region has to be related to production, consumption and the systems of distribution. The complexity of the picture obtained leads us naturally to the question of how to organize the evidence and thus perhaps not simplify it, but at least save it from the chaotic state in which we found our early observations enmeshed. The recognition that we have to observe production in its primary forms (that is, the agriculture, the industry and the crafts of the region) introduces one principle of order. In studying this aspect of organized activities, we obtained evidence indispensable to a general economic appreciation, and we were also led directly to the solution of many questions arising out of the market.

We shall here record the preliminary results we have obtained thus far. Ethnographic data referring to production in the region studied must be placed within the context of importation from outside the region. As regards primary production, we know already that maize is the primary staple food of the people. The consumption and production of wheat is increasing. The black bean still remains of great importance, especially in times of maize scarcity. The various types of chilli are more than a condiment to the Mexicans. They are both a condiment and a nutritive contribution to the diet; that is, an integral part of the diet. Vegetables, fruit and flowers are also indispensable, and a substantial contribution from the soil and human labour to the local consumers' needs. Although our study of agriculture in various aspects constitutes perhaps the most rudimentary and incomplete part of the work done, the following tentative generalizations can be formulated.

The Indians from the surrounding mountains contribute largely to the supply of fruit, nuts and potatoes; while from one or two of the tribal regions considerable quantities of chillies are brought to the markets. The staple agricultural produce comes from the Valley, where several types of peasant smallholders cultivate maize, black beans, sugar-cane and vegetables. Vegetables and flowers are very largely grown round some of the townships and in the low fertile marshy regions between Zimatlán and Zaachila and round Ocotlán. An important contribution of these districts consists of onions and garlic, which are also exported to other parts of the republic.

As regards staple contributions in agriculture, more of the production by far is done by smallholders. Land has been allocated under various systems of tenure. A more precise assessment of producers with regard to the size of their holdings still awaits full inquiry on our part. A full social and legal study of agricultural production necessitates a detailed analysis of land tenure, the organization of labour and the technology of the work carried out at present. For all this we only have the data in a rudimentary form so far. We know that land tenure is to be found in several forms. We have the old traditional holdings in private ownership dating from colonial days. A certain amount of land was confiscated from large holdings, especially from ecclesiastical holdings, in the middle of the last century. Under Benito Juarez the government intended that this land should be distributed to the peasants in the form of communal tenure. More recently, under the laws of expropriation dating from the third decade of this century, another communal type of ownership was established. We have found in Oaxaca that in some cases part of the expropriated lands are rented out to enterprising individuals by a group of owners. Some villages have refused to accept any lands under this tenure, since experience shows that a considerable amount of disagreement and rivalry is usually connected with it. Much fuller research into this complex and delicate problem will be necessary before detailed facts can be presented.

De la Fuente: *Private and communally held lands have existed since the colonial period. The Reform Laws* [those promulgated by Juarez in 1859 – Ed.] *affected only communally held land.* [This meant that lands held communally by Indian *pueblos* were affected. Ed.] . . . *Communal property which survived was registered in the name of certain reliable persons. This must have been the prevailing situation in the small localities of Oaxaca.*

A few days ago in Oaxaca, a law was passed which denounced 'hidden ownership'.[1] *This could affect the communal landholdings even though these are now legally recognized.*

*[With respect to land ownership by individuals.] The most general case, as I understand it, is that the landowner continues to live in the same town. The characteristic institution of half-profit lease (*medianería*) occurs when land is leased to the cultivator and the profits of cultivation are divided between the owner and cultivator. But two types of* medianeria *are found in Oaxaca. In the first and more frequent type, the landowner lives in the same locality as the cultivator. In the second case, land is owned by an absentee landlord who resides in a town or another part of the republic.*

[The history of landholding in the Oaxaca Valley is complex and not yet fully explored. Taylor (1972) concludes that during the colonial period the Oaxaca Valley did not suffer from the creation of large Spanish-owned farms and ranches to the same extent as northern Mexico or the valleys of Mexico and Morelos. The larger estates which did exist in the Oaxaca Valley were not inherited for generations within a single family as occurred elsewhere. On the contrary, Taylor claims (1972, p. 201): 'Individual Indians and Indian communities controlled about two thirds of the valley's agricultural land during the last 200 years of Spanish rule.' Taylor also writes (p. 201), 'The priesthood made the most significant gains in land ownership during the late colonial period; usually at the expense of the local Spaniards rather than Indians. Secular priests and regular orders acquired many of the best haciendas . . . between 1680 and 1770.'

The lands of large farms, ranches and church estates were all theoretically subject to division under the Reform Laws. However, the communally held lands belonging to Indian communities were often first and most disastrously affected (see Gonzales Navarro, 1954, pp. 121-31).

A new form of land tenure called the *ejido* has been created by the Agrarian Reform Laws derived from the National Constitution of 1915. Both individual and collective ownership of *ejido* parcels is possible. However, the outstanding feature of *ejido* ownership is that parcels of *ejido* land can be inherited but may never be sold. This form of tenure was created specifically to avoid the formation of large landholdings. Solis (1970, Table 5, p. 203) publishes data which show the total land area divided into *ejido* parcels between 1930 and 1960 in the various states of Mexico. Land area in the state of Oaxaca held in *ejidos* increased from 87,072 hectares in 1930 to 1,128,493 hectares in 1960. An increase from 87,072 hectares to 666,347 hectares had taken place by 1940. This does indicate that the Oaxaca Valley was probably undergoing radical reform in landholding during the time Malinowski and De la Fuente were in the field.

Although in theory *ejido* land was meant to be cultivated in small parcels by individuals and their families, the form of registered landholding in Oaxaca does not necessarily give a clear indication of the organization of agricultural labour. In the Oaxaca Valley (see Iszaevich, 1973) it does often indicate smallholdings. This is not necessarily true throughout the state. It is also the case that *ejido* land is on occasion sold (see Iszaevich, 1973). Ed.]

As regards labour, the bulk of it is done under the present system by the owner and his family. Agricultural hired labour is fairly frequent. There is a class in every village whose own lands are not sufficient to feed the man and his family, and such people hire out their services during the intensive period of work in the fields, usually receiving their keep and a small remuneration in money, ranging from 37 centavos to 1 peso daily.[2]

As regards technology, we find the widest range, from digging stick and hoe to the iron plough drawn by oxen. The prevalent agricultural implement is the old Spanish narrow plough, consisting of a substantial wooden head with a narrow iron cutting prong. The iron point has to be renewed frequently.

The horticultural type of production to be found in the low-lying, well-drained half of the Valley is carried on by small enterprises. The vegetable gardens have to be watered by hand. Water is drawn from the several deep wells scattered throughout the garden by means of large pails of tin or earthenware. Seasonal vegetables and flowers are grown and usually marketed by the producers.

Turning from agricultural production to local industry and crafts, we might start once more from those which are traditional, carried on by small enterprises and sold more or less directly in the market to the local consumer. We know already that earthenware plays an important part and is of great interest both to the antiquarian and to the functionalist. Ironwork, such as finds its way into the household, the workshop and the agriculture of the local peasant, is nearly all produced in the Valley. The raw material does not come from local mines, but is all provided by ironmongers from the city of Oaxaca and from scrap. The old, disused railway branches, among other sources, are of considerable importance. The craft of the tinsmith is expanding, since tin receptacles and utensils are beginning to replace earthenware, which previously was used almost exclusively.[3] Leather prepared in local tanneries is made into the traditional sandals (*huaraches*), shoes, straps and harnesses. Saddles are mostly imported from other districts. The carpenter and joiner, together with the wheelwright, supply ox-carts and doors, chairs and tables. Wooden troughs and large wooden spades are a local industry of some villages and the products can be seen in the market.

De la Fuente: *The ironmongers of the city sell nationally produced iron and also iron imported from the international market.*

Saddles come mainly from the Chontal region near Yautepec or the Isthmus of Tehuantepec. Burro saddles come from the Mixtec region, above Etla, and ox-carts[4] *are a special product of Sole de Vega.*

Weaving, as already mentioned, exists in a few communities which use the small, pre-Columbian handlooms. It has also developed on much more advanced patterns as a cottage industry in Oaxaca and elsewhere, and is rapidly becoming transformed into factory work. Dairy produce appears in the markets principally in the form of cheese, the best being produced in and around Etla.[5] Milk is rarely consumed by the peasants or Indians, but appears in the market, particularly in Oaxaca.

Among the purely local and characteristic crafts we have to mention, naturally, the extensive and complex industry in maguey fibre (*ixtle*). This is grown in the mountainous regions north-east of Tlacolula and in the Caxonos region of the Sierra. The production of rope, string, nets and bags, which formerly was carried out almost exclusively in the region of Caxonos, is now shifting towards some centres in the Valley, especially to Oaxaca. Natives of the region of Caxonos have now opened several workshops in the state capital, receive the material from their villages, and manufacture, it in the market town. [See photo 16.]

De la Fuente: *Historical sources suggest that the* ixtle *industry is extremely ancient.*

Another extensive set of industries is connected with the paraphernalia of religious cults. Candles, scapularies, votive offerings of tin or silver, rosaries and small printed pictures and texts are produced in Oaxaca and other Valley towns or imported from Puebla and Mexico. A few selling sites appear in every market place, and they blossom to an incredible extent during a fiesta market. On one occasion, at San Martín Tilacayapan, we counted six selling sites within the church, twenty in the church atrium, and some six to eight outside. An even greater number appear during the festive markets in Oaxaca and Tlacolula, at the feast of All Souls, during the feast of the patron saint of the capital, or on patron saints' days in the smaller towns.

The production of charcoal and firewood, this latter especially in the form of highly resinous pieces of pine, is one of the staple industries of the poor Indians from the mountainous regions.[6] The peasants from a few villages in the Valley also own communally parts of the mountain. They make expeditions from home in order to collect wood from the mountain. On a rough calculation, we estimate that during a period of five to six days, some nine loads (*cargas*) of wood are collected. This yields eighteen nets full of charcoal, which then are sold at a profit of 50 to 75 centavos for the load. This would make some 4.50 pesos for five days, or 90 centavos per day. From this gross profit we have to deduct certain working expenses and to consider that a load is usually the work of more than one man. On the production of pitchwood our data are incomplete.

An important native industry is the distilling of *mezcal* (an alcoholic drink distilled from the fermented juice of the maguey). In most of the villages there are one or two, sometimes many more, illicit stills (*palenques de contrabando*). In such cases the craft is a home industry, never very profitable and always subject to government raids. A year or two ago one of the villages was severely 'punished' and several people killed during a raid on a *mezcal* distillery. There are a number of legitimate small-scale distilleries, especially in the region of Tlacolula and Ocotlán. There are also some fifteen or more industrial firms employing half a dozen people each.

This brings us to a distinction which is always very easily made in the arts and crafts and industries of our area. So far we have mostly enumerated small-scale production, usually carried out by individuals or families within the household or, as in the case of the charcoal and wood providers, by people going out with some domestic assistance or in a group. However, the line between an incipient industrial enterprise and a case of household production is not very easy to draw in some cases. Thus, we have in Oaxaca and in some of the other towns the production of articles which need electric power or else an internal combustion engine. Ice, aerated water and lemonade and castor oil cannot be produced without some additional power. This is now also employed in many of the mills producing the coarse maize flour used for making tortillas, *molinos de nixtamal*. Such mills are increasing in number and output, as a supplement to the pre-Columbian *metate* which, as we know, is by no means displaced. We have already spoken of the large-scale production of earthenware in Oaxaca. In an establishment like the one described, the mills and mixers in which the clay is prepared are mechanically operated. In Oaxaca we find also motor-driven mills for wheat and bakeries on an industrial scale. Industrialized production occurs in the tanning of leather, and in several textile, hat and soap factories. Obviously, the production of electricity is itself an industry; giving employment to a number of workmen and producing power for the capital and one or two of the towns such as Ocotlán and Ejutla.[7]

We have seen throughout that native production has to compete against, and becomes in many ways supplemented or even supplanted by, importation from abroad. If we consider the market system as a mechanism of exchange, we have to treat imports and objects locally produced as two 'equivalent' sources of supply. To study the market without being aware of the two channels by which it is fed would obviously be incorrect. The inventory of the articles sold, the insight into the consumers' needs, the economic and social role of the middleman – not to mention the wholesale importers and exporters – would be distorted if we did not consider both factors. From the point of view of the fieldworker who studies the economics of the region, a clear distinction between imports and local production must be made. Local production must become the subject of careful and detailed study in its own right. The ethnographer interested in the Valley of Oaxaca must devote as much attention to agriculture and native crafts and arts as he does to the market itself.

Yet it is necessary to see that under present conditions of international trade, worldwide culture change, and interdependence, even the peasants in the Valley of Oaxaca are affected in what they do and eat, think and wear, by what is happening in Japan or England, in India or Germany. The standard of living of a Japanese worker or a Chinese coolie, as well as the industrial mass production of Germany, the USA or Great Britain, allow certain articles to be effectively marketed in Ocotlán, Tlacolula and Etla. Thus, very distinct factors and forces may affect the standard of living of our peasants and also influence their income and mode of life. In one way they may increase their real income, while they may affect adversely their actual wages. On the other hand, a careful ethnographic study of the standard of living in any part of the world is a piece of research which, if multiplied and integrated over considerable areas, might become an important contribution towards solving some problems in international economics. Even during our preliminary study, we were impressed by two facts. First, the influence of foreign imports is still astonishingly small; second, this influence is decidedly on the increase.

As a problem of culture change, it is interesting to note that adopting foreign, unfamiliar, artefacts, techniques, modes of life and standards of existence is not a simple process. What the ethnographer usually calls diffusion is not a matter of having a new trait 'presented' by an alien culture and 'adopted' by the indigenous one. Our study shows that clear-cut and simple but often disregarded dynamic elements enter here as main determining factors. The foremost factor, of course, is the purchasing power of the culture into which 'diffusion' has to make inroads. The standard of living of a mountain Indian or a Valley peasant is a system of needs to be met by a supply of material goods, services and objects of spiritual value. Economically speaking, the system of needs is the cultural and sociological basis of what is called in the textbooks 'the demand'. The supply, if it arrives in the form of a traditional flow of goods and services, is simply the result of organized local activities gradually built up round the satisfaction of these needs.

Under conditions of culture change, however, there enters also a supply of articles and practices not previously known. New needs or wants have to be created, new suggestions are made to the community as a whole, successfully or not. Yet the link between the range of needs, including the potential ones to be developed, and the scale of old satisfactions and new temptations, is essentially economic. The commercial traveller, the agent, the advertiser – all spearheads of diffusion – are not so much interested in raising the native standard of living as they are in obtaining native cash.

The duty of the ethnographer, therefore, is to determine the exact context of traditional needs. Putting this in concrete terms for our region, we find that there are traditional systems of housing, of dress, of diet and of intellectual and spiritual requirements, all of which produce a system of definite demands.

We have tried to establish what this system is by studying a typical household in a village, another in an urban community and a third in a mountain region. At this stage of research, however, the ethnographer can only insist that the standard of living of an Indian or a peasant community is conservative for two reasons. In the first place, the range of goods which have to be purchased regularly on a definite family budget is determined by such well-organized and traditionally founded institutions as the household, the village community, the church and the occasional feasts.

In the second place, such items as food, dress, furniture and cooking utensils cannot be changed piecemeal. They are related to one another through the institutions mentioned above. The Indian or peasant has, for example, a high demand for fireworks. With these he worships God, glorifies his community and satisfies his sense of the dramatic and supernatural. To replace fireworks and a whole range of 'miraculous' or religious objects would mean a complete transformation of the spiritual universe.

'Conservatism', 'apathy' and 'traditionalism' are useful labels, but to interpret their meaning correctly we have to state that they all cover the intricacy and interdependence of the various forces – spiritual, customary and technical – within each institution, and that they also represent the interdependence of the various institutions within each municipality, each district and each region.

Another and equally potent determinant of the 'conservatism' of 'cultural lag' is economics. The well-to-do Indian in the Valley lives in a house built of sun-baked brick and lives with his family on something like 1 peso a day. The poorest Indians in the mountains have been estimated to exist on 3 dollars a year by Steininger and Van de Velde. This, I think, is perhaps a sensational rather than a correct estimate, because allowance has to be made for 'real income' in terms of free lodgings, a great deal of free food and a number of services for which no payment is necessary except in terms of reciprocity. Indeed, the calculation of 'real income' in our region and in ethnographic areas in general is a problem to which we do not pretend to have a solution. None the less, if we assessed the value of the food consumed by a poor highlander at 10 or 20 centavos a day, this would not be an exaggeration. Such facts tell their own story. To attempt to transform the standard of living by education, advertising, commercial blandishments or any other means of 'free floating diffusion' is simply absurd.

The main prerequisite of diffusion is purchasing power. This was recognized by the Mexican revolutionary reformers, who had clearly before them the principle that the Indians must be given more land. In some cases the reforms proved successful. In some cases they were not feasible, because, as in the mountainous regions of Oaxaca, there were no large estates and no church property to be allotted to the natives. In other cases still, the reform has to be gradually translated into the effective working of a new system. Here, perhaps, nothing is as necessary as a few ethnographic investigations carried out, not by partisans of conservatism versus progress or vice versa, but by students inspired by one passion only: that for full and detailed understanding of the mechanisms of economic production in relation to land tenure and to the social organization of groups.

Turning now from this theoretical digression to the facts at hand, it will be necessary briefly to indicate some of the mechanisms used by foreign trade in the creation of new needs. In the market they are still to be found only in the most rudimentary form. Perhaps the most powerful way in which new requirements are created, and the sale of imported goods is gradually introduced into the region, is by the process of usage percolating from the higher and wealthier strata to the poorer people.

For the analysis of economic demand in general, and demand in the market more particularly, we have to establish a number of social strata and classes. We find in the region a few hundred families with annual incomes above 10,000 pesos. These can be classed as the well-to-do bourgeoisie. None of them belongs to the colonial aristocracy of Oaxaca, of whom, to our knowledge, not a single survivor exists on the spot.

De la Fuente: *A few marquesses are said to be 'floating around' Oaxaca City and a few people pretend to be of the old aristocracy. Also, and in a similar manner, some Indians of Zaachila, for example the Velazco family, claim descent from the indigenous aristocracy of that locality.*

The bourgeoisie are rather the main industrialists and wholesale merchants, mostly Spaniards, also one or two other foreigners, the highest government officials and a few mine owners. The confiscation of the large landholdings (*latifundios*) and of foreign property has eliminated most members of this class. Those who exist combine a Latin and North American standard of living. Some have motor cars, most have large, comfortable houses, well furnished and provided with bathrooms. They dress, eat, and in some cases read and amuse themselves, in a manner which combines the cultural appetites of the Anglo-Saxon (*gringo*) with those of a cultured Latin. There are among them one or two prominent intellectuals, notably Sr Solano y Gutierrez and Sr J.F. Iturribarría, who play a part in the creative life of Mexico. We have expanded on this class because through it the influence of Western culture permeates our district.[8] If we made an inventory of their purchases, we would find that they own and use many imports from the USA, notably the motor car, the sewing machine, the radio and many of the books they read. We find also that members of this class make a great many purchases in Mexico City, and import such articles as they need from several other centres, such as Puebla and Monterrey. Nevertheless, for their domestic table and for a number of articles of common use, they or their servants still frequent the market place. There is not a single butchers' shop in Oaxaca outside the markets. Fruit, vegetables and even earthenware may be purchased in the market for even such a prosperous household.

Another class consists of the town-dwellers with incomes ranging between 5,000 and 10,000 pesos, who would differ on minor points from the previous group. They still purchase most of their clothing in local shops, but for groceries and objects of domestic use they rely even more on the market.

A third group are the urban mestizos: the teachers and the smaller shopkeepers, the wealthier artisans and the large class of government or commercial employees. We have made one or two detailed investigations about the budgets and standard of living of representative examples in this group. We deal here with people whose incomes range between 2,000 and 5,000 pesos.

The poor urban population of Oaxaca and other towns may live on anything from 500 to 2,000 pesos. They are the small artisans, the employees, and those who, living in town, gain most of their living by the cultivation of gardens or lands. They differ in their mode of life, requirements and dress from the peasant. Their clothes may be worn and tattered, but they constitute the livery of Western civilization. Their food is very much like that of the peasant. In their budget we would find items such as cinema tickets, an occasional newspaper and a subscription to some local society – items not to be found in the budget of a peasant or mountain Indian.[9]

In passing to the fifth group, the peasants, it is interesting to note that in many smaller towns there is a clear-cut distinction between the Westernized, indigent townsman and the peasant who may live beside him. There is a current Oaxaca expression defining the 'civilized' people as *gente de razón* and the genuine indigenous group as *naturales*. This corresponds to the distinction found by Robert Redfield in Morelos in 1930 between *los correctos* and *los tontos*. A parallel distinction is made between *gente de castellano* or Spanish-speaking people, and *gente de idioma*, or people who speak a native language. There is, moreover, a current expression in Oaxaca which characterizes all the culturally indigenous Indians as *yopes*.

The line of division is clearly and palpably marked. The indigenous group speak a native Amerindian language as the mother tongue: Zapotec, Mixtec or Mixe. The *gente de razón* speak exclusively or predominantly 'Castilian' [Spanish]. Men of the first group dress in shirts, white or coloured, and in loose trousers. They wear sandals, and are engaged primarily in agricultural pursuits. We have already distinguished the urbanized people of Ocotlán from the 'indigenous' population of San Antonino. Nevertheless, in the latter place a few people would probably qualify as 'reasonable' (*gente de razón*). In such large half-villages, half-towns as Zaachila and Zimatlán, the difference runs along boundaries between village sections (*barrios*) where we would find groups of brick or stone houses clustered in one part, and typical peasant dwellings, each within a fenced garden (*solar*), in the other.[10]

The fifth group, the peasants, though they may live in towns, reside predominantly in the many villages scattered throughout the Valley. There is a uniformity in peasant housing and furniture, in domestic implements and clothes. The characteristic diet consists of coffee, chocolate or *atole* with tortillas in the morning; tortillas and occasionally meat or soup at midday; and in the evening a dish of black beans or soup with chillies and tortillas. Meat may be eaten once a week or more often, according to the wealth of the peasant. The poorer peasants may have a much plainer diet. Their clothes are more tattered or mended, and furniture is simpler.

Roughly speaking, people in the villages of the Valley live within a budget of between 25 centavos and 2 pesos a day per person. The latter figure will apply to wealthy individuals. We know of some individuals whose fortune is valued at about 50,000 pesos, and at least one famous genuine Zapotec peasant who has the reputation of being a millionaire. His nickname is Chindino, and he is said to live according to the standard of living of the average Indian.

In many of the peasant communities an Amerindian language is spoken exclusively or predominantly. There are still communities in which we are not able to converse with most men and with hardly any women. Near them are villages inhabited by peasants who do not know any language other than Castilian. In villages where Amerindian languages are spoken there are marked differences in custom, outlook and in certain habits and domestic equipment. The peasants all dress alike, as we have previously described. They have certain characteristic customs and mannerisms. A meal taken with such a peasant group would reveal that, while men sit on diminutive chairs or benches, women invariably sit on the floor. Meat and soup are served in bowls. The tortilla is rolled up and used as a combined fork and spoon. Otherwise fingers and teeth are used. Good table manners include noisy belching as a sign of satisfaction. Some peasants sleep on primitive bedsteads; most, however, use mats spread on the floor. The daily toilet follows a characteristic routine of a somewhat rudimentary nature. Soap is now generally used and maize husks function as effective sponges. The sanitary arrangement consists usually of a hole dug in the ground somewhere in the *solar*, or else a convenient area of the earth's surface conventionally reserved within the precinct without too much regard for privacy.

Peasants are also set aside from other groups by their economic occupation, which is agricultural work. Most peasants are deeply religious in the traditional, Mexican sense. The attention given to the domestic altar, though formal, is scrupulously observed. The festivities of saints, especially of the patron saint of the village, have to be observed, and they demand a considerable outlay of money and energy.[11]

An important sociological characteristic of this group is their strong sense of village community independence. Each community regards itself in many ways as sovereign. Although quarrels between *barrios* in larger units such as Zaachila are frequent and bloody, when it comes to alien control or interference the members unite to form a hostile front.

When, recently, a murder was committed just on the outskirts of Oaxaca in a political feud between two sections of the village of Xoxo, the aggrieved party strongly worked against placing matters in the hands of the police. They regarded the traditional institution of vendetta as more efficient, appropriate and honourable. In a community in which one of us (B.M.) spent some ten days, the village of San Sebastián Abasolo, we frequently met cases in which some legal malpractices and even felonies and crimes were well known to the inhabitants. They were discussed, and adjudicated by public opinion, and adequate punishments were prepared by the aggrieved party. In no circumstances would the inhabitants think of bringing matters before a court or administrative agency.

The same village has a definite policy in its attitude towards the church and the school. It has followed this policy for years, and neither state authorities nor the federal government have been able to exercise effective pressure against the intervention of the church in the school.

We mention this fact because such detailed observations, if carried out and confirmed in other areas of the Mexican republic, would give a very important set of indications in matters of social reform and political planning. The communal sense of autonomy that the Indian villages have is in reality a highly important democratic asset of the country. It means that local public opinion is extremely important when it comes to carrying out any planned systems of education, economic improvement and other elements of culture change.

This, indeed, was recognized by President Lázaro Cárdenas, whose success was largely due to the fact that during his journeys across the republic he was able to win and mobilize local public opinion in most Indian areas.

There is a sixth group of consumer-producers who are constantly met in the market and who, in some ways, are one of the most important factors in its vitality. These are the hill Indians from the surrounding mountain ranges. One of us (J.D.L.F.) has worked previously in the Zápotec region of Yalalag and visited the tribal region of the Mixe. We were also able to obtain second-hand information about this latter district from one of our best educated informants, Professor Unda, who worked in the various districts for years. It is necessary to distinguish here between several Mixe sub-groups, some of which are still but little affected by recent changes in the republic, by education and progress. These groups have also remained somewhat outside the Latinizing influence of the colonial period.

Let us start with possibly the poorest, least Latinized, and least economically organized group, the Indians of the south-western range. Steininger and Van de Velde (1935) give an interesting picture of perhaps the poorest communities in this group. Our observations of economic aspects of life in this Indian group, which we know only from the market places, show a satisfactory concordance with the data collected in much greater detail by the authors. Although the standard of living of that region is extremely low, people consume and need a number of articles which are mainly supplied by markets in the Valley. They like to have coffee, chocolate and sugar. For their thin porridge and tortillas they do not grow sufficient grain in the region. They need to purchase at least double the amount they produce. Occasionally, also, they like to have bread for some of their festive occasions. They also have to acquire a substantial range of fresh vegetables and citrus fruit, which, with chilli peppers, probably supply the necessary vitamins in their diet. Their clothing, poor as it is, must be purchased for money, with the exception of some woollen items of clothing which are locally made. Most of their household utensils, the earthenware, leather goods, hats and such articles made of iron as they need have to be procured in a market or a shop.

If the nearest market in the Valley disappeared overnight, the Indians from adjacent mountain districts to the west would either have to walk a much greater distance to another purchasing centre, or forfeit some of their necessities. Indeed, they would be on the verge of starvation. It is well to discuss here the manner in which they obtain purchasing power as consumers of necessities. The region which they inhabit allows them to collect and, in some cases, to produce articles badly needed in the Valley. They market pitchwood and charcoal; wool from their sheep; fruit such as apples, peaches and pears; and also *amole,* a root which grows wild in the mountains and is used as a substitute for soap. These articles are brought to the market and sold or exchanged, largely through barter, for other articles they need.

The details of barter will be discussed later. Some of their transactions have to be made in money, because coffee and sugar, maize and earthenware, as well as clothes and leather goods, have to be purchased for ready cash. It is easy to see that to this type of participant the market is an extensive and elastic means of acquiring immediate purchasing power, through both barter and cash sales. The market and the local shops are also an emporium, vast and varied from the point of view of the Indians' standard of living, in which the full range of their needs can be readily satisfied.

A somewhat different role is played in the market by the Mixtec Indians. Here our information is even less complete. None of us has visited this part of the country, in which the situation is very much more complex. The region is certainly not wealthy as a whole. Some districts have to buy in an additional quota of the staple food, maize. Native craft items, such as earthenware and many of the textiles, as well as the products of maguey fibre, and some basketwork, are imported from the Valley. This region, however, is vast, and some of its northern districts are supplied principally from the large industrial centre of Puebla.

The influence of Mixtecs on the market of Oaxaca is due to many importations from that region. Products of palm leaf – principally straw hats, mats, small woven baskets – certain types of chilli, blankets, wool as raw material, wheat and medicinal herbs are the imports which allow the Mixtec Indians to command the necessary purchasing power for their acquisitions. Many Indians from this region have settled in the capital, Oaxaca, and in other towns and act as agents, especially in the importation of straw hats, but also as minor or major brokers in the import of wheat and raw materials and in the export of Oaxacan goods mentioned.

Compared with the south-west mountain range and its relationship to the Valley, we have here a somewhat different picture. We could say that the Valley and the Mixtec region are two interdependent economic producers, exchanging goods and services and each supplementing the production of the other. The greatest complication for our study probably arises from the fact that certain goods manufactured in Puebla or in Mexico City, as well as some raw materials, pass through the Valley into the Mixteca, but they are also sometimes imported into the Valley via the old trading routes going across the Mixtec region. Eastern and southern parts of the Mixtec region are by no means poor. The soil is fertile. Large quantities of maize and wheat are produced, and the country is well stocked with cattle and other animals.

De la Fuente: *In reality it is the northern part of the Mixtec region which is poor in the neighbourhood of Huahuapan, Silacoyapan, Teposcolula and Tlaxiaco. Nochixtlan seems somewhat more prosperous, as do the eastern Mixtec Highlands which border on Etla and Zimatlán.*

All this is preliminary information to put us in the picture, and was gained from contacts with agents and middlemen dealing with the Mixtec region, but settled in and around Oaxaca. Also we had information from those of our friends, principally Professor Unda, who know the Mixtec at first hand.

Passing now to the region of the Mixe Indians, we obtained a picture not unlike that of the poor inhabitants of the western mountains. It refers primarily to the Mixes inhabiting the district adjacent to the eastern valley of Mitla and Tlacolula, and it is these people who are the main participants in the Valley markets.[12] These Mixes have to supplement their production of maize with considerable quantities, which they buy on every visit to the market. They usually also purchase meat in the Valley, groceries, bread and vegetables. They hardly ever leave the market place without consuming some strong liquor in addition to what they carry in their travelling bags. Although there are two or three Mixe centres where earthenware is produced, the Mixe buy large quantities of good pottery, especially that of Atzompa and Oaxaca.

De la Fuente: *I would be unable to check the affirmation that the Mixe hardly every leave the market place without consuming some strong liquor.*

In order to purchase all this they bring, first and foremost, the fruit which grows better in high altitudes, mainly oranges and peaches. They also sell potatoes and chillies, which grow primarily in the warmer regions, but are traded by the Mixe from high altitudes in the market of Tlacolula, their principal emporium. In season they sell a type of broad bean (*alubia*), and *pixtle*, the seed of the fruit of *mamey*. They sometimes carry coffee, collected from their neighbours with a warmer climate. Much of the earnings of this poor but hard-working nation are due to the services which they render as carriers of heavy loads. Their remuneration is about 50 centavos a day, from which they have to purchase their food and deduct their net income. The same forces and the same mechanisms which we found underlying the western mountain Indians' participation in the market obtain here. The Mixe does depend for some staple food and for the minor luxuries, such as meat, groceries and hard liquor, on the Valley market. He can offer certain goods for which there is a ready sale since they are not produced in and around Tlacolula. On the same day and in a series of transactions (some of which once more consist of barter) he obtains necessary goods and a surplus of money, with which he makes his purchases on the market or around it, and starts on his return journey.

De la Fuente: *The dependency of the Mixe on the Valley market is not absolute. In fact the Mixe provide some Zapotec with cattle. The major part of their liquor and groceries are carried to the Mixe by Mitla traders through Ayutla. My impression is that the Mixe attend the market places, and are just beginning to develop as traders with some ability. . .*

The Zapotec Indians of the Sierra Juarez, who undoubtedly are more prosperous than the Mixe, also depend to a certain extent on the markets of Tlacolula, Oaxaca and Etla. In some of their districts they need to supplement their production in maize. In most places they have to buy fresh vegetables (including onions), earthenware, groceries and clothing. In all this, the distinction must be borne in mind between the districts adjacent to the Valley and the parts much further distant which rely on other market places. Several of these are located in the Sierra itself. Nevertheless, many of these other markets draw upon the Valley system, and import some of the more modern products coming from abroad, as well as the articles already mentioned. For all this, the northern region pays in wheat, coffee and such fruit as apples, quinces and pears. In this vast area many distinctions would have to be made, for some of the especially fertile districts send their surplus of maize to the Valley.[13]

We shall see that the type of economic necessity which makes the market important, even indispensable, to the Indians of the outlying and surrounding regions applies also to the peasants in the villages around Oaxaca. Most of these villages can and do produce the staple food, maize. Some of them are highly specialized, like Atzompa and Coyotepec with their earthenware, Tlacochahuaya and San Antonino with their vegetable markets, or the villages round Etla with efficient bakeries and cheese production. They bring important articles to the market. But they have to sell their goods or barter them in order to supply themselves with necessary food and manufactured goods. We have already discussed in some detail how this mechanism covers a very small section of the food requirements of Atzompa.

We could study the problems of consumption in a village from the point of view of the household. We would find a weekly or fortnightly family budget appropriate to the wealth and prosperity, as well as the intelligence of the family. On the day of the week when the nearest market is held, the household members have to mobilize their resources. They gather a few *almudes* of maize, a sucking pig, a few dozen eggs, in the case of the agricultural producer, or the earthenware finished during the week, or the vegetables ready for sale and collected during an analogous period. These are brought to the market place and the net cash obtained is then invested, first and foremost, in the items of the commissariat: coffee or chocolate, sugar, meat, liquor and necessary utensils. Twice in the year the wardrobe may be replenished or a new hat purchased, usually in connection with a festivity. The same principal market mechanism – a place to obtain purchasing power and a large range of opportunities to exercise this to fully satisfy all current needs – shows us how necessary this institution is for the peasantry of the village.

Only a few words can be said here about the other classes of consumer. The poor urban population, or the *naturales* who live in the larger settlements, live with the same short-range budget as the village peasant. We estimate that by far the larger proportion of purchases made by these people are made in the market. In other words, we would find that a considerable proportion of their income is spent in buying from market vendors. The main difference between poor urban dwellers and peasants consists, first, in the somewhat different range of needs already indicated. In the second place, people can use the market every day if they live in the capital; indeed, according to where they live, they can supply themselves from one of the four functioning daily markets. In these they can purchase any foodstuffs and also a range of other consumer goods. Moreover, urban people frequently purchase goods in small shops which are open the whole day within a very short distance of their homes. Here, however, there is a differentiation according to the articles purchased. Many market articles are not to be bought in the shops, or else are to be bought only at a much higher price. Our information about this type of consumer is very deficient; indeed, this is the class we have so far been unable to study. We have obtained an occasional indication, not integrated into any clear picture, and we have no budgetary evidence.[14]

The bourgeois class with incomes above 500 pesos per annum we know better. One of us (J.D.L.F.) has undertaken research in a few households. Members of the bourgeois class still rely principally on the market for food. They buy some textiles and objects of daily use in the market, or else in the smaller shops. As regards more sophisticated articles, they may have a sewing machine, one or two pieces of furniture, maybe a gramophone, all articles imported from outside the region and not to be found in the market.

We have already spoken somewhat extensively about the well-to-do classes, and we know that these rely to a much larger extent on many articles imported from abroad.

To the above discussion concerning the relation of supply to the market places and its two-fold sources, local production in the Valley and importation from the outside, a few concrete remarks might be added. We distinguish here between the market and other commercial establishments. In the latter we would find a good many articles not produced in the state of Oaxaca, or in the republic of Mexico. Motor cars, sewing machines, gramophones and radios come principally from the USA. That country, as well as Germany and, to a lesser extent, Great Britain and France, supply kerosene and gasoline lamps, electric torches and a whole range of articles connected with lighting, and heating and more elaborate cooking apparatus. Hardware pots and pans, very little used by the Indians or peasants, come principally from the USA and Germany. As regards textiles, most goods are manufactured in the district or in the republic, and only finer qualities come from abroad. Musical instruments and a number of chemicals and pharmaceutical products are imported from abroad. A quantity of canned goods and some table delicacies, such as saffron, are imported from Spain, while a few of the best grocers and liquor shops sell wines, liqueurs and brandies, imported from France, Italy and Spain. Canned goods come mostly from the republic, but also from the USA, France, Germany and Spain. We were impressed by the small quantity of cheaper Japanese objects to be found in the region, excepting a few celluloid objects such as combs, mirrors and toys.

Hardly any of the foreign imports, however, affect the actual market place. Having formulated this problem earlier in our research, we were especially interested to discover any non-Mexican produce marketed. We can register few items definitely traceable to a foreign source.

De la Fuente: *In general terms one might say something like that. We have already discussed it several times. Nevertheless, I remember English thread, foreign satins and a good deal of other haberdashery in addition to the celluloid objects. For the sake of precision I would suggest that this phrase be modified to be consistent with the tone of other observations relating to the same topic: i.e. there are few foreign articles in the live market.*

The most significant import, however, is that of staple food. Our data indicate that under normal conditions the region is self-supporting as regards maize, wheat and cattle. Indeed, these articles are normally exported from Oaxaca to other parts of Mexico.[15] At the same time, during years of drought or blight, when the price of maize soars to tenfold the average value, while elsewhere in the other Mexican states or abroad the crop is good, this staple food would be imported. This would affect the economics of the market and of the whole district to a considerable degree. During the summer that we worked in the Valley, the crop was by no means disastrous, but it was below normal. Maize was imported from other Mexican states.[16] We could see that it was sold at lower prices than its local equivalent.

There are definite consumers' preferences for the local product. This is due to the fact that the local types of maize are suitable for its various uses in the *atole*, a highly appreciated beverage, in the tortillas, which play the role of bread in the Mexican diet, and a great variety of rolled or compressed forms in which it is used. A keen distinction is made here, for unless the difference in price becomes considerable, the natives of the Valley will pay perhaps 5 centavos or more for the local corn over and above the price of the imported one.

At this point we would like to state that the preparation of the various dishes, the tastes of dishes, and the assessment of these – the relation of food preparation to supply, price and market transaction – should be further studied. Another important point is that on the subject of staple food and its preparation the work of the ethnographer or the economist in Mexico and that of the student of international trade will have to be co-ordinated. The price of importing maize depends on railway tariffs, the overheads of large importing businesses, at times subsidies from the government, as well as on the progressive development of the standard of living and the consumers' taste. Ethnography can be of use to the economist here, but it has also to rely on the economist's co-operation. The problem of maize is unquestionably of national importance in Mexico. It is the staple food of Mexico; it will not be replaced and should not be replaced by other cereals for sentimental, historical and economic reasons. To study it in detail within a small Indian or peasant household is essential. To put it within its larger framework of national economy and international trade is indispensable.

De la Fuente: *In this section it is said, in essence, that foreign imports only affect the market slightly. There is obviously a partial contradiction here, given the later description of the importation of maize. But it seems to me that the affirmation is wrong in general and that precisely at this moment we have proof of the error. Although there are no large quantities of imported goods in the market place itself, the shops around the market place and the larger commercial establishments [carry imported goods]. This, together with the scarcity of maize, the export of maize [as opposed to local consumption], the insect plague, etc., must be seriously influencing price rises in the market place itself. We can see this is another case of the interdependence of the market place and strong commercial movements like price rises and the absence of certain goods, as well as the lack of control [over prices] and the authorization of commercial dealings which are prejudicial to the poorer people. This happens throughout the country. In my opinion the idea that foreign imports only affect the market slightly is incorrect and should be amended to assume precisely the contrary.*

We have spoken on various occasions of the export of grain and other products out of the Valley to Mexico. It would be interesting to know if thirty years ago similar export occurred. I think that the export of goods, which (unlike cochineal and certain other goods) were not traditionally exported from Oaxaca, has begun relatively recently. The existence of a maize deposit, which functioned up to the last century and was a means of safeguarding the poor against speculation and famine, indicates that maize was accumulated locally rather than exported. I believe that the export of chicken, eggs, pottery and other goods in addition to maize is decidedly recent. I observed in the Sierra that sudden exports from one region to another provoke local disturbances which are very evident. In the Sierra, for example, the rise of a mining enterprise called Natividad provoked imbalances in a large number of markets when hens, eggs and many other products were taken to the mine because a good price was paid there. The purpose of all these observations is merely to call attention to the possibility that these exports from Oaxaca, despite their complex organization through agents, may be of very recent creation.

In connection with this, we are fully aware that the data contained in this section are only an approximation to full economic treatment. The presentation of a true economic record of production, exchange and consumption would obviously require numerical assessment of the activities in each phase. We propose, however, to study agriculture more fully in its economic aspect. We need data concerning the value and quantity of land held and used by the average peasant. We would wish to classify these according to a few categories of wealth and efficiency. The economic assessment of labour as a factor in production implies some standard of comparison between the use of domestic labour and that of hired assistant, again, if possible, in numerical terms. We have an approximate idea of several family budgets, although we have no definite data to present. All this is mentioned because the purpose of our memoir is to suggest and stimulate, to indicate the scope of this research, and to define the main theoretical problems of a type of combined ethnographic, sociological and economic fieldwork in Mexico.

7 Market transactions under the microscope

We still had to take a closer look at some typical transactions in the market, observe the display of wares, the methods of attracting a customer, the inevitable hither and thither of bargaining, the sale and the appropriation. In this, our methods consisted not in asking what the price was, nor yet in discussing matters with buyer or seller. The principal approach on a busy market day, when trade was brisk and the visitor attracted little attention, consisted in registering what actually happened and thus obtaining data of behaviour and performance rather than verbal indications of intention and hope.

This does not mean that we would not discuss problems, ask questions, and obtain as full a commentary as possible of what was going on. But the solid realities of the transaction, the price asked and the price offered, the sum paid and the method by which the buyer judged the quality and quantity of the articles, these were observed. As a rule we observed first, before the conversation was started. At times one of us would sit down on a small chair near a well-disposed and friendly merchant. Clients would come, look at the wares, inquire about prices, examine and walk away without buying. Others would actually make purchases. The transaction was usually, though not invariably, woven into a prolonged conversation of bargaining, advertising eulogies and deprecatory remarks.

At times we would follow the buyer, and thus be able to compute the range of his interests and needs as a consumer. This was a complex and difficult task. But it could be accomplished, and was done especially by one of us (B.M.) when the excursion to market was made in the company of a good friend from one of the neighbouring villages. From the friend we obtained a detailed and accurate account of the manner in which quality and quantity are assessed, and the final choice made. The general problem which underlies all such observation is obviously to obtain a clear idea of the essence of haggling in the market. In other words, we observed in all this the concrete, specific working of the interplay between supply and demand as it occurs in typical transactions of a regional market in Mexico.

We were able to reach a few interesting and, we believe, firmly established general principles. The fair and correct price of each commodity is known by buyer and seller alike.[1] As regards bargaining, we observed several important differences and established conceptual distinctions. In some goods – first and foremost, in maize – the interplay of supply and demand and also the actual bargaining in performance are economic realities. In other words, people do not bargain here within the range of 2 to 5 centavos for the pleasure of verbal interchange or any other psychological reason, but because throughout a market day the price of maize rises and falls, within narrow limits, it is true, but in a manner which is definitely determined by the need of the consumer and the financial requirements of the producer. The effective mechanism of the price change consists of the integral fact of the infinitely many, infinitely small acts of bargaining which actually occur.

De la Fuente: *Here I would question if the buyers, or the majority of the buyers, have an exact idea of the fluctuations in price which occur during the day. Do they know what is happening? It would be possible, perhaps, to investigate whether the fluctuations are seasonal or if they occur throughout the year. This and subsequent information would throw more light on the affirmation that bargaining occurs because of daily fluctuations in price.*

As opposed to maize prices, which fluctuate during the day, we found that there are articles sold practically at fixed prices. The buyer approaches, the seller mentions the price, the transaction is effected or is not effected. No haggling occurs and for these articles, obviously, the price becomes fixed early in the market day. Among such articles we might mention chillies, cheese, leather goods and perhaps some fruits such as bananas, pears and pineapples.[2] Most other articles are sold with the more or less extensive latitude of offer and counter-offer, of bargaining and argument, at a price, however, which in reality is not very much affected by the initial statement and the counter-bid. The widest margins, perhaps, are found in native-made blankets, in the *rebozos*, and also in *huaraches* and textiles.

De la Fuente: *Here price fixing is discussed. It is true that the price is sometimes fixed early in the day or even weeks before, and there is relatively slight variability in prices. Bargaining is then done not for the amount of money, but over the quantity of merchandise. For example, the number of pieces in a heap will decrease. What is said here about bargaining must be related to the affirmation made several times in the manuscript, that the price is known to both the seller and to the vendor.*

To what extent is this affirmation true?

It seems over-emphatic. I would say that often the price is known, for example, of a heap of some particular goods . . . but the market is absolutely inconsistent on this point. Ignorance of the price, and the well-known fact that ignorance of the price can be turned to the vendor's advantage, has a great deal to do with the phenomena of bargaining.[3]

In the manuscript, the relationship between vendor and buyer is mentioned as an element which serves to facilitate transactions, but the differential value of goods at different places is also mentioned. I believe this is recognized by the vendor who is looking for the opportunity to take greatest advantage of his client by giving him less merchandise or giving it to him for a higher price.

In essence I think that bargaining is an economic reality, not only with regard to maize, but in many other articles in which it appears to be only a psychological phenomenon. Can it be said that the price of wagons, or saddles, is known to the consumer? I don't think so. Nets and other products, too, have seasonal changes in price. Perhaps these observations may have clarified the point. But aside from feeling that the phrase is over-emphatic, the question is too important to let it pass without further observation.

The problem which we had in mind in orienting our observations on haggling, bidding and bargaining refers to the determination of prices. Our general conclusion is that prices are determined by real economic factors of the market: by supply and demand in such articles as maize, cattle, vegetables, fruit and other produce. In many other articles the cost of production puts a minimum selling price on the article, which would include also the cost of transport, taxation and gain. Here, undoubtedly, great variations occur between such people as the sophisticated sarape makers of Teotitlán, or the potters of Atzompa, on the one hand, and on the other the Indians who produce and bring charcoal, rope or firewood to market. Even here, however, it is not impossible to calculate the economic motives of either side. We have made several attempts at such calculations, which will be found in the following detailed descriptions. Our data clearly show that however near the subsistence level an Indian lives, he will not carry on trade at a loss, but will replace it by some more profitable occupation. This and other important problems, for which we have some data, await much fuller elaboration. The study of the calculations made by the buyers and sellers is one such problem. We have met some Indians or peasants such as our friends Manuel Andrés Jarquín of Abasolo and Antonio Sumano of S. Juan Chilateca who are able to observe directly or learn from hearsay, and know the fluctuation of prices throughout the whole system. With remarkable clarity and astuteness, Manuel was able to foresee and calculate the probable trend in the price of maize. He could give us exact information about what was likely to happen the next week in Zimatlán or Zaachila, and his forecasts usually were confirmed. Incidentally, it is to him, perhaps, more than anyone else that we owe the rapid progress of our work.

The same clarity, astuteness and keenness of calculation can be found in a great number of the professional shopkeepers, middlemen and *regatones* of the Oaxaca Valley. On the other hand, the middlemen who work semi-professionally and make frequent trips from some surrounding districts into the Valley, are not as well able to calculate. Examples will be given presently in which one of us (B.M.) attempted to calculate for a *regatón* of S. Agustín Yatareni the approximate net gain obtained in one trading trip. To gain such a man's confidence a very good trick consists in asking him how much he has paid in municipal contributions. When, on examination of the ticket, it is found that the contribution levied amounted to as much as 50 centavos, the ethnographer expresses his astonishment at the size of the figure and presents the trader with the amount. Given in this form, it is easily acceptable – for the taxed Mexican Indian feels, like any other taxed human being, that he is being robbed – and it gives a fair assurance to the native that he is not dealing with a government agent. They often suspect even *gringos* of being agents. This procedure allows the anthropologist to obtain a much greater flow of sincere information than could be secured for double or triple that amount in an unvarnished tip. This latter would simply arouse suspicion. As will be seen from the data, the man proceeded in his trade more or less empirically. He knew that at the end of each journey he cleared so many pesos and that he could live on it. He was, however, generally unaware that for certain articles it was definitely more profitable for him to buy in the market and to resell in his village.

The class of people who do not calculate at all, who do not think in figures and who are easily cheated and exploited, are the Indians from the outlying districts, more particularly those characterized by their inability to speak Spanish and their extreme poverty. Also they cannot manipulate figures, since most of the schools in their villages are of recent date, and they do all their marketing with certain well-established traditional habits. Even here, however, taking the ingenuousness of these people into account, it is not impossible to assess their behaviour in an economic framework. Taking their role in the market into account, not as isolated individuals, but as a group, they contribute, exchange and carry away goods on the basis of certain principles of equivalence, which the ethnographer can and must observe and even formulate numerically. The detailed examples which follow will show at least some samples of how such calculation was done, and establish general principles on which we propose to continue our work.

De la Fuente: *I would object to the way in which 'the class of people who do not calculate . . . cannot manipulate figures, since most of their schools are of recent date' is described. The correction is purely stylistic, but the way in which the idea is expressed gives the impression that the natives do not have a means of counting in their own language.*

With regard to these people, exploitation, economic pressure and extortion as well as direct cheating are phenomena which the ethnographer cannot neglect. We were able to list three types of extortion and economic ill-treatment. In the first place, and most vociferously denounced by the market public, is the question of taxation, to be discussed more fully in our analysis of transactions. Second, it has already been mentioned that the buying up of large quantities of produce at artificially low prices under pressure, economic or political, is an abuse not necessarily perceived by the peasant or Indian, but unquestionably affecting him in that he receives less for what he sells and has to pay more for what is purchased. Third, there is small-scale, systematic exploitation and cheating of the less educated Indians by the various classes of middlemen, shopkeepers and even ordinary buyers and sellers. This cheating, of which we will see some examples in performance, may be plain petty thieving, *sub rosa*, of which the Mixe are especially afraid, and rightly so. Beside this are the differential handling of measures, cheating in quantity, in quality, in calculations and even in money. All this, once more, enters as an economic factor which affects certain transactions and not others.

This brings us to another general problem, which must be stated here, as it was formulated by us in some of the theoretical discussions which punctuated our fieldwork. Every economic transaction of sale and purchase obviously has two sides. A piece of merchandise is offered.

It has to be in one way or another measured or qualitatively assessed by the buyer. He in turn, gives either the value in money or else the equivalent in some other form of merchandise.

In all trade, on every market place, therefore, how the goods are weighed or measured, or else how they are qualitatively appreciated and their value determined by certain standards, is an indispensable problem of observation. To put our results briefly and definitely, we have found that the use of weights and measures is extremely limited. The officially accepted metric standards, which imply a precise definition of weight or cubic capacity, are used in only a few butchers' shops in Oaxaca and for relatively rare transactions in maize.

A few things are weighed or measured in a manner which contains no definition whatsoever that could be put into terms of numerical equivalents. We have seen a vendor of copal incense with a pair of completely unstandardized balances made of wood, string and pieces of gourd, weighing his produce using two or three stones on one side and resinous bits of the copal incense on the other. Salt, locally processed near Tlacolula, is at times 'measured' by being crystallized in a little wooden case and thus assuming a definite, but hardly measurable, solid form. This type of measuring and assessment becomes even less defined when dried shrimps are sold on little plates, or fried grasshoppers are doled out in bowls, or dried peas are sold in arbitrary plate measures. The meat, which in most cases is sold not entirely fresh, but salted, is divided in a complicated manner into long strips, those being subdivided into smaller pieces, the length and thickness of which are known and assessable to buyer and vendor alike. The subdivided meat is offered in some places, notably Ocotlán, bound up in large parcels from which so many pieces are then extracted. In Tlacolula, the meat is displayed in long strips. These are subdivided by the vendor who names the quantity as he detaches pieces from the long strip at each sale. [See photo 13.]

The staple produce, maize, and also black beans, peas and broad beans, are still almost universally measured by the square, wooden, fairly shallow case which corresponds to the *almud*, or its various subdivisions. This measure, at present, is not the legal one. Yet it is the one preferred by seller and buyer. The problem of 'traditional conservatism' has occupied our attention, and below we shall discuss the various, mostly sound and well-founded, reasons why the *almud* does not readily give way to the litre or the kilogram. [See photo 30.]

The fruit, nuts, vegetables and other goods for direct consumption are invariably displayed and sold in *montones*, heaps of traditional size in which the quantity, as well as the quality, can be readily seen. Here we deal with the purely intuitive appreciation of quality and quantity. The reasons why this does not lead to any chaos in the economic sense are not difficult to give. From the point of view of each class of buyers, the range of articles purchased is limited. They know quite well the amount of tomatoes, bananas, nuts or salt fish which they need for a meal or two. They are allowed not only to see the articles, but to handle, poke and even to smell them. In many cases, when small quantities can be abstracted, as in the sale of cheese, bread, grasshoppers or nuts, the vendor spontaneously and graciously gives a tasty morsel to the buyer. This is characteristic of many transactions. The buyer takes his time, perhaps deliberates with his friends or members of the family, and the decision is taken according to knowledge, appreciation and experience in buying.

When it comes to meat, the fullest examination is the rule of the market. Fingers, nose and tongue, even, are freely used. In the case of fried bacon and pork, or barbecued and other prepared meats, small pieces are cut off to tempt the buyer. Thus, there is little doubt about how the assessment is made without weight or measure. In all cases, the seller and the buyer alike know perfectly well the monetary equivalent in terms of quality, size, thickness, tenderness or freshness.

Another point never to be forgotten is the personal relationship between buyer and vendor. The goodwill, especially of the peasants who come from villages surrounding a centre, is a determining factor. Our friend Manuel told us that he always buys his meat from two or three butchers' stalls in Tlacolula. He calls the women vendors *comadre*,[4] and is on friendly terms with them. He informs us that these people know perfectly well that they are dealing with a regular customer and do not attempt to cheat him. Similar relations obtain frequently between various middlemen or producers and regular customers.

Exceptions to this type of relationship between vendor and buyer are the *naturales* (Indians) of the surrounding regions. The Mixes have to fight the buyers and they are fair game, we are told, when it comes to their purchases. Their defence in selling is to cover the bag of fruit, push away the crowding purchasers and take out a handful of peaches or apples, selling each handful to one purchaser at a time. In buying, they go from table to table in the butchers' gallery, surveying other articles carefully from a distance. They buy only after long and careful deliberation. Since they do not speak either Spanish or

Zapotec, their verbal bargaining is often limited. At times, when it comes to a somewhat larger purchase of maize, they are directly cheated. Both of us have observed transactions in which the number of *almud* sold and those charged for did not tally. Again, it is against these people that the various cheating tricks in measuring are most frequently perpetrated. These consist of pushing off some of the grains when the flat measure is straightened, or in letting a few grains drop back into the vendor's bag when the measure is emptied into the Indian's bag.

We have now to pass to the other side of the transaction, the value received for the merchandise sold in terms of money or other goods in barter. In each economic situation which is different from that of our own – based on bankers' credit as the principal means of exchange and on more or less perfectly controlled uses of banknotes and specie – the problem of money as currency has to be studied in some detail and with consideration of general principle.

In the region of Oaxaca and as far as the market situation is concerned, we have only to deal with the Mexican federal issues of banknotes, and the various types of silver, nickel and copper coins. As regards paper money, the banknotes of 5 to 10 pesos and certainly those of higher denominations have a very limited currency in the market place. This is related to the fact that a large part of the market public do not accept paper money, for it has apparently no currency whatsoever in the outlying districts and it is regarded with suspicion and used with difficulty even in the villages of the Valley. When our friend Manuel, in the company of one of us (J.D.L.F.), went to buy some cattle in the great market of Tlacolula on 10 October, he had to carry 250 pesos in silver specie. This is a symptom of the fact that banknotes are not accepted as payment in the surrounding district.

The reasons why paper money is so limited in its effectiveness are largely historical. The district of Oaxaca, like most other parts of the republic, has experienced since 1910 a number of financial crises, apart from the fact that on one occasion Oaxaca became an independent state with its own money during that period. On various occasions, therefore, the inhabitants, rich and poor, found that banknotes lost their value, completely or partially. The sophisticated members of the community, who understand the reasons and mechanisms and who could sustain losses with greater equanimity, have adapted to the present currency, which is valid and stable. Not so the Indians. Even the foreigner who wants to have some purchasing power in the market, or who would make an excursion into the surrounding regions, has to provide himself with a sufficient quantity of silver.

When it comes to smaller quantities, there are nickel and copper coins, all based on the metric system, with coins for 1 centavo in copper, 5 and 10 centavos made of nickel, 20, 50 and 100 centavos (or 1 peso) made of silver. The student of the market place has to become accustomed to a whole set of expressions referring to amounts not coined now, but used in familiar assessments. Three centavos are familiarly called *cuartillo*; 12½ centavos is a *real*, hence 25 centavos become *dos reales*. Two *cuartillos* are still called *medio*. Another expression often used is *tostón*, meaning 4 *reales*, or 50 centavos. The diminutive for a centavo is *vito*. There was a time when this 1-centavo coin used to be cut in half and used as currency in the market.[5]

One of the problems which obviously had to be posed and solved by our observations was that of the manner in which an article of merchandise, assessed at its proper value, was exchanged for its equivalent in the market. In other words, it was necessary to define, with as much detail and precision as possible, the types of transaction. We have found here that two main categories have to be established, since both are still in practice. Barter still exists – that is, the direct exchange of commodities for commodities and, very rarely, for services. Although less frequent than actual monetary sale, barter is still important and is still determined by economic needs. Barter is the form in which the major part of the transactions of the poorest Indians is still carried out. It is also predominant in the small market town of Atzompa.

De la Fuente: *It seems to vary according to market place (*plaza*). For example, I would say that the natives of Sta Inez del Monte and others barter a good deal in Zaachila, and sell more in Oaxaca. In other words, there are market places with more or less barter. It is perhaps of interest that I was told in Ixmiquilpan (an Otomi market place) that before the revolution, around 1905, barter was very frequent, and that it ended with the revolution.*

The other type of buying and selling is the purchase of goods for money. We have discovered very few cases of credit. The one on record refers to the sale of ready-made clothes in the market of Oaxaca. People personally known to the vendor, as a rule themselves established in the market, either permanently or at least once a week can obtain goods on credit and will make instalment payments once a week. We are not listing here cases of credit given by shopkeepers, since our attention is focused on the market place. We know that credit is occasionally given, and have one or two concrete observations from Etla and Tlacolula, but here our material is certainly incomplete. In most cases, the money is paid directly in full, and only after the payment is made can the buyer take away the article purchased.

In a fuller elaboration of the subject of credit, barter and the direct exchange of goods and services for money, the student of economic and sociological conditions in the district would have to list one or two interesting cases of gifts to be repaid later, as well as the customary pooling of services and goods. The institution of *guelaguetza* consists of gifts received during a large festival. The gifts are carefully listed and are repaid when the donor has to organize a similar enterprise. This custom has already been noted by several ethnographers; [see Parsons (1936) and De la Fuente (1939, 1949); also Beals (1970)]. One of us (B.M.) was able to study the performance with minute detail during a *mayordomía* in the village of Abasolo. We both saw it at work at a large feast in Coyotepec.

We now pass to a more detailed study of some concrete behaviour in the market place. We may as well begin with barter. [See photo 32.]

In many markets we would find that on a hot day a number of obviously poor people each carry round a large jar of water and a glass. They offer their services to various vendors, especially to those who sell articles of small value. For a glass of water they will accept any small remuneration given them in commodities as well as money. A small apple or peach, a couple of nuts, a few beans, will repay the service received. It could be called a type of begging-barter, in which something is offered in the expectation of a small repayment. We have also seen old women offering small parcels of salt and receiving a centavo's worth of various articles.

It may be added here that actual begging hardly ever occurs in the region. None of us has ever been approached with a demand for coins except, of course, by small children who treat it as a game, and who have probably been encouraged by some stupid tourists.

De la Fuente: *When we discussed this I said that in contrast to Veracruz, for example, the number of beggars (*limosneros*) is minimal. It does increase a good deal on fiesta days. It would be convenient to study 'the day of the beggars' in which the beggars go from house to house, and shop to shop. I believe the day is a Tuesday, but I am not sure.*

Passing now to more serious types of barter, let us take our stand on the south-eastern side of the market at Ocotlán, where the poorest Indians from various regions traditionally settle down to display their wares and carry out their precarious business. Among them, we would find a group of people who have come from one of the villages to the east, San Miguel Tilacayapan, and brought with them dry wood for fuel. This article, which can be collected by the members of the community, represents only the value of labour and the price of transport. Usually donkeys transport the wood in loads which we estimate roughly at a value of 1 peso per load. The vendor of such an article will squat and place his firewood in heaps valued at 3 or 5 centavos. Presently, people approach him or her and bringing such articles as chilli, apples, peaches or prepared grasshoppers. A careful inspection by either side takes place first. The initiative comes from a merchant in fruit or vegetables. Usually a handful of the articles to be bartered is offered for inspection. The equivalents are then discussed. The fruit is delivered and the wood collected.

After a time, if all the wood has not been sold, the vendor takes the initiative. He or she will get up, leave somebody in charge of the remaining supply and, taking only a few bundles, go to the meat stalls. There, late in the morning, large heaps of dried wood and other articles can be seen accumulating in the street under the eye of the butcher's lady. These are the goods to be bartered for pieces of meat. In such transactions, the initiative is taken by the wood-seller, who offers a bundle and is, in turn, presented with an appropriate equivalent in meat. The Indian will thus go round the market and offer his wares for any other article he needs – onions, salt, sugar-cane or other vegetables. We suspect that during the morning some of the wood has also been sold for money. In so far as money has not been accumulated, the Indian may take articles obtained through barter to his village and resell some of them for a better price or barter them for such commodities as he still needs. [See photo 18.]

Although we have incomplete material on this type of barter, we have been able to ascertain certain interesting generalizations. For reasons not quite clear to us, these Indians find barter preferable to sale. A woman of San Antonino told one of us (J.D.L.F.): 'The people of San Miguel, they like to barter; they do not like money, instead they like barter, even when you offer them money.' The most probable explanation of this is that, like some other traders, they prefer to acquire merchandise at Ocotlán which they can then resell at a better price in their own locality.[6] This follows the pattern which we find in the large-scale commercial journeys to Tehuantepec, and which we also observed in most of the smaller trading enterprises of this region.

The good woman of San Antonino also confessed that she gives 3 centavos' worth of dirty salt or of shrimp powder for 5 centavos' worth of firewood. And this brings us to an interesting point. In the assessment of the value of articles sold and purchased, there is obviously a distinction to be made between the Indians' own locality and the centre of Ocotlán. The firewood is collected free. We would have to calculate the amount of time expended in the collection and in the transportation and also the price of the transportation. This latter includes an assessment, in percentage terms, of the value of the beasts of burden, of their maintenance and of the special expenses in tethering and feeding the burros at Ocotlán. The Indian has an assessment, no doubt intuitive, of the value of the wood which he brings to Ocotlán. This differs from the value as assessed by the people of Ocotlán. Hence, the frank statement that 3 centavos' worth of salt buys 5 centavos' worth of wood. It represents the difference in the respective calculations. On the other hand, the 3 centavos' worth of salt or shrimp powder will be realized at 5 centavos in the Indian's own village. She or he may make less profit than calculated, but the profit is there.

De la Fuente: *I suspect there may be no subsequent resale in the village if, as I was told, the settlements of the Chichicapa region are dispersed and not compact. Of course, the possibility of resale in a market place does exist.*

Even more important and interesting is the fact which we have clearly ascertained that most of the wood bartered goes to middlemen (*regatones*). A woman who has brought firewood from a nearby village sits a few paces from a group of Indians who have brought apples or peaches, nuts or chillies. Yet barter never occurs between these primary producers. Invariably and inevitably the middleman enters; he makes a profit by buying some goods, and then barters these articles for wood. The explanation of this behaviour can be found by further inquiry. The people who bring fruit or nuts from the mountain will not barter it for wood. They have an abundance of it in their own surrounding woods. They need articles which the middleman can give them. There is no possibility of barter between the two groups who bring different articles but cannot find a common measure in goods for the transaction. Firewood has no purchasing power with regard to the producers of fruit or of most vegetables. Hence, the middleman is indispensable. He makes his meagre living through his ability to negotiate with the other sides of the tripartite transaction.

De la Fuente: *In my judgment, the reseller (*regatón*) buys more than he or she barters and barters later. The first process is purchase, and the second is barter (*trueque*).*

*In the following affirmations: 'most buyers are middlemen (*regatones*)', 'there is no exchange between primary producers' and 'the middleman (*regatón*) is indispensable', the middleman's role is emphasized as indispensable because he exchanges with both parties. Aside from the plausible explanation that there is no common measure by which to judge the transactions, there is a simpler fact. The inhabitants of those places which lack wood and forest are led (by their lack of fuel) to accept the offer made by the wood-dealers of Chichicapa. Because of the differing value of the goods exchanged in the different places where the goods are to be used, there is an advantage in not using money. Here, as in Ocotlán and Tlacolula, it is possible that on one day of the week barter occurs, and on another day goods exchanged initially in barter will be sold.*

In the same market place we observed another type of barter between peasants from two neighbouring villages, a barter also typical of this market place. To take a concrete example, we stand near a woman from San Pedro Guegoreche, a village about one league distant from the centre of Ocotlán. She sells quicklime, an ingredient necessary in the preparation of maize for tortillas. A man from Santa Lucía de Ocotlán approaches her with a basketful of tortillas. They barter. Four tortillas of a yellow, thick type are exchanged for four 'measures' of quicklime (*cal*). Each measure consists of a fairly large, standardized chunk with a small piece added as a tip (*de pilón*).[7] The woman has brought her quicklime, about 1 peso's worth, on a burro, and she displays it in three standard sizes at the values of 1, 5 and 10 centavos. She has also brought some twenty or thirty small cheeses. The man informs us that he prefers to barter his tortillas, since he knows what he needs and receives better value without using money.

We shall rapidly survey one or two more examples. In Zimatlán the main street of the village is lined with two rows of obviously poor Indians in dirty, tattered clothes. They sit on the edge of the pavement displaying their apples, pieces of pitchwood and peaches. On inquiry we find that they are from the villages of Sta Catarina and Magdalena Mixtepec. They are among the poorest Indians of the Mixteca. The local people, both middlemen and consumers, approach with vegetables and ready-made food. Among the articles acquired by the Indians by barter we noted cooked young corncobs, cooked squash, tortillas and tamales (steamed and filled maize bread); also quantities of raw onions, squash, lemons and garlic. In the transactions we found that little bargaining took place. Vegetables and food were offered to the Indians in the palm of the outstretched hand. We noted once or twice that they rejected such articles as lemons and quicklime. They never refused cooked food or vegetables. The value of an onion (1 centavo), garlic (three for 1 centavo), a tortilla (1 centavo), tamales (2 or 3 centavos each, according to size), a corncob (1 centavo) are standardized and there is no discussion in terms of money. The goods offered by the Indians had to be defined in monetary terms. They were selling four large apples for 4 centavos, the actual value of which would be 6 to 8 centavos in the main market as sold by re-vendors, while the smaller ones were two or three for 1 centavo. Thus, barter here proceeds on both sides on well-known lines of customary, standardized value.

Another scene of barter, observed in some detail, included a woman who came from San Antonio de la Cal. She was offering the standard produce of that locality, quicklime, in standardized pieces. This is displayed in 'measures', which are solid pieces at the value of 1, 3, 5 or 10 centavos; at times, also, smaller pieces are accumulated in a small basket and given in a piece of paper or a large leaf. For her wares the woman would receive fried grasshoppers measured out in small earthenware plates at 1 centavo per measure. With each transaction she would add a small *pilón*, and would receive a small tip in grasshoppers or other articles. She was observed leaving her selling site and doing the rounds, offering pieces of quicklime and attempting to barter them for peanuts, without much success; also for pitchwood and fruit, equally unsuccessfully. She informed us that she tries to barter and to sell for money. Indeed, she was seen buying peanuts for money. [See photo 24.]

These data are given here as noted down in our field books. They are obviously incomplete. One of the problems connected with this type of small-scale barter is that we have hardly ever observed poor vendors of the type here described, either Indians from the mountain or small-scale vendors like the woman with quicklime, selling their goods for money. Yet they undoubtedly have money, because we have seen them buying objects in shops or from market vendors. The main object of the Indians from the mountain is to purchase maize in grain, which they apparently cannot do by bartering their goods. For the present, we have put forward one or two hypotheses and we hope to follow them up. It is possible that these people carry the wares procured by barter in the market back to the villages. There they might sell them at a profit for money. Thus, they would arrive at the market next time with some cash as the result of the transaction.

Another possibility is that these bartering Indians may sell for money, not in their own villages, but perhaps in some small local market. This type of problem may be solved by further fieldwork. These Indians can be followed to their own locality and the transaction observed at the other end. It would then be possible to calculate the profit resulting from the different values of articles according to where they are bought and sold. This type of small trading journey might correspond closely to what happens on the big overland trips from the Valley to several outlying regions, a form of commerce which we have studied in detail only with regard to the journeys to the Isthmus.

As regards the woman with the quicklime, the costs of production of this article could be studied without too much difficulty as the locality is very near to the capital.

The case of the woman with quicklime brings us to another broad economic problem on which our data are copious, but neither fully digested nor yet precise. It refers to the quantity of the goods brought by a vendor – whether he be the poorest of the poor or a well-to-do middleman – and the surplus left unsold. Direct inquiries of people who sell in the market elicit invariably the stereotyped, 'It will be sold in the end' ['Se vende']. There is almost a superstitious attitude in the market towards the possibility of a large surplus being left. Direct observations show that there are various ways of dealing with surplus which, on a 'bad day', may be substantial, even at four o'clock in the afternoon. When the vendor is a local person with a house and store rooms in the market locality, he packs up his goods, puts them on his back, or calls one of the market porters, and carries them home. Not so a vendor from the outside. The wealthier type of middleman, who has a varied and rich display of earthenware, textiles or leather goods – that is, articles which do not easily perish – will have a number of receptacles in which all the goods are packed and then transported to the railway station, bus or ox-cart and thus carried to his residence, which is very often in the capital. Breakable goods, like earthenware, are often stored in a room hired for the purpose. We know of a number of middlemen who have such stores in Ocotlán and Tlacolula, paying some 2 pesos a month rent. Thus, they are able to have their merchandise ready every Friday and Sunday respectively. All this, of course, enters into the economic calculations and has to be allowed for in any computation of profit.

Poor Indians who bring to the market fruit, firewood, brooms, vegetables or flowers try to dispose of the unsold surplus in several ways. They will first walk round the market offering the goods for barter at every selling site where articles which might be useful to them are to be found. This is not often successful. They will then go round the local shops, offering their articles at prices considerably lower than their value in barter or market sale. They also may try to sell it from door to door at private houses. And then there are the middlemen. These, however, would be more likely to buy at the beginning of the market than at the end. The prices which they offer in the afternoon would be nominal, for at that time there is not much chance of resale.

[De la Fuente here comments on reports about the proportion of barter to sale. He finds that the Indians of Sta Inez and the vendors from Zimatlán and Zaachila report that they barter more than they sell. By contrast the mountain people and the vendors in Oaxaca and Tlacolula report that they sell more than they barter. Ed.]

There are some interesting distinctions which we tried to confirm regarding the nature of the barter transaction itself. In some cases, especially barter observed in the Atzompa market, money definitely enters as a measure of value. In other words, both sides in the transaction inquire about the price of the articles. They come or do not come to an agreement, and if the goods change hands, the difference is paid in cash. Thus, if the price of a little jar is finally settled at 18 centavos, for which the other side trades three articles of food, each at 5 centavos, 3 centavos in cash would be added. We could speak here, therefore, of barter on a firm monetary basis as regards the definition of value, although the transaction is principally carried out in goods.

In other cases, the traditional equivalents of the two types of articles seem to be so well-established that barter takes place without any reference to the price of the two articles. Here, as we have seen, the two series of articles exchanged are from a relatively limited range. They are articles of small value and quick 'turnover'. That is, they are one of a great quantity of transactions. The price of onions, garlic, tortillas or corncobs is so definite and fixed that these articles may almost be regarded as currency. Their character as currency is also due to the fact that they are permanent, constant and ever-recurrent necessities of typical Mexican consumption.

In Atzompa, by contrast, we deal, especially on the side of the potters, with a relatively wide range of articles, the price of which varies according to type, size, quality and possible defects. These articles, though of great utility, are not the type of consumers' goods wanted by everybody at any moment and with a constant recurrence.

De la Fuente: *I think that there are appreciable variations in the price of the articles mentioned (garlic, onions, corncobs) according to the season and place of origin. I don't believe that there are traditional equivalences, or that the prices of goods like tortillas, maize cobs, garlic, etc., are sufficiently fixed that they could function as currency. I suspect that was the situation some thirty years ago and might continue to be so up to a certain point. At present the oscillation in prices refers always to money.*

It will be obvious to the ethnographer who has read the preceding pages that we are as keen on defining the inadequacies of our results as on recording some interesting discoveries made. Our demonstration of the method adopted here, though only partly successful, may be useful to those engaged in similar researches, even when these centre on a different problem.

8 Concrete data on selling and buying

Having given a brief analysis of barter, we pass now to the transactions in which money changes hands, as well as goods. We shall not try to cover the whole field, either by describing fully each type of article sold and bought, or by entering into a detailed discussion of the various types of business found directly in the market place or as collateral mechanisms. We sift our data, and do not select them on the basis of completeness in preference to unfinished points and problematic subjects. We have data on the production and exchange of maize, on cattle, and on butchering and the sale of meat, which, if presented fully, would take up more space than is available here. Our selection will be made in order to define our method of research and to indicate some problems of primary importance at various stages of solution.

The interplay of crude observation, with the registering of what actually occurs in the market, on the one hand and the theoretical analysis on the other is, in our opinion, the most important principle of sound fieldwork. We wish here to bring out the importance of guiding fieldwork by a set of theoretical principles and interests; of digesting facts in the light of such principles; and of translating such principles into a point of view from which further observation can be made. Thus constant constructive re-handling of the subject matter can be achieved during fieldwork. All this we have been doing during our work in the Valley, and we want to show the results even when these disclose the deficiencies of our initial way of treating the problem and show the lessons which we were able to draw from our own errors.

Let us begin with one of the characteristic products of our region, present in every market place and economically important, that is, earthenware. There is hardly a shop in a remote village, however, small and poor, in which we failed to note a few jars, bowls or pots, as a rule from Atzompa. The mixed permanent market sites in such daily markets as those of Totolapa, Miahuatlán, San Antonino or Mitla have, as a rule, a few pieces of pottery side by side with vegetables, fruit and aerated water.

Earthenware is displayed in the markets in a variety of ways. We shall, for the time being, ignore the varied and well-stocked permanent stalls in the market of Oaxaca, and the displays belonging to professional middlemen who, on a market day or any other occasion, are to be found in some of the market streets of the capital. Let us make a few observations in the market place of Ocotlán. A row of combined selling sites runs from the north-west corner, in which the earthenware is placed directly on the ground. At one of these sites, the vendor is a middleman of the wealthier type. The buyers may be recruited from townspeople, peasants and Indians. The poorer the buyer, the more time he will take over the examination of the article. A pot will be picked up, tapped in various places, carefully scrutinized with an eye for defects of shape, glazing or colour, and also for an exact assessment of size and volume. Then the mouth will be applied to the opening, if this is not too large, and the buyer will blow into the pot or jar to detect any crack or small hole. Finally, many a buyer looking for a possible defect will apply his tongue to it, because wetting the surface of earthenware shows up the defects which are darker, when wet, than the perfect surface.

After this examination the bargaining begins. As a rule, the price will be given within a 10-centavo margin on articles up to 50 centavos; 15 centavos will be added to the acceptable price on articles between 50 centavos and 1 peso; and maybe some 20 or 25 centavos on more expensive ones. We have made one or two concrete observations. A woman buyer, told that the article is 35 centavos, offers 20. She is told: 'There are no pots at twenty now.' She hesitates and goes away. We assume that had she gone up to 30 she would have obtained the article. On other occasions, we have seen the time-honoured custom of bargaining proceed with an initial difference of 10 centavos, ending with the article being purchased at the intermediate figure.

We shall not describe here the great number of detailed observations made in which we recorded the conversation, the range of prices and the very careful way in which the article was scrutinized. The above summary covers our data. However, the economic aspect of the whole transaction still awaits solution.

We were not able to assess with any degree of detail the gains of wealthier vendors of Ocotlán and Tlacolula or those with better-stocked selling sites at Oaxaca. That is, we cannot yet derive from our data an exact statement of the prices at which he or she buys for the expenses of running the establishment, the gains as regards various classes of articles, and the amount of sales on ordinary or market days. We can, for example, calculate the overheads of a merchant who permanently stores some of his goods at Ocotlán and has another store in the capital. We know that an article which can be purchased in Atzompa for 15 centavos will be found in Oaxaca priced at 18, in Ocotlán 20, in Tlacolula 22, and still further away, in places such as Mitla, Miahuatlán or Totolapan, with increments of about 2 centavos for each unit of distance. We have found also that when it comes to a large and very expensive article, say an enormous cauldron or a cooking pot which he will use in his *mayordomía*, the peasant from the Valley has to go to Atzompa, order it, and pay the price of between 5 and 15 pesos in cash directly to the producer. But a view of the manner in which the actual distribution through middlemen takes place has still to be integrated.

We have some data concerning lower-grade earthenware produced in Ocotlán and Coyotopec, in which the economic points are more fully dealt with. One of our friends in Ocotlán told us that he produces during the week, but sells extremely little, except on Friday in the market place. There, he admitted, he will earn some 15 to 20 pesos on an average day, as little as 7 or 8 pesos on a particularly bad occasion, while on especially good days – that is, during the festive periods early in November, in December, and during Holy Week – he may gain as much as 50 pesos or more. This, of course, is his gross profit. We have to deduct the expenses of carting the clay, the cost of firewood and the small sum of 2 pesos per month which he pays for the right to excavate the clay. Exactly how much this amounts to we are unable to say, but we estimate that it would be about 20 to 25 per cent of the sale value of the articles. Hence, if we take the average as 20 pesos per week, we might estimate the net gain at 15 pesos, or 2 pesos per day, which would be a normal income for a man, his wife, maybe an assistant and the children of the household.

Another piece of calculation connected with this concerns the time people are employed. While we were observing manufacturing technique we found that it takes about ten minutes to make a small piece of pottery, which would be sold at 20 centavos, from the moment the lump of clay is taken from the mass till the product is ready for baking. At this rate, in order to gain the 50 pesos in the course of an especially busy week, about 250 or 300 articles would have to be manufactured making allowance for breakage and defective pieces. For such production the women's work, which is the moulding, would occupy some nine to ten hours of each of the five working days, deducting Friday and Sunday. Meanwhile, the men would have to be busy bringing the clay, procuring the wood and firing the articles.

This calculation is provisional. It will have to be checked by more careful observation. We also have the question whether these people ever produce in advance and store their goods in the expectation of an important market. Also, at the season of feasts and general increase in food consumption, many more earthenware articles are needed. We do not know whether the potters of Ocotlán have any organization for distributing their produce to other markets through organized agencies.

The buying and selling of the earthenware from Coyotepec brings us to transactions between direct producers or, at worst, the first of a series of middlemen, on the one hand, and usually Indians on the other. On one occasion in Ocotlán we met two of our friends from Coyotepec. They brought two loads, that is, four large nets full of the substantial jars very much in demand by peasant and Indian alike. They told us that they would sell the larger jars for 25 centavos each, the smaller for 20 and 15. They made no secret of the fact that they would ask 35 centavos for a large jar, hoping to sell for 30, and that they would part with the jar for no less than 25 centavos. Observing the transactions for some time, we found that what they said was essentially correct. Articles which they would sell at 20 centavos were initially priced at 25. When discussing the price with buyers, they would always utter such sentences as: 'This much we ask; how much do you offer?' 'Let us bargain; we are here in the market place.' If the buyer insisted on a lower price for a better article, they would say, 'We cannot reduce this, but we have articles here for 25 centavos.' Such articles, of course, would be sold at 20. They told me that if, in two or three hours, they had not sold their whole stock, they would then get rid of the remainder at about 5 centavos less on each article to a local middleman, their usual partner in such transactions.

In this case we failed to calculate precisely what the value in production and the transport of the four loads amounted to; hence we cannot say how much these people gained during the day. Incidentally, on that occasion they were able to sell all their articles in the market. The two men were wealthy producers from Coyotepec. They could afford to put a definite time limit on the market sale, and they told us that they would not wait till late in the afternoon in order to gain 1 or 2 pesos more, for the time was more valuable to them. We know that they were going to buy certain articles, probably vegetables, from the market place, and carry them back to Coyotepec, but the details of this side of the transaction we also failed to register. Here, however, with our knowledge of production in the village and the rough cost of transport by donkey, we hope to complete our information.

One of the cheapest types of pottery, considered 'inferior' by the natives, although it looks attractive and is apparently quite durable, is made in the village of San Marcos Tlapazola. Observing a number of transactions between these people and buyers, we found the same systems of bargaining, that is, within the range of 5 and 10 centavos difference. A small earthenware basin was priced at 20 centavos originally. The counter-offer was 15, the sale made at 18. There are two main articles which the San Marcos people produce; the large, flat dishes (*comales*) used for baking tortillas, and the pots and basins in which are cooked various sauces and stews. The price range is narrow, the largest article being effectively sold at about 35 centavos, the cheapest at between 5 and 10. The price might be some 2 centavos lower in Tlacolula than in Ocotlán. The exact economic calculations on this earthenware were never made, although there would be no difficulty in observing the production in the village, which we never visited, and comparing it with the sale.

The type of economic analysis suggested here, with the methods of solution clearly defined but with only a few cases already solved, would be much more difficult to carry out in the cases of some of the larger and more complex businesses in earthenware. Were we to inspect the self-contained wooden stalls in Oaxaca, we would find in them a full range of products made in the capital, those of Atzompa also, some articles from Coyotepec, but hardly ever any of the poorer earthenware of San Marcos Tlapazola. Such a middleman buys extensively, stocks permanently, and his sales, considerably more effective on market day, are lucrative because they are carried on day by day from morning to nightfall.

Here the calculation which we planned – but carried out only piecemeal – would consist in an assessment of the middleman's overhead expenses, including the capital investment in the small wooden structure, in the stock in trade, and perhaps also in the risks of theft or breakage. Above all, however, we would have to find out from whom the middlemen buy and how much they pay. The probability is that, since they are stationed in Oaxaca, they buy at the lowest prices from the potters of Atzompa. Such permanent middlemen have storing places in their homes and are able, therefore, to purchase the surplus stock from an Atzompa potter who comes to town on a Saturday, strikes a bad market, and has to sell his wares at two thirds of the market value. We have seen such transactions taking place early in the afternoon, in which the very facial expressions and manner of the primary producer were a testimony to the bad bargain which he was forced to make.

Another important problem which brings us for a moment outside the market is the general organization of export from the village of Atzompa and from the town of Oaxaca. As we know, both these centres supply the whole region, and Atzompa pottery is exported from Oaxaca to many parts of the republic. We know for certain that the producer uses an agent who sells for him at a relatively low price to an agent from Oaxaca, who buys in the village. There is also an exporter in Oaxaca who puts the product on the train, as a rule in large nets for short journeys, so that the breakable article is not protected, though careful handling is recommended. For longer distances pottery is enclosed in baskets or other packing. Then there is an importer in Mexico or Puebla, who again has agents or middlemen who sell to market vendors in the capital or elsewhere.

We have seen Atzompa articles in one of the markets of the capital and also in Puebla, selling at about double the price for which we could have obtained them in Atzompa or Oaxaca. Between the producer and the consumer there may be five or more intermediaries. To determine the number of intermediaries and their activities is a problem not easy to solve, but from the data already obtained it is surely by no means insoluble. It is a problem of great theoretical interest and also of practical importance.

Attempts have been made already by one or two enthusiastic local teachers to organize the potters of Atzompa into a co-operative enterprise which would manage their exports directly. At first sight it might appear that such an organization could only be a blessing. So far it has not succeeded, owing to local rivalries, lack of the necessary initial capital, and the feeling of the producers that unless they could control the negotiations they would be cheated by the officials or clerks entrusted with the manipulation of business. We would like to study this problem more fully without any political or economic bias. The elements in the situation to be investigated would be, obviously, the obstacles already noted: absence of capital and the question of who might supply it; the local commercial organization, which should not be dominated by one or two individuals; and the possibility of finding suitable officials for such a co-operative. We have seen types of communal enterprise on a similarly large scale, involving tens of thousands of pesos, in another village. The result was that one individual of outstanding ability and commercial keenness was able to concentrate complete control in his own hands. The rest of the community suspected him – and they had unquestionably good reasons – of having diverted most of the money to his own profit. The benefit of the enterprise had been, at that time, practically nil, and the amount of money lost by the Indians enormous.

This sort of research on the possibilities for contemporary economic improvements, the difficulties as regards native commercial ability, the formation of an economic caucus, and the general inability of a group of natives to control their controllers, might lead to the adoption of a slower tempo in projected improvements and reforms, but also produce firm plans for long-range and all-round reforms.

An example of another attempt at such reforms, economic and social, is the straw hat industry of the Mixteca.[1] In every market place we find two types of Mexican hats sold: those made of wool, which are principally a local industry of the Valley; and those made of straw, which, so far, are mostly imported from certain districts of the Mixteca, notably from Nativitas. 'Straw hats' really means hats made from a palm leaf.

Walking through the northern square in Tlacolula, we come across some three or four selling sites of such palm-leaf hats. A woman, who after the usual bargaining has sold a couple of hats to an Indian family, informs us that she herself is a native of Nativitas. She has settled in Oaxaca and is acting as an agent for her family, her friends and other producers. She confirms a fact we had already known, that a few years ago the Mixteca Indians were only weaving the hats up to a certain stage of manufacture. All the articles had then to be sent to Tehuacan, where a few Spanish entrepreneurs did the finishing work and secured by far the larger profit. After the formation of extensive co-operative organizations, machinery for the shaping and smoothing of the hats was acquired by the Indians, and now their gains and standard of living have been considerably raised.

Previously they were able to obtain only 20 to 25 centavos per hat. Now they may be gaining double. Such hats sell in the Valley, the price ranging from 75 centavos to 1.50 pesos. Discounting one third of the value for transport and the gains of the middleman, there is still a substantial increment to the producer. Since this industry is organized and probably subject to some sort of accountancy, it would not be very difficult to translate our approximate estimate into a reliable calculation. It would be an important testimony to substantial progress.

De la Fuente: *As far as I know, the co-operatives were not in fact co-operatives, but another type of private institution which, in so far as the objectives of the programme were concerned, has been a failure. The co-operatives have developed into replicas of the Spanish pattern. The bank itself has totally failed in the Mixtec region, and some agents have made a good business out of the Indians.*

About profits from the hats: buying from a weaver, one pays on average 6 centavos for the unfinished hat. Each producer makes three per day and spends 3 centavos on palm leaf, so his profit is 15 centavos. For a fine hat 18 centavos is paid, less 3 centavos for the palm. One can make a single fine hat in one day.

*The reseller (*acaparador*) finishes the first type of hat, adding 7 centavos' worth of material and labour, and sells it for at least 25 centavos.*[2]

Walking along the market of Tlacolula on the northern side, we enter a part reserved for the vendors of ropes, nets, articles of harness, all made from the fibre of the maguey plant. The vendors are primary producers from Huila, one of the villages of the Valley. It takes them some four hours to traverse the distance from Huila to Tlacolula. There are also producers from the Sierra, notably from the complex villages called Caxonos. Besides these producers, there are also regular middlemen, either local or from Oaxaca. The producers try to sell their wares in the morning; they sell the remainder to middlemen at lower prices in the afternoon. The bargaining is 'psychological', that is, for the pleasure felt by the buyer as he beats down the price, which is fixed and well-known to the vendor. On one occasion we saw a number of articles moving with arithmetic precision within the 10-centavo limit. The vendor would ask 30, be offered 20 and sell at 25. Or else the bargaining might start at 65, go down to 50 or 55, and the transaction occur at 60. After we had observed such a course of bargaining for half an hour or so, the man, in this case friendly and good-natured, told us his place of residence (one of the mountain villages), disclosed the minimum price at which he would sell the article, and discussed in roughly estimated figures what it costs to produce and how much he thought he gained.

De le Fuente: *I was unable to check that the middlemen for maguey fibre in Oaxaca were buying in Tlacolula. Those vendors we have noted* *are manufacturers of Caxonos, and they do not buy fibre in order to resell it later. Don Abundio, who is quite a liar, buys fibre in Tlacolula, but the middleman (*acaparador*), Sr Sanches, receives it directly (from producers) as well as buying it from intermediaries.*

Such data, however, are never sufficiently reliable. To check them, one of us (J.D.L.F.) made a fuller investigation of an interesting group of natives from the Sierra district of Caxonos, who have settled in Oaxaca and, importing their material from the district or buying it in the market place of Tlacolula, carry out a somewhat more fully organized type of production in the capital. From a detailed calculation of their expenses, as stated by themselves, somewhat contradictory data were obtained. One establishment was found to produce ropes for 4.40 pesos. They allege that in this the expenses amount to 3.83 pesos. Thus, their net gain would be 57 or 60 centavos per day. Since this establishment consists of about three working people, they would each earn 20 centavos per day, which is certainly not plausible. We are giving this example to show how difficult it is to rely on the statements of a manufacturer or of a merchant unless these be collaterally controlled.

Like every other businessman, the Zapotec minimizes his gains and exaggerates his outlay. We hope, however, to control these figures more fully, especially if a visit to the producer's district can be carried out. These people, nevertheless, gave some interesting information on the earnings and cost of production in the villages. Thus, we learned that the women who specialize in net making earn, at piecework rates, 5 centavos for making two small nets. Since they are able to produce six or seven daily, their earnings would be about 15 to 17½ centavos a day. Women who make finer nets receive 10 centavos per piece and can produce about three pieces, which makes a higher earning of 30 centavos. Small and rough hammocks are paid for at 12 centavos per article and two can be produced daily, earning 24 centavos. This work is paid in cash, and the woman also receives her keep, which may amount to half the price mentioned. Women who make large and fine hammocks may earn as much as 80 centavos a day, since they receive 2.23 pesos for three articles, and can perhaps produce one article a day. They are not given food. All these figures are certainly plausible, since they are characteristic of the wages available to the poorest Indians. They might be too low, since they were obtained from the natives of the district, whose tendency would always be to exaggerate the value of the produce and to underrate all the profits made by every link in the chain of production, distribution and sale.

To turn to another sociological aspect of the market system, we have already mentioned on one or two occasions the phenomenon of migration. People have moved from their native towns and villages – important industrial centres – to the capital. These include people from the Mixteca, with its palm-leaf hat industry, from the maguey fibre producing region just described, from Ejutla and Yalalag where leather goods are manufactured, and from San Antonino de Ocotlán.

In some cases they are plying their native trade for which they have a better market in Oaxaca, directly at their front door. In other cases they act as agents in circumstances where their personal relations of kinship, friendship and knowledge of the people in the producing centres is extremely useful.

We have, thus, an economically determined tendency for people from the outlying districts gradually to drift to the industrial and commercial centre of Oaxaca, and take up agencies or expand industries in the main market place. We know also of people coming from Zaachila in order to act as butchers, since in that region cattle are cheaper. Over and above this, the concentration of means of transport in the capital has induced many enterprising, keen and relatively well-educated individuals from Tlacolula, Ocotlán, Zaachila and Ejutla to move to Oaxaca.

The capital, on the other hand, has lost a great many of its inhabitants, especially among the wealthy and enterprising, owing to two reasons. Two terrific earthquakes, which occurred about 1930, shook the nerves of some, especially when they lost their homes and part of their fortune. Again, the same centripetal tendency, which operates in our district, in the whole republic and, indeed, all the world over, is pushing people with commercial, political and literary ambitions to move to Mexico City, or to such places as Puebla and Guadalajara. There is, thus, a gradual shift both vertically and horizontally. Oaxaca is becoming populated by less wealthy, less educated, yet enterprising and promising people from outlying districts who probably, in the future, will gradually move up the social scale. It is becoming depopulated as regards many members of its higher strata (who are moving, presumably, to Mexico City).[3]

Returning now to the market, we might visit a section which occupies a vast area, extending in space, time and number of transactions. This is the fruit market. Here, as we know, a rapid survey of the selling sites in a market place like that of Oaxaca on Saturday, Ocotlán on Friday or Tlacolula on Sunday would disclose a whole set of distinct categories. We would find the Indians from the surrounding ranges in every market, either bartering their fruit – a transaction already described in as much detail as we possess – or else, like the Mixes in Tlacolula, selling their fruit for money. We would find that category of impecunious, small middlemen, or here usually middlewomen (*regatonas*), who have bought from the same Indians some of their fruit, and also some other types of fruit from the neighbouring peasants. These women resell this produce at a small profit and at great leisure.

Then come the local fruit vendors, who provide themselves during the week from the producers who come specially to sell a considerable variety of articles. On this point we have substantial data about producers from Zaachila, Zimatlán and San Antonino, who either send fruit to small merchants in Oaxaca or bring it on Friday evening in order to carry on rapid transactions in the homes of their partners or in the hostelries (*mesones*). We have some calculations on this subject, from which we estimate that the producer receives about two thirds of the market value.

Finally, there is a special subject for ethnographic and economic study in the importation of tropical fruit. Pineapples, bananas and, to a smaller extent, coconuts, are imported into the Valley. Pineapples, which do not grow in the Valley at all, are now brought in by rail, but a certain quantity enters the Oaxaca Valley from traditional journeys made to the Pacific coast, mostly to the district of Pochutla. On this subject our information is very rudimentary.[4]

We will give an interesting calculation on fruit selling and buying, which had some importance in our own fieldwork because it was perhaps the first occasion on which we were able to obtain reliable numerical data covering a whole transaction. This calculation showed us the way to proceed in the field, and was a proof that economic problems are capable of being approached and even solved. A group of Indians from the neighbouring district of San Agustín Yatareni, which lies on the slopes of the Sierra Juarez, were selling quinces on the corner of one of the streets adjoining the market. These vendors were obviously not of the poorest class, and a brief conversation disclosed that they were semi-professional middlemen whose business is to buy up quinces in their neighbourhood and bring them to the market. After the quinces have been sold at a profit, the middlemen purchase articles which they can resell with profit at some market in the Sierra, or perhaps by hawking from house to house. Having gained the confidence of one of these vendors by the means described – of reimbursing him for his market tax – an inquiry was made about what he and his fellows were purchasing with the cash collected, and what profit they made. He and the others informed us that they buy salt meat, small sausages and earthenware in Oaxaca. When asked on which of these articles they obtained the best financial result, they were not able to answer. A suggestion then was made by the ethnographer that a rapid calculation might give a clear answer.

Here are the results: We were told that one load of quince averages 300 items of fruit. For this the buyer has to pay in his district about 7.50 pesos. Thus, one quince costs him about 2½ centavos, or a little less. The additional expenses are 60 centavos for the transport, 40 centavos for the meals purchased and 30 centavos for market contributions. Thus, the whole cost of a load of quinces amounted to 8.80 pesos.

They sell their quinces – and this was noted during some thirty to forty-five minutes' observation – at 5 centavos each. We are told, however, that when the best quinces are gone some of them may be sold at 4 or even 3 centavos. At 5 centavos the net gain on 300 pieces would be 6.20 pesos, at 4 centavos 3.20, and at 3 centavos 0.20. Discounting for some exaggerations as to the price paid at home and for the cost of transport and market contribution, we might assume that a net gain of between 2 and 3 pesos is made on each load.

Let us for the moment, however, consider our Indian entrepreneur with the gross receipts from his transaction, and follow his further manipulations. Assuming that for one load he has received 10, 11 or 12 pesos, he then purchases one of the four standard articles of his trade. Were he to buy salt meat, he would pay 4 pesos for one 'piece' (that is, a long strip of meat of a standard unit). According to his own statement, he can resell this for 9 pesos in his district. Here his net gain would be 5 pesos for each transaction in which 4 pesos was the outlay. If he brings two loads of quinces to the market and finishes with 24 pesos gross on a good day, net gain on the return journey would be six times five, or 30 pesos. Deducting from this his expenses on the homeward journey, which might amount to 1 peso per load, his gain might be reduced to 28 pesos.

A similar detailed calculation on sausages has indicated that the gain was smaller, about 3.50 pesos for a transaction of 4 pesos' outlay. Hence, on a total transaction we would have 21 pesos gross and maybe 19 net profit. On the two types of earthenware which he buys, the profit would be larger per unit of outlay than for either meat or sausages. As regards the smaller or cheaper earthenware, the gain amounts to 5.50 pesos, on the more expensive 5.60. Here the gross profit would come to 33.60 pesos.

One or two points emerge from this inquiry. The observation described here was made in the middle of our fieldwork. Afterwards we were deflected by other, even more important information gained during the observation of maize trading. The data, however, show that it is possible to interest some of the less sophisticated middlemen in calculations concerning their business. There is no doubt that a trip to the district of such a vendor would be indispensable in order to check the price at which he assesses his wares at the starting point.

[The authors go on to calculate the profit made by a vendor who was dealing simultaneously with quinces – produced in his home district – and meat, sausages and earthenware – which he imported into his home district.

The figures are not of special interest and the text is confusing. However, the authors observe that (1) the vendor appears to have exaggerated the price he paid for the quinces in his home district; (2) there was a great difference in the profits made in the resale of each of the three types of commodity bought from the Oaxaca markets; (3) the commodity which provided greatest profit was earthenware and that which provided practically none was sausages; (4) the vendor seemed to be unaware of the different profits made on different commodities and that he almost lost money on the resale of sausages.

Higgins (1974) shows that cooked food prepared for sale may bring no other profit than that of maintaining household consumption, and similarly it is possible that the vendors dealing in meat and sausages were doing so simply to ensure their own or some other group's consumption of sausages. Ed.]

When pressed with questions as to why he did not import earthenware alone, he was somewhat puzzled and said he has to import such goods as are demanded, and that usually he would distribute equally among the various other articles the cash at his disposal after he sold the quinces. Were we to follow this indication, add the three profits and divide them by three, we would figure 8.80 pesos (identical, by chance, to the cost of one load of quinces) as his total net gain on a journey with two loads. The total transaction may take about five days, which would make the net profit 1.70 pesos per day – not an unlikely figure.

We have now to review more briefly a number of other scenes in the market. From the descriptive point of view, the sale of *sarapes*, the native blankets, is interesting because it reveals psychological bargaining in its most decorative aspect. The sale here is carried out, we suspect, mostly by specialized vendors from the producing centre of Teotitlan del Valle and Santo Domingo del Valle. They usually have a fixed place where a quantity of *sarapes* is put on a mat, sometimes on a table. In some towns, especially in the capital and in Tlacolula, the vendors walk around in search of buyers, especially tourists.

When it comes to a sale to an Indian, the vendor would try to attract the buyer's attention by spreading out the *sarape*, shaking it, showing the attractive designs or colours. Some of the articles are produced in several shades of grey, brown and black. Aniline dyes are already prominent in many articles. The buyer approaches, he examines the blanket for size, thickness, texture, smoothness and the percentage of cotton mixed with the wool. After he has approved the article, the question of price is broached. The price asked is, in a special case we observed, 6.50 pesos. The buyer responds, after he has been encouraged with the words 'Tell me, how much do you consider this type of blanket should be?', with the counterbid of 2.50. The vendor: 'This is the price till here.' (He shows the central dividing line of the blanket.) 'Open it out completely to see that we can not give it for 2.50; see the width and length. We demand a very cheap price. How much can you pay? What I have told you I have told. I wish to exchange words with you over this price. I want to sell. We are all children of God. How much do you offer, in truth?'

The client smiles. He examines the blanket again, touches, strokes, assesses the thickness, looks at the tints and then offers 2.50. The vendor 'That would be the price of this side. Look at the other side – let me know your views. Your word is like that of a king. I have my word. You have the money. I have the blanket. Therefore we are in the market place, to buy and to sell. You set the price.' The buyer repeats: 'Two-fifty.' The vendor: 'No more. It is impossible. You want to get it for a mere nothing.' He then tries to attract other buyers and the prospective buyer increases his bid. The vendor comes down, and finally they agree on 4.50 pesos, at which price the article changes hands.

We have quoted this as an example of the wide-margin bargaining which is primarily encountered with this type of article. Similar types of wide-margin bid and counter-bid are found in transactions concerning shawls, where several pesos, up to 4 or 5, may separate the first offer and the counter-offer, and yet a friendly and pleasant conversation may lead to a final meeting half way. On the outskirts of some market, especially in Ocotlán, we would find more extensive transactions, in which ox-carts, yokes, wooden troughs are sold and bought with similar wide-margin bargaining. It is important to note that in all these cases the bargaining does not very much affect the final price. In many cases, both vendor and seller know what the real value of the article is. The bargaining, perhaps, is not altogether a merely verbal by-play. At times it is a means of indicating to buyer or seller that the other party is not in real need of the article or the money respectively. In other cases the price is not known to the buyer and the long bargaining process is necessary to establish an acceptable price. Our observations show that sometimes even a professional vendor may give almost identical articles at different prices. Yet, on the whole, bargaining for articles whose price is determined by the cost of production is very largely the result of a traditional convention that the buyer should be as impressed with the fact that he has achieved a reasonable bargain.

The sale and purchase of chillies is a subject on which we have good data. Chillies change hands with a relatively small amount of raising and bidding down of prices. Although a perfunctory manipulation of weighing occasionally occurs, our general conclusion is that these articles are sold on the basis of a thorough familiarity by both parties with size, quality and market value. Were we to describe all the varieties of chillies with their native names and uses, the distinctions in size, colour and condition – for chillies are sold fresh or dried – we would fill several chapters of this memoir with detailed data. Suffice to say that several kinds are grown in the Valley itself; much is imported from the adjacent regions, both the mountains and the semi-tropical valleys. Except for the fresh and dried chillies produced in the Mixe region, the other imported chillies are dried. The chillies are displayed in little heaps containing from two to ten items, according to size and quality. At times chillies may be measured out or conventionally weighed, as mentioned. Usually the buyer has a good look at the heaps, asks the price, is often allowed to exchange one item in a heap for a better one, and the transaction is accomplished or is not. Here also we have at least one group of professional vendors who have emigrated from one of the important producing regions, the Mixteca. They buy the various types of chilli in several markets, moving from

Oaxaca to Etla and from Ocotlán to Tlacolula, and sell at a profit.

The Mixtecs who sell chillies are not from the region in which the chillies they sell are produced. These *regatones* pass through their own area and continue (southwards) almost to the coast, in order to acquire chillies.

The aesthetically attractive subject of flower selling we somewhat neglected. One of us (J.D.L.F.) has made a rough calculation concerning a vendor from the village of Huayapan. The man sells flowers and aromatic herbs gathered in the surrounding woods and glades. He admits to a gross income of 1.50 to 1.75 pesos on a market day. His expenses amount to 10 centavos of tax and 20 centavos on the return fare on the bus. This seems a plausible calculation, netting a gain of 1.20 to 1.45 pesos, for the man probably has other occupations during the week. An income of 1.50 pesos per day would be excessive for a very poor man without capital or property, but this is only one day a week.

We also have calculations on the cost of the production of flowers in the gardens surrounding the capital, but in this case the ethnographer (B.M.) failed to relate the cost of production to the system of marketing and the profits obtained.

Flower consumption is determined almost exclusively by the necessity to place fresh flowers once a week, usually on Sunday, on the domestic altar; also on various altars in the local church, and when festivities occur. There are vast floral displays on festive days in the forms of garlands, crosses, hearts and enormous flower-decorated baskets.

A very extensive trade in flowers obtains between Zaachila, San Antonino and other horticultural districts on the one hand, and the capital on the other. Our observations have revealed interesting aspects of this trade without, however, any quantitative data. There are agents in Oaxaca, natives of San Antonino mainly, who appear to control the flower trade. Great quantities of flowers are brought from Zaachila on a Friday afternoon and evening to be sold in the Oaxaca market by two middlemen.

The antiquarian, as well as the sociologist interested in culture change, would not miss the principal pre-Columbian article which appears in the modern market: the grinding-stone or *metate*. There are usually a few of these to be found in every market. The seasonal variation in sales is connected with the custom that at every marriage a *metate* painted and decorated in gaudy colours has to be presented ritually to the bride. We were told that in the period between January and May – that is, the time when we have not studied the markets – a much larger quantity of decorated *metates* is to be found. When buying a *metate* on behalf of the donor, the woman – for grinding is women's work – would examine the surface, assess the size, and carefully look for any defects in the three feet which support the stone or on its surface. A handful of maize is usually supplied by the vendor, so as to make a trial assessment possible. For certain uses a rough surfaced stone is necessary, for other uses relatively well-polished ones. Bargaining within the latitude of 2 pesos usually obtains. The price of the small articles varies from 1.50 to 2.50 pesos; the larger ones are sold at between 4 and 6 pesos. For the painting, 50 centavos extra is charged.[5]

This decoration is indispensable on bridal *metates*. The godfather of the bride, who is the usual donor, will dance ritually at a certain stage of the marriage ceremony with the *metate* held on his back. This was actually observed by one of us (B.M.) at a marriage ceremony in the village of Abasolo. [See photo 27.]

We shall briefly examine two more articles, both primarily of antiquarian interest. In the market of Oaxaca six or eight selling sites for medicinal herbs can be found every Saturday, fewer in the daily market. The vendor displays his wares on a large table covered with baskets, in which various dried flowers, leaves or roots are contained. Scrutiny would disclose horns of deer, dried little birds and desiccated skins of vipers or snakes. Dried insects are an important item sold as an aphrodisiac. Invariably, also, we found a few marine products – the shell of a sea-urchin, shells of molluscs, pieces of coral – all of them brought in the traditional journeys from the Pacific coast. Little earthenware bowls of Atzompa ware filled with aromatic, resinous paste are displayed as a remedy for rheumatism and other pains.

The herbalists and pharmacists of the market usually sell the substance specifically asked for: a centavo or two of dried rose flowers, some well-known herbs, the decoction which serves as a tonic for the stomach or a laxative, a remedy for fevers or a sleeping draught. The vendor, however, is always ready to give medical advice, to listen to a description of the complaint, and to advise what ought to be purchased.

We have followed independently several series of transactions. Bargaining does not occur. The price of some of the articles is fairly high, but it is well-known to the buyer and seller alike. The shell of a sea-urchin is worth 50 centavos, and might perhaps be given for a little less to a good client or a friend, but the margin would not be great. The balsamic, resinous substance sold in Atzompa bowls is valued at 25 and 60 centavos, according to size. The horn is sold in small bits, and the reptile skins in small quantities. We have observed transactions mostly averaging between 1 and 10 centavos.

One of the old women who became quite friendly with both of us represents the third generation in her trade. One of her nephews, incidentally, is studying medicine at the University of Mexico. She affirms that she does not sell medicines for any magical purpose or any type of sorcery. The question put to her was whether people could use some of her herbs as cures in the same way that people are cured by rubbing themselves with blessed flowers from the altar – a practice universal in this and other parts of Mexico. She assumed that the only influence of any of her medicines was to attack the illness directly. Of this we need more collateral evidence.

The illegal part of the herb trade consists of selling drugs which provoke abortion, are supposed to cure dangerous or venereal disease, or else act as aphrodisiacs. We have data on this trade, including extensive inventories of the stock-in-trade, but the above summary gives information which in our opinion is reliable on the salient points of the trade.

Some of the articles mentioned here – for example, the marine produce – are the result of long trips taken by people from the Valley to the Isthmus, the southern coasts, and the regions of Pochutla and Juquila.[6] Some other articles, imported in the same manner, were found by examining the ubiquitous selling sites in which the local inhabitants purchase their salt fish and dried shrimps, and by looking at the stalls with tropical fruit. The transactions here are carried out in the usual way. No weights or measures are used. The fish is sold in conventionally defined 'pieces', usually of considerable size. The prices range from 40 centavos upwards. The shrimps are retailed in small gourds, or measured out in cups, or weighed in imaginary units. All the products interest us primarily because they are carried on the often-mentioned overland trips – a trading custom dating undoubtedly from pre-Columbian days and carried on through the colonial period up to the present.

Our information on this subject is very extensive, somewhat chaotic, interesting from the point of view of sociology and economics, but completely devoid of any relevant numerical data. We cannot even say how much the people actually gain on each journey. We suspect that the gain must be, if not substantial, at least sufficient; and sufficient gain in the region of Oaxaca would amount to 1 peso per day per person.

The organization of such enterprises is, at present, in the hands of individuals and groups of individuals. We have some information that before 1910 one or more well-organized enterprises, no doubt with some capital, existed in Oaxaca and were conducting the overland trade along traditional routes systematically and on a large scale. At present there are in several centres men who make it their business to travel from the Valley, through the various passes and valleys, via Totolapa and the district of San Bartolo Yautepec, to the Isthmus. These people may also be producers and take some of their own vegetables or other articles with them, but they buy products in the neighbouring villages to increase their load. At various centres in the Isthmus they have partners or agents who take over from them the bulk of their load, and who have also accumulated other goods which the travellers will bring back to the Valley. We have not examined the organization of such agencies, but we are told that the partners or agents are often people from the Valley who have settled at the other end – another example of commercially determined migration.

The main centres from which the trips are undertaken are San Antonino, Ocotlán, Zaachila, Tlacolula, Mitla and a few centres in the district of Tlacolula. Such merchant-travellers have their beasts of burden, usually donkeys, for there are very few mules in the district. A man may go with two or three donkeys. As a rule, a party of several men go together for company and security.

The articles exported from the Valley appear to be primarily onions and garlic; also non-tropical fruit, earthenware and large wickerwork baskets. The time taken for the outward journey may be between six and twelve days. The length of time varies according to business transacted on the trip. We suspect that, as they go along, the merchants sell and buy at certain places.

On arrival at their destination, they undoubtedly attend some of the local markets, in which they can obtain much better prices for their goods than for those offered for wholesale by their agents. We were told, but have no means of verifying this information, that most of the articles exported from the Valley are sold at double the price. After they have disposed of their goods, the merchants load again with salt, fish – dried or still damp – shrimps, marine shells and also coconut, tamarinds and other tropical produce. We may note here that during such trips the travellers come very near to the frontier of Guatemala. Even now, and certainly in the old days, some of the travellers would go as far as the famous shrine of Esquipulas, and probably pilgrims to that shrine would carry on some collateral trade as they travelled.

We may add that the best organized system of trade is carried out by the semi-professional merchant-travellers of San Antonino. We have noted several different groups of traders who go from San Antonino to the Isthmus: the professional merchants, and the peasants who make the journey once or twice a year; the traders who have agents in the Isthmus and those who have to trust to luck in selling in the market or from house to house.

One of our informants told us that there are as many as 300 or 400 people who go to the Isthmus. From other sources we learn that the number does not exceed a dozen. The former figure seems more probable. One of us (B.M.) was assured by an entirely disinterested informant in Totolapan, the local grocer and school teacher, that practically every day a few travellers pass through his village, and that at certain seasons a much larger number would be seen on the road.

There is another discrepancy in our information. We were told in one place that the journey is accomplished in ten days, and in another that it takes thirty.

We have already mentioned that cash is never carried on the return journey, but always sent by mail, the safety of the roads being questionable. The precaution is necessary owing to robbers, who apparently do not threaten the merchandise but who make the carrying of money inadvisable.

We shall not describe other traditional routes which run directly to the south through Ejutla and Miahuatlán, or those which go to the state of Guerrero or the shrine of Juquila. Our information here is less complete. In all these journeys trade is carried on in several ways. There are partners and agents at either end and some sales are made on the trip.

9 The maize market

We cannot leave the description of what happens in the market places of the Valley without making at least a general survey of what happens in those streets, corners or sections of the market where maize is sold and bought. We do not find them in any privileged position. In Oaxaca only a few selling sites are under cover at the south-eastern corner of the small market of San Juan de Dios. Even here on a day when wind and rain lash in, the vendors have some difficulty in protecting their valuable goods from being damaged. The main exchange in the staple food takes place in the street which runs along the southern side of the small and older market place, and where the producers (*propios*) squat on one side and the middlemen on the other. Their numbers are not impressive. This is due to the fact that many producers sell their relatively small quantities early in the morning and are replaced from noon onwards by other vendors. In Ocotlán we would find all the transactions in maize in the small street running to the west of the new market. The street is badly paved, and the gutter runs down the middle. It divides the two rows, the producers seated on the east side, the professionals on the west, each beside his storehouse, of which there are some six or eight on the west side of the street.

De la Fuente: *The majority of those who line up to sell maize on the south side of San Juan de Dios are middlemen (*regatones*), but occasionally one finds producers (*propios*). The majority of those I know are* regatones *from Zaachila, San Antonio de la Cal and that neighbourhood. I therefore suspect that the* propio *finds it more convenient to sell to the* regaton *from his own village, or another village, than pay the necessary taxes in Oaxaca.*

In the afternoon here, also, the *propios* disappear and the *regatones* appear on both sides of the gutter. In Tlacolula the maize exchange occupies an extensive part of the larger square to the south-east of the church. Here we have drawn, as in other types of market sites, a number of detailed plans, and on the average we reckon that there are some forty to sixty selling sites at any time.

Were we to walk beside such a display of maize some time earlier in the morning, let us say at nine o'clock, we would find a variety of quantities and qualities exhibited. At times a peasant may come with as little as two or three measures of Indian corn, especially if he resides very near the market place. Usually the neighbouring peasant producers bring about five to fifteen *almudes*, and the quantities displayed by middlemen are very much larger. Very often, in order not to encumber too much space and accordingly pay a high municipal contribution, a vendor or even a producer might keep the bulk of his merchandise in the *mesón* or in his store, and bring only a small quantity to the market, replenishing it as the sales proceed. The largest site, such as we find in Oaxaca, would contain some half a dozen bags, and a few types of maize spread out on mats or displayed in baskets. Each vendor has one type of measure or another, and the larger ones also have standardized weights. [See photo 23.]

The distinctions in quality are complex and a full list, with all minor subtleties, would be too long to give here. The main principles on which maize is classified are according to the type of plant. They can be summed up according to form, size and colour. Over and above this, there are distinctions referring to the soundness of the corn, to its age, that is, humidity and dryness respectively, and to the question of whether it is grown in the Valley or imported. On this last point we have already commented to the effect that the local varieties are preferred because they are adjusted to the local consumers' needs and tastes.

As regards colour, we have white, yellow, 'black' (really purple) and blue maize. Some of the characteristic shapes are related to colour. Thus, *maiz bolita*, a roughly spherical variety, is always white. This is the maize which fetches the highest prices in the Valley. It can be used for the best tortillas and for a variety of drinks (non-alcoholic, prepared from maize meal). Two other shapes occur also in white maize, the thick and the thin. They are less appreciated by the consumer, and fetch a lower price. A thin-grained yellow variety is used similarly. It is favoured on the mountain range and among the Mixes because of its 'strong' taste. It is not appropriate for the preparation of maize drinks, but can be used for many other purposes. The varieties classified as black or blue occur mostly in substantial thickness. They are liked in some districts in the mountains and are used almost exclusively for tortillas.

De la Fuente: *The adjective 'strong' does not refer to the taste of the maize, but to the quality of the kernel, which when prepared allows the consumer to 'resist' longer. That is, he does not need to eat again for a while, which is not the case if he has eaten white maize. In such cases the individual needs to consume more tortillas and to eat more frequently*.

The so-called 'old' maize, which simply means maize from the previous harvest, is dry, gives more meal or porridge for the unit of volume and, if it is not eaten up by insects, fetches a higher price. In our district, maize does not last more than one year to eighteen months, after which time it is usually attacked by insects. If this process has not gone too far, the grain can still be used for human consumption. After that, it will be given as fodder to animals.

Thus, even the qualitative distinctions introduce a considerable variation in the appreciation and the price of maize. The complexity of this market is increased by the somewhat anarchical variety of measures used. The Mexican government has been, for some time past, exercising a more or less persistent, and at times energetic, pressure for the general introduction of the metric measures. So far, success has been limited; indeed, in some ways it complicates the picture and introduces one more element of confusion and elasticity in the standard of comparison. From the point of view of the whole system of maize marketing, this usually means that the poorer and less educated or less keen market agent is exploited by one who can manipulate figures, as well as measures, more rapidly and skilfully, and who has the whip hand of more capital at his disposal.

The traditional measure still by far most prevalent in actual use and observed by us in most of the transactions is the old Spanish *almud*. In its concrete forms, it appears as shallow, square, wooden measures of 1 *almud* ½, ¼ or ⅛ in volume. It would be difficult for the ethnographer to say with certainty whether all the measures are identical. We suspect that they are not. Certainly they are used in a manner which makes them essentially elastic. Nevertheless, the natives in most walks of life and degrees of prosperity insist on using this measure. The poor Indian and peasant prefer the *almud*, not because they are 'conservative' or 'dislike innovations', but because this measure enters into all their domestic calculations in a manner which has been standardized for centuries, and they are accustomed to calculate with it. Thus, they know how many tortillas can be produced from one *almud*, or how many cups or bowls of *atole* (maize drink); in short, how many *almudes* per week their budgets require. Thus, they prefer to buy in terms of this old measure. Since they know it well and are able to calculate the grain received, they are also able to calculate what can be spared and so they prefer to sell by this measure. Moreover, according to our best informants, grain can be seen more easily in the *almud*, which is a shallow measure. This gives a greater sense of security to the buyer than the tall, narrow litre measure. For all these reasons, buyers and sellers are even more opposed to measure their produce in metric units.

The equivalence between the *almud* and the litre is not even known to most of the vendors. In reality it is simple. The *almud* is 5 litres. When we asked about the equivalence we received the most fantastic answers in the market, proving how little the metric system has penetrated into the mental and manual habits of the people. An additional complication is the kilogram. It is increased by the fact that weight and volume do not correspond with regard to the various types of grain. Round and solid grain weighs more per unit of volume than other types. Thus, an *almud* of the best maize, bolita, weighs 4 kilograms; of thick maize only 3.75 kilograms; of the thin, 3.5.

Four kilograms have acquired a familiar name in some of the more sophisticated markets, and have become a unit called *pesada* (one weight).

The traditional measure of Spain, the *fánega*, consists of 24 or 25 *almudes*. In Oaxaca the distinction is regional. In Tlacolula and Etla we have the smaller *fánega* of 24 *almudes*. In Oaxaca city, and all the other markets on our list, the *fánega* contains 25 *almudes*. We shall not enter into further complications. It is quite clear, and it was made very obvious to us in actual transactions, that the larger the vendor's stock, the more advantage he can gain from buying in a form in which he gets more grain for his money and selling it measured so as to give less for a corresponding amount. And this is, of course, apart from the matter of cheating in measures and computation.

Let us turn now to an actual transaction, and start at the selling site of a primary producer. He has brought some 5 to 10 *almudes* to sell at the price which obtained during the last market, hoping thus to realize some 2 to 4 pesos. We engage in conversation with him and find that once a week, on a Sunday if he lives in Tlacolula, or on a Friday if he is from the district of Ocotlán, he takes out from his stock of corn an amount calculated to cover his weekly budget. According to whether he has a few men working for him whom he has to feed, or if for some reason he still has old stock, he will bring a smaller or larger quantity to the market. In maize he has a staple commodity which is always negotiable and which he produces, if he is a typical, average peasant, in a quantity sufficient to cover his needs all the year round.[1]

Having stationed ourselves with the producer in the maize market and determined to concentrate on it, we find that some producers arrived early in the day, maybe at eight o'clock or even earlier. They will remain, selling in small quantities of one *almud* directly to the consumers. On closer scrutiny we find that the poorer the producer-vendor, the longer he will remain, trying to sell directly to the consumer. If he is well-off and values his time, as well as his comfort, he will remain for an hour or so in the morning, and then go to a middleman and sell the remainder, losing some 2 centavos per *almud*. Whichever way he has obtained his few pesos, he then will make a round of selling sites and shops and purchase meat, sausages, sugar, coffee and other groceries and articles needed for the week. This type of transaction is one of the most important in all our market places. We know of a whole set of people who can thus keep to their weekly budgets throughout the year. For them the market is indispensable for the acquisition of purchasing power, as well as for the provision of necessary commodities.

The somewhat wealthier and more substantial producer will still have to cover the weekly budget by such small sales. Our friend Don Federico Aquino, who is valued at 50,000 pesos or more and is, therefore, a local capitalist, we first encountered stoically selling his maize per *almud* in the market of Zimatlán. At the first shower, however, he picked up his bags and went home, thus showing that for him comfort was preferable to a few more *almudes* sold, and that he did not depend on such weekly sales.

De la Fuente: *I should like to remind you that Don Federico on that occasion was more worried by the arrival of more maize than by the water. He commented that there was getting to be a lot of competition, and that it was no longer worth staying.*

Another friend, whose income we afterwards assessed at what is for our district an astronomical figure of 10 or even 15 pesos per day, was discovered seated behind a large heap of maize during a fiesta market at Teotitlán del Valle selling to the local peasants and Indians. Nevertheless, this type of wealthy producer accumulates considerable quantities of maize in his home store, calculates how much he has sold at a weekly market, and speculates on the rise or fall of maize prices during the coming months. Our best informant, Manuél, was keeping something like 2 tons of maize, reckoning that the price would rise from 45 to 50 and perhaps even to 75 centavos per *almud*, owing to the expected bad harvest in 1940.

We can only indicate more briefly the somewhat complex transactions of the middlemen and the *acaparadores*. These purchase according to their own financial capacity directly from the producers, always paying a substantially lower price than would be paid elsewhere, and at times cheating. They also buy maize by the *fánega*, and even by the ton. The data obtained here would enable us to write up a full account, but this brings us to the collateral transactions outside the market and to the somewhat delicate subject of the procedures by which a few larger capitalists corner and export the grain. How far this actually affects the retail price is not easy to say, and we want to continue our researches. We would have to study the manipulations of the wealthier mill owners, most of whom are of Spanish extraction. We would also need to observe the exporters and importers of maize, the various agents and the 'regulating commission', which is a semi-official board, somewhat influenced by the interests of the larger merchants. Over and above this there are, as we have already mentioned, one or two individuals who combine politics with the business of cornering, certainly to the advantage of the latter.

It is necessary to add a few words on the purchase of maize, since so far we have mostly dwelt on the sales. The buyers are the Indians from the mountains, about whom we have already spoken; the urban population in the centres; and probably also those half-peasants, half-artisans who, like the sarape makers in Teotitlán or Santo Domingo del Valle, live mostly by their industries. Considerable quantities of maize are also destined for purchase by the industrial districts of the Mixteca, especially in the markets of Etla and Oaxaca.

Owing to the differential production of the staple grain in the Valley, some districts are richer in maize in certain seasons, while in others the supply may be deficient. Thus, at times, even peasants may be purchasing maize in the markets.

We can now pass to the important problem of price. Price depends upon the annual harvest in the Valley and it varies within the normal range of production between 25 to 30 centavos per *almud* in an especially good year and 40 to 60 per *almud* during a poor harvest. The corrective to these figures consists in the fact that were the harvest to be exceptionally good, grain would be exported from Oaxaca, thus preventing the price from falling below, say, 20 centavos. On the other hand, we have data about a disastrous year, 1925, when the *almud* had to be bought at three silver pesos, and 8.50 pesos for the especially good grain to be used for sowing. Apparently 1925 was bad in the whole republic. If only Oaxaca had a very bad harvest, maize from the other provinces would be imported.[2]

During the summer of our investigations, production was certainly deficient. The average price at Oaxaca swung round the figure of 45 centavos for the *almud* of dry, perfect bolita maize. It is, of course, necessary to take a standard product as unit of comparison. As regards seasonal variations in the market, these depend on the two harvest periods. The first occurs in May to June, and is the smaller, early harvest of the maize sown in February. The growth season of this maize depends on the natural moisture in the ground, and the early maize grows well only in the districts with somewhat marshy soil, or where irrigation is possible. The main harvest depends on the rains (June-September) and occurs in October and November. The price always rises before the harvest, that is, in March or April and again in August, September and early in October. This price rise, however, depends very much on the prospect of a good or a bad harvest, and also on the supplies which remain from the previous harvest. At the times of sowing, in February and again in June and July, the prices of the best grains rise sharply.

There are also almost permanent regional variations. We have computed such tables several times largely from our own observations, but also from comments from, and discussions held with, a few of our best informants. Under normal conditions the cheapest price, that of 43 centavos, obtains in Ocotlán. Our information is for a specific date in the middle of August. In Etla and Oaxaca the price at the time was 45 centavos per *almud* for the best product. At Ejutla and Tlacolula the price was 50 centavos, and at Miahuatlán, 55. In a normal year this degree of regional price variation would occur whatever the level of prices. It would only change in an especially wet season. The valleys of Tlacolula and Ejutla, which are exceptionally dry, might have a better crop than the marshy regions if these were to become swamped.

The differences in price are primarily determined by the prices which the producer has to accept because of the relation between supply and demand. When the best maize stands at 45 centavos in the capital, the middleman will readily give 43 centavos in Ocotlán, since transport is easy and 2 centavos per *almud* repays him for his trouble, overheads, and transit costs. The middleman will charge 50 centavos for the same article in Tlacolula, since he has to repack it and probably transport it to that place, giving the local producers of that district the possibility of selling their maize at this high price.

Our observations show, in a way, the interdependence of the market system. That is, they show how middlemen can flourish even through local transactions. Also, one can see how the general price level has to move in accordance with the general harvest in the Valley or else with differential production in the various districts.

The point at which the variations start, where the effective bargaining between producer and consumer or between producer and middleman give the tone to the whole market, would occur at any time and in any year in the district with the best harvest. In this place the supply, as well as the necessities of the other, less favoured districts, determine the first upward and downward movement. Normally this occurs in the district of Ocotlán, more especially in the small but important market of San Pedro Apóstol. This market, and to a certain extent also that of Zimatlán, usually determines the movements which have repercussions in the market of Ocotlán and in the remaining places of the district. Knowledge of these variations is common among all middlemen, even the smaller ones, and among many peasants. Initial variations may result from a few showers during the week, or else from some visible deterioration of crops in one of the drier valleys. As we moved through the valley of Tlacolula, we were shown in the summer of 1940 the places where maize fields which might have been harvested in the following October had been completely ruined by drought. This was one of the elements which influenced the movement of prices.

We are able here only to skim the surface of our data on maize, a subject to which we have devoted a good deal of time and attention. We also have substantial data on the way in which agents for the larger buyers proceed in collecting and cornering maize. On this subject we hope to obtain fuller information next summer, especially since we have a few good friends among these very people, and we also know a few of their competitors. From the facts we have, however, it is clear that the maize market is in many ways the determining aspect of the whole system. It is very complex, but it also gives an insight into the real needs of the consumers and the producers. The maize market is also a subject on which the ethnographer interested in the application of his data has a rich field for study, which is as relevant to the welfare and progress of the Indians as it is sociologically and economically interesting.

10 A comprehensive look at the market

In the previous sections we have presented in a brief manner and with many omissions some of the results obtained from our fieldwork. We have also tried to disclose the method by which we proceeded and to show the theoretical implications of this type of work. It will be worthwhile, now, briefly to formulate some of the points of theory and method contained here, and to link questions of practice in the field, general analysis and the practical value of this type of result for applied anthropology.

The essence of our method lies in the constant interplay between observation and theoretical treatment. The collection of data through actual participation in and study of commercial transactions has always and avowedly been inspired by definite theoretical and, at times, practical aims. At many stages of research the economic, sociological and practical relevance of the material thus far collected was scrutinized. This guided our further research; it suggested the more selective and wider ranging collection of new data, and thus allowed us to organize our evidence, as well as to direct it. In all this, we were obviously not guided by 'preconceived ideas', but by the formulation of problems which naturally emerge out of previous observation. We were primarily interested in the economic aspect of the phenomena; that is, in the influence which the market has on the welfare of the Indians, peasants and townspeople, as well as on the livelihood and vested interests of commercial agents in the district. We studied the market also as an agency which organizes some groups and through which specific differentiation of an economic class or a group becomes evident. The market, in many ways, integrates the inhabitants of the Valley into interdependent social groups and individuals. This aspect was touched upon when we demonstrated the unity of a centre and its surrounding region; the migrations and resident agencies linking towns and districts; and the economic dependence of the surrounding districts upon the Valley and of the subdivisions of the Valley upon each other.

The unit or isolate of our research was the market system as a whole institution. This wider unit consists, as is always the case in such phenomena, of component institutions, in this case the specific market places of Oaxaca, Ocotlán and Tlacolula, etc. This is not the place to define the concept of institution as it ought to be used in cultural analysis. For a summary see 'Culture' in the *Encyclopedia of the Social Sciences* edited by E.R. Seligman and Alvin Johnson; also 'The Scientific Basis of Applied Anthropology' in the *Transactions of the Volta Congress*, published by the Royal Italian Academy; and the article 'The Group and the Individual in Functional Analysis', in the *American Journal of Sociology*, May 1939, all by B. Malinowski. Suffice it to say that the study of institutions requires analysis of the social organization, the rules and norms, as well as the material substratum in each system of traditionally standardized human activities.

That there is a distance between the stated, written or professed norms of conduct and their actual performance is one of the important implications of our concept. The reader will have noted that this was a constantly recurring theme of our analysis. The two important concepts characteristic of institutional analysis are those of charter and function. By charter we mean the system of values laid down by law and custom, by tradition, and by sentimental associations which surround an institution in the mind of its members. Charter, thus, is the traditional definition of the market place as we find it in native psychology, in the aims and purposes of more sophisticated merchants (whether capitalistic exploiters or ordinary middlemen), and in the interplay of progressive reform and conservative usage.[1] Function, on the other hand, is the integral role played by the market place in the culture we are considering. Both concepts, of charter and function, will have to be concretely defined and more clearly presented.

Let us start, however, with the more concrete and more fully discussed aspects of our market system as a complex institution made up of component parts. In thinking about the social organization, let us think first of the administrative aspect. This consists primarily in policing and keeping order, as well as in the taxation levied by the municipality, the government of the state and the federal authorities. We have seen that, as regards actual policing, very little intervention from any administrative agencies is practised or needed. Instead, traditional custom and usage define the placing of men, beasts and commercial articles in the market. Minor conflicts such as one vendor encroaching on the habitual selling site of another sometimes occur, but they are usually settled in a more or less amicable manner. We have observed vendors who objected to someone else opening a small selling site in front of their row, and complained to the municipal tax collector. Once or twice the interloper was removed. In other cases the plaintiff, with a shrug of his shoulders, accepted the situation, promising that he would see to it that the trespass did not occur the following week.

The main official administrative activity is taxation. Here, as we know, the situation is somewhat complex. The municipality collects the bulk of the taxes. These are defined as payment for the space occupied by the vendor. The taxes vary with the extent of this space and the quantities of merchandise displayed. The government of the state also levies taxes on the sale of cattle. The federal authorities, as well as state and municipal authorities, have the right to issue licences, stamps, documents and permits for the sale of liquor.

In this aspect of the market place the divergence between strict law and practice is considerable. The vendors, especially the poorer ones, complain of a whole set of abuses. The municipal collectors are able to explain their difficulties. Very often a poor Indian who enters the town has not a centavo on him. He promises to pay after he has sold his wares. The collector knows quite well that once the goods are sold and the money spent, the Indian can walk out of the market unobserved. Hence, illegally but under pressure of necessity, the collector tries to abstract from the native some articles, such as his blanket, his hat or any object which he can keep as a guarantee of payment.

Some Indians, especially those not accustomed to town markets and unable to understand that they are penalized for others' misdeeds, object. Feeling sometimes runs very high over such conflicts. During our stay in the month of July, a tax collector was actually stabbed and killed by a native from the Sierra. A number of arbitrary means of evasion on the one side, and means of compulsion on the other, have been developed, and a skilful game of hide-and-seek is played by both parties. The municipal collectors often place themselves at the entrance to the town and try to collect taxes then and there. This, again, is a usage to which the Indians and the peasants very much object, and which is not in strict accordance with the legal provision that only the use of a selling site should be taxed. Nevertheless, here once again, the collector cannot be blamed, nor yet the municipality. We hope that from further study of this problem, and from a sympathetic consideration of both points of view, some practical suggestions may emerge from our work. Some clear statement to the effect that no vendor should be allowed to enter without paying for his prospective site, and a legally defined system of collecting some guarantee of payment, would be better than the present haphazard usage.

When it comes to the social organization of a weekly market place, this has to be defined in terms of professional quality, economic function, ethnographic character and economic relation to the market as a whole. The reader will see that we have constantly had to distinguish between groups of consumers, types of producers, and the various strata divided by capital and type of business. Taking into account the various roles played in the market, as well as in the processes of production, exchange and consumption, we may distinguish the regional Indians, mostly from the mountain, the peasant producers from the Valley, the artisans and independent industrial producers, the town proletariat, and the professional middleman. In this last group we made several subdivisions, such as between the impecunious small-scale middlemen, who range from extreme poverty to a fair competence; the native agents and distributors acting for larger businesses; the shopkeepers on a small scale; large-scale business, mainly run by Spaniards; and a few really important types of financial enterprise.

When we pass to the material substratum, we have the problem of the various objects which enter [to provide the tangible aspects of the market system]. And here we have to study the objects in terms of property; legal and customary rights to use; and effective use. Most of the buildings, as well as the soil on which the market is held, are owned by the municipalities. They are, through the system of taxation, hired out for each occasion; however, when it comes to more permanent booths or butchers' tables, the payment may be monthly or even annual.

The municipality renders certain services and draws its income from them. Here, after a fuller study, we may be able to suggest certain practical points as regards hygienic conditions and means of gradual improvement, both economic and cultural. The sanitary services of the market present an interesting problem. In each market place large notices exhort the native and remind him of the need for cleanliness: 'Cleanliness is the luxury of the poor.' They suggest, in print, very often unintelligible to the Indian, that microbes, disease and other calamities can be avoided through the use of soap and water. We cannot yet say how far such general exhortations are really efficient, and how far they merely offer moral satisfaction to those who paint them.

As regards the analysis of the various goods, of their definition in terms of weight and volume, and also as regards the character of money and currency, the reader will be aware that we have discussed the material substratum of market transactions at some length, always with reference to the social groups or individuals involved, and with reference also to the economic character of the proceedings as a whole.

We have tried to refer to the official point of view, although we have not quoted many official regulations in the text. We have shown where they are actually enforced and performed, and where usage is at variance with law. As regards the unwritten code of the market, we have noted its validity on many points and also shown where it fails. We have stressed in many of our descriptions the fact that personal acquaintanceship between agents and vendors, the necessity of maintaining lasting goodwill, and the ability of vendor and buyer to agree on quality and measure, secure on the whole a flow of honest and adequate economic performances. But we have also described and suggested the extent of cheating and exploitation.

In all this it will be seen that the essence of the institutional approach consists in the treatment, using sociological techniques, of material objects, rules of conduct, as well as actual behaviour, always in relation to one another. Mere inventories of what is sold or displayed without considering what part the objects play in consumption and also the manner in which they are produced will always give incomplete and, at times, worthless information. The reader will also probably be aware that in the course of our fieldwork we started from general impressions and superficial observations as to the manner in which the articles and money, or articles and articles, changed hands. Step by step we inquired into the assessment of value on either side of the transaction, and this led us, through an analysis of the mechanisms of supply and demand and of market haggling, to regard exchange as the crucial phase in the process of production, exchange and consumption.

Gradually it became clear that the market is primarily connected with the short-term budget of the average member of the community inhabiting the Valley. Or, to put it more clearly, taking the majority of peasants and Indians who form the bulk of the population, we would find that each household produces enough and can part with a sufficient amount of its production – agricultural or industrial – to supply itself with a week's budget. This refers primarily to those Indians and peasants who grow vegetables, collect fruit, firewood or charcoal; to those who make earthenware or live by the making of ropes and other *ixtle* products. The producer of maize might perhaps sell his whole harvest in bulk. But in such a transaction he will always receive a smaller price and he is fully aware of the fact. He prefers to store his maize, to allocate his grains week by week, and to sell a few *almudes* on the main market day in his district.

The vast majority of the people thus carry their produce to market each week, and obtain their weekly income. As producers they benefit from the market as the best source of obtaining purchasing power. It is an always ready, always accessible and amenable bank. As consumers they use the market and the surrounding small shops as a vast emporium, from which all necessities can be supplied in a manner familiar, easily acceptable, and easily manageable to them. Thus, the main use of the market place to the vast majority of inhabitants is its two-fold character as source of purchasing power and convenient supply of consumer goods. The market, in its weekly concentration of buyers and sellers, represents a large-scale emporium; it also supplies a relatively large amount of ready money. The market, as it were, in one day plays the part of an extensive commercial establishment with facilities which would be spread over the week.

We have on several occasions already brought out this general function of the market as it works, especially with reference to the very poor Indians from the mountain regions. We have shown how it benefits the peasants from the surrounding villages. It is clear that the artisans working during the week in such centres as Ocotlán or Tlacolula, or in the villages of Atzompa, Coyotepec or Teotitlán, depend upon the market place for the sale of their produce and the satisfaction of their consumer needs.

Let us look at the other side of the picture. To the large-scale importer and exporter, the Spaniard, the foreigner, and to the one or two Mexicans engaged in substantial commerce, the market is equally indispensable. It presents opportunities for buying at the cheapest rates, with or without economic or political pressure. It is the best distributing centre for some of the imported goods, although these, we know, play a much smaller part. Nevertheless, since all such organizations, those of the capitalist, the entrepreneur, and his agents, are vitally interested in the market, they also contribute to its vitality under the dictate of their vested interests. The municipalities, the state government and the federal authorities receive income, derive profit and, as regards the municipality, also gain prestige. They are eager and instrumental in developing and maintaining the market place. Nor are the religious and conservative interests of our district in any way opposed to the market place. The markets, especially those held in conjunction with calendar celebrations of saints and with sacred occasions, are events closely related to their vested spiritual and material concerns.

In defining thus the integral function of the market system of Oaxaca and listing the various interests, reasons and motives which contribute to its vitality, we are clearly aware that our formula probably also applies, with certain modifications, to other markets of the republic. Yet it is through the concrete and specific study of the institution that we can construct generalizations like the present one, which are based not on armchair intuition, but on observed fact. The functional approach takes its stand on the existence of general principles. It equally insists that principles must be constructed on the basis of detailed fact and inductively formulated with reference to culture as a whole.

What is the charter of this institution and how can we construct it from the detailed facts observed? The concept of charter is closely related to function. But while the latter contains the scientific formula derived by the sociologist, the former embodies the doctrines, values and sentiments of the participant. We have already supplied the reader with most of the necessary facts. We have shown why the peasant or Indian goes to the market, and the manner in which he defines his motives. He is deeply convinced that in the market he will obtain all that he needs at better prices, and also that he will be able to sell his produce more advantageously, than elsewhere. That his belief is only partially correct could easily be shown. We have discussed at one point or another the advantages, for instance, which might be derived from co-operative selling and buying. It is here that a full understanding of domestic habits, of the ability of the natives to calculate and of their liability to be cheated, will show why the piecemeal, somewhat clumsy, and, in many ways, wasteful sale and purchase in the market is still the principal manner in which the natives carry on their life.

The fact that an Indian or peasant will usually refuse to sell his produce on the way to the market, that he insists on going there and selling it in a customary manner, has often been observed by us and by others in various regions of Mexico. In our district, the middlemen very often try to waylay the producers coming from the surrounding districts and buy the produce in bulk. They are usually unsuccessful. The Indian knows from experience that he may obtain a better price if he goes to his usual site and sells his goods piecemeal. He also wants to turn the cash into goods on market day. Hence, he refuses to sell it prematurely on the previous evening or too early in the day. He has also the goodwill of habitual customers to consider. Thus, his refusal is not due to any 'traditionalism' or set of irrational motives, but to an integral attitude derived from experience, and on the whole well-founded.

At the beginning of our inquiry we discussed and formulated a question as to why people went to the market. Did they go for purely economic reasons? Did they go to market for amusement, social reasons or any collateral motives? Our final conclusion is that the market is almost exclusively an economic mechanism in the conceptions and ideas of the natives themselves. We were unable to find a single person who did not come to a market place with something to sell or something to buy. The amusements, the participation in the crowded market place, some religious motive for entering the church, and many social occasions, alcoholic or not, are always there. Yet no one ever goes into the market, we found, without having as the principal motive of the visit a purchase and a sale. (In rare cases only one of these two transactions takes place.) We also inquired into this in the villages. We have not made a complete or even a semi-statistical survey, but we can say that not a single inhabitant of a village would go into a market unless he needed to for an economic reason. The answer which we always received when asking 'Why don't you go to market?' was, 'Why should I go, since I have nothing to sell and since I do not need to buy anything? I prefer to remain at home and work.'

Another problem with reference to the psychology of the market place, to the value and habitual preference for the market as against purchasing in shops, also has a bearing on the problem of charter. We find that the vast majority of both Indians and peasants buy everything they can in the open market place. In Oaxaca, Etla and Zaachila, even groceries are sold in the market. In other centres, such as Tlacolula, Ocotlán and Zimatlán, some articles have to be purchased in the adjacent shops, mainly such groceries as sugar, coffee and cocoa. Liquor may be bought in a shop, but usually the poorer peasants buy directly from the legal or illegal producers. The preference, however, is general for goods obtainable in the market or else in the smaller shops surrounding it.

A careful inquiry into the reasons shows that these are primarily connected with the manner in which the transaction is performed in the market, as against buying in a shop. The market booth or site displays the full range of articles. They can be seen and compared readily. The habit of examining, touching, smelling and even tasting is universal in the market. In the shop the Indian does not have the textiles, groceries or loaves of bread actually displayed before his eyes and accessible to his hands. He is accustomed to the careful, slow procedure of making up his mind, of examining and testing. He likes the privilege, fully granted to him in the market place, of going away when he is not satisfied. He is also accustomed to the long and extensive bargaining which the shops, especially the better ones, do not readily grant. We have reason to assume that sometimes the vendors in the market place sell at a lower price and, at the same time, cheat on the full measure, which probably leads many of the poorer Indians or peasants to believe that they can buy cheaper in the market. Actually, on comparing prices, we did not find any difference whatsoever.

Our statement that the market functions primarily as an economic mechanism raises a difficult problem of how to draw the line between economic and non-economic activities. Without entering into a theoretical discussion, we want to state our conviction that the best way of approaching this problem from the ethnographic point of view is to define as economic any activity which is connected with the processes of production, distribution and consumption of goods. Wealth, obviously, consists of goods, either consumer goods or instrumental goods, which have to be produced by human effort and labour and which acquire value through the mechanisms of exchange and through satisfying the needs of the producer and consumer. Hence, a definition in terms of wealth and value leads us back to the processes of making, exchanging and using.

Applying this point of view, we are able to isolate the economic aspect from all the others. When you find a table laden with scapularies, candles and votive offerings in a church, you obviously have a mixed phenomenon of a religious and an economic nature. In so far as these goods subserve a type of consumption connected with religious belief, we can define its religious aspect. At the same time, the transaction of buying and selling is a contribution towards the maintenance of the church itself, of the priest or sacristan and perhaps of the agent who is acting for them. The increment to the income of the priest, which gives him additional purchasing power as a consumer, is economic. The economic definition of the processes can, therefore, be given in assessing those material advantages which are derived by all concerned, and also in satisfying the consumer needs of the buyers. The religious aspect consists in the distribution of objects of cult, which satisfies belief and ritual needs.

Another difficult problem which has been running right through our analysis refers to the determination in economic terms of such transactions and of such conditions of living which still remain outside the monetary economy. When, for instance, we are told that some very poor Indians in the mountains live on 3 dollars a year, and on examination we find that this means that their annual monetary income amounts to 15 pesos, we are faced with the question of whether this is an economically correct statement. Obviously, these natives enjoy a great many 'free goods', since they can collect their fuel and fruit and hunt their venison without any monetary outlay. Here we might approach the problem by assessing labour in terms of money, since there is hardly any district in Mexico, now, where opportunities for paid work are completely absent.

We might also assess the value of certain goods which are free in the mountains but have an exchange value in the Valley. This could be done by deducting from the price in the Valley the cost of transportation in terms of labour and time spent. The problem is not insoluble and it is important. Raising the standard of living of Indians and peasants, townsmen and artisans ought to be in the mind of the anthropologist as the lode-star of his investigation. Now, when most communities are on the verge of being drawn into our economic monetary system, it is necessary to attempt an assessment of production and consumption, of the value of labour and the consumer's needs in numerical terms. This is a preliminary step towards solving the next question of how to improve – within the limits of local possibilities and by simultaneous development in education, in capital assistance, in hygiene, and in the reduction of infant mortality – the general condition of the Indians in our district.

We believe that the type of research undertaken here may contribute to the establishment of practical, constructive and, at the same time, scientific, ethnographic research in Mexico which will follow the example given by Dr Manuel Gamio, and continued in the work of Dr Robert Redfield and Dr Alfonso Villa, and also by ourselves.

Appendix

The memorandum reproduced here in its original form, showing the signatures of B. Malinowski, Julio de la Fuente, Luís Chavez Orozco, Alfonso Caso, Moisés Saénz and Manuel Gamio on the reverse side, is translated into English below.

This is, as far as I know, the first written agreement between an anthropologist and representatives of the nation in which his fieldwork is to be undertaken, which provides for the disposition and publication of research results in the host country. As such the memorandum is of interest beyond its relevance to the 1957 publication in Mexico, of *The Economics of a Mexican Market System*. It marks a step in the history of anthropological fieldwork.

Susan Drucker-Brown
University of Cambridge

MEMORANDUM.

ASUNTO:- Estudios e investigaciones que realizará en México el Dr. Bronislaw Malinowski.

El Instituto Indigenista Interamericano se complace en reconocer la gentil disposición del Dr. Bronislaw Malinowski para realizar en México algunos estudios e investigaciones de orden científico, relacionados con nuestra población indígena, y de conformidad -- con lo tratado con el citado hombre de ciencia, así como con el señor Prof. Luis Chávez Orozco, Jefe del Departamento de Asuntos Indígenas de México, asienta lo que sigue:-

1.- El Dr. Malinowski, determinará los estudios que va a - emprender y los realizará en el tiempo y circunstancias que estime - más convenientes aceptando la colaboración del señor Julio de la --- Fuente, a quien comisionará para el efecto, en calidad de ayudante, ~~el Departamento de Asuntos Indígenas.~~ El Dr. Malinowski no incurrirá en ninguna responsabilidad económica por causa de la dicha colaboración del Sr. de la Fuente. Por otra parte, el Dr. Malinowski ha - expresado al Director del Instituto Indigenista Interamericano, que sus propios trabajos no implicarán carga económica ni para el Instituto ni para el Departamento de Asuntos Indígenas.

2.- El Dr. Malinowski ha pedido que se constituya un Comité integrado por el Sr. Chávez Orozco, Jefe del Departamento de Asuntos Indígenas y por los Doctores Manuel Gamio, Alfonso Caso y Moisés Sáenz, Comité que servirá como organismo consultor y del Proyecto de estudios de que se trata.

3.- En su oportunidad el Dr. Malinowski pondrá a disposición del Instituto Indigenista Interamericano el o los materiales -- provenientes de los estudios de referencia, destinados a la publicación. Una vez que el Instituto Indigenista Interamericano y el Departamento de Asuntos Indígenas hayan tomado nota de dichos materiales, se procederá a su publicación en la forma que se estime conveniente.

Estando de acuerdo con el contenido del presente Memorandum, firmamos de conformidad.

(A la vuelta)

México, D.F., a 20 de julio de 1940.

MEMORANDUM

Subject: Studies and research to be
carried out in Mexico by
Dr Bronislaw Malinowski

The Inter-American Indianist Institute recognizes with pleasure Dr Malinowski's kind desire to carry out research of a scientific nature in Mexico, with reference to our indigenous population. In agreement with the said scientist and with Professor Luís Chavez Orozco, Head of the Department of Indian Affairs in Mexico, the following is here set down:

(1) Dr Malinowski will decide upon the research to be undertaken and will carry it out in the space of time and under the circumstances he deems most convenient. He will accept the collaboration of Mr Julio de la Fuente who will be commissioned as his assistant by the Institute of Anthropology. Dr Malinowski will incur no financial responsibility as a result of his collaboration with Mr Julio de la Fuente. On the other hand, Dr Malinowski has assured the Director of the Inter-American Indianist Institute that his own work will not cause any economic burden either for the Institute or the Department of Indian Affairs.

(2) Dr Malinowski has asked that a Committee be composed as a consultative group for the Research Project. The Committee is to be made up of Mr Chavez Orozco, Head of the Department of Indian Affairs, by Dr Manuel Gamio, Dr Alfonso Caso, and Dr Moisés Saénz.

(3) At an opportune moment Dr Malinowski will place the material gathered from this study and destined for publication at the disposal of the Inter-American Indianist Institute. Once the Inter-American Indianist Institute and the Department of Indian Affairs have taken note of said material, it will be published as seems convenient.

In accord with the contents of this Memorandum our signatures indicate our collective agreement.

Luís Chavez Orozco
B. Malinowski — Julio de la Fuente
Alfonso Caso
Moisés Saénz — Mexico, D.F., July 20, 1940 — M. Gamio

Notes

1 The actual problem of fieldwork in Mexico today

1 Parsons (1936) also comments on the consuming interest which her friends in Mitla expressed in the prices of a wide range of goods, even those which she described to them but which they had never seen.

2 The 'plans, diagrams and numerical computations' referred to were not published in 1957, nor were they found with the typescript of the essay. However, the field notes which contain additional data referred to in the essay are presumably among the Malinowski papers which now belong to Yale University.

3 The 'plans and photographs' refer also to material which was not complete or prepared for publication at the time of Malinowski's death (verbal communication from Prof. R. Waterbury).
Maps and diagrams which illustrate the text were prepared by the editor.

2 General aspects of trade in the Valley, and a visit to the market place of Oaxaca

1 In the pre-colonial markets of the Aztec Highlands (from whence came the first indigenous settlers of the Spanish town, Antequera, subsequently Oaxaca), an indigenous market system was highly developed. Carrazco (1978, p. 55) cites Sahagun's description of periodic market places (Nahuatl: *tianguis*) which operated in cycles of five, nine or thirty days. Carrazco writes: 'all transactions were watched by "merchant lords" [Spanish: *señores mercaderes*; Nahuatl: *pochteca*] who formed a tribunal with jurisdiction over the market and decided *in situ* all cases presented there' (Trans.).

2 Marroquín (1957, p. 211) writes,

> [The market of Tlaxiaco is] a tranquil market . . . [which is] frankly surprising in an agglomeration of two or three thousand persons, some of them smelling intensely of alcohol and ether. There are no fights or discord. There are no typical aboriginal authorities such as we find in other markets but at all times the market is patrolled by municipal police who are in charge of keeping order. Their efficient zeal, severity and frequent excesses in dealing with the Indians is perhaps a primordial factor in keeping the peace. An Indian who commits some disorder is conducted immediately to the public jails where he will be kept locked up for several days without the authorities bothering about feeding him. He is, moreover, obliged to perform certain public works like sweeping the square and public offices. (Trans.)

3 1 and 2 November, also known in Mexico as 'the days of the dead' (los dias de los muertos).

3 The Valley markets in their cultural and economic interdependence

1 The population figures at ten-year intervals, from 1940 to 1960, are given for the municipalities containing Valley markets in Table A-2 of Diskin and Cook (1976, p. 288).

2 See Evon Z. Vogt (ed.), *Handbook of Middle American Indians* (1969) for descriptive summaries of Mixe, Mixtec and Zapotec ethnography.

3 The Cultural Mission preceded the Centro Coordinador as a centre for local development programmes (see Aguirre Beltrán, 1976).

4 A 'permanent road' in Mexico is one which is not regularly washed away, or made otherwise impassable, during the rainy season.

4 A brief survey of the surrounding district and townships

1 See Chapman (1957).

2 The Pan American Highway was completed to Oaxaca in 1943 and paved as far as Tehuantepec in 1948. In 1980 it reached the Mexican border with Guatemala.

3 Although the text here contrasts religious and patriotic festivals as alternative spurs to market activity, there is some ambiguity in the reference to 'the celebration of the hill near Oaxaca (connected with memories of Benito Juarez)'.

Hills are often celebrated in Mexican Indian religious ritual. In pre-Columbian religions certain deities were identified with hills and mountains. Temples were often constructed on mountain peaks. The most widely known Catholic shrine in Mexico, the Basilica of the Virgin of Guadalupe, is constructed on the site of a pre-Columbian temple which was located on the hill of Tepeyac. Among the pilgrims who come annually to Mexico City on the day set aside for the celebration of the Virgin there are some who come to celebrate the pre-Columbian deity associated with the hill. For a fascinating, if speculative, analysis of the role of mountains and hills in contemporary and pre-Columbian Indian cosmology, see E.V. Hunt (1977).

5 Problems and methods in the analysis of market transactions

1 Waterbury and Turkenick (1976, pp. 212-13) note the same continuity in the placement of traders at the Oaxaca market. Transport is presumably more efficient.

> The night before principal selling days in the city plaza (Tues., Fri. and Sat.) a truck makes its way up and down San Antonino's streets loading baskets that are left in front of each regatona's home. . . . In spite of the number of individuals involved the trucker and his helpers know exactly where each regatona sites on the Oaxaca City street reserved for San

Antonino marketeers (. . . even though there are no marks on the pavement to indicate the approximately one square meter occupied by each vendor). When the regatona arrives between 5:00 and 6:00 a.m. her goods await in her spot.

2 Plans drawn up from this phase of the study were not published in the 1957 edition. Like those referred to in the preface, they were incomplete at the time of Malinowski's death and remain among his papers.

3 This woman selling eggs is behaving in a fashion typical of the *regatonas* to be met with in the region of Tlaxiaco. She is engaged in purchasing produce from numerous individuals which she pools and resells to another individual. This latter buyer also purchases maize for later resale to the producers of maize. (He is the typical *acaparador*.) The alliance described here, of tax collector, *regatona* and *acaparador*, is an example of how pressure is bought to bear on the producer to provide goods for a specific network of intermediaries. It is this pressure which underlies the bitter tension which could be seen in the 1950s in some markets (i.e. Tlaxiaco) between the *regatona* and the *propio*, particularly in markets where maize was being resold to the producers.

The same tension underlies the frequency with which relations of ritual co-parenthood (*compadrazgo*) are established between producers and particular buyers. The networks of economic exchange may thus be buttressed by ritual, and certain moral obligations are supposed to enter the relationship between the parties to the exchange.

4 See Charlotte Stolmaker (1976, pp. 189-207) for a detailed study of Santa Maria Atzompa. She notes continuity in the forms of pottery with pre-Columbian ware. As in 1941, 'the household continues to be the production unit; its members dig clay, temper [the material], fetch kindling and procure wood . . .'. Stolmaker found that the potter's wheel (the kick wheel type), although introduced in 1940, was infrequently used, and produced a type of pottery inferior in quality to that formed by the coil method used traditionally.

Changes had also occurred in the type of pottery made, including types specifically designed for the tourist and folk-art trade. New types of glaze had been introduced. Wood was still the basic fuel used for firing the pottery.

5 Iszaevich (1973) notes the sale of livestock in 'lean months' from the village (*pueblo*) of Las Margaritas near Etla. Here the sale of livestock forms part of a farming economy in which 'the cultivation of alfalfa to feed cattle, the rearing of cattle, the use of milk for cheese, and the use of "suero" as feed for pigs' (p. 53) link the village with neighbouring villages and to specialized outlets for these goods. The outlets through which these goods are sold do not form part of the Market System as an institution in the definition used by Malinowski throughout this work.

Iszaevich writes that cheese is sent regularly to 'established businessmen'. Pork is sold locally or sent to Mexico City. Cattle are sent to the butchers of Oaxaca. Maize is bought from the national marketing board (CONASUPO).

6 Economic background of the market place

1 'Hidden ownership' refers to the practice by which large holdings could be preserved or created through false registration.

2 Steininger and Van de Velde (1935, p. 111) give the exchange rate of the Mexican peso as 'slightly less than fifteen cents' (of the US dollar) noting that there is 'a fluctuating foreign exchange'.

3 The increased use of tin recorded here was shortlived. At present the use of plastic utensils is widespread; and plastics, together with aluminium, tend to replace earthenware when replacement occurs. Artificial fibres have also replaced, to some extent, leather, palm and *ixtle*.

4 By 1978 ox-carts had disappeared entirely from the Oaxaca market and from the roads. Wooden goods were few.

5 See Iszaevich (1973) for a description of the development of dairy production in one Valley community.

6 Berg (1974, p. 219) confirms that this was still the case for parts of the Zapotec Highlands in the 1960s.

7 Beals (1975, p. 109) mentions the increased use of electricity in Oaxaca. However, he makes no systematic mention of the presence or absence of electricity in the market towns. Atzompa received electricity in 1969 (Stolmaker, 1976, p. 204) and the Zapotec highland village of Zoogocho was electrified in 1970 (Berg, 1974, p. 19). Beals's only conclusions about the introduction of electricity to Oaxaca is that the presence of electric light may lengthen the working day.

8 By 1978 the bourgeoisie had been re-established in Oaxaca though few could be considered members of a landholding class. However, people whose high income derives from the tourist industry or government bureaucracy, local businessmen and resident foreigners (many living on income from abroad), and tourists themselves, constitute an influential segment of the population of the Oaxaca Valley. The characterization of the 'bourgeoisie' given in the text, though outdated in some respects, still accurately reflects the position of this group as a source of the influence of Western culture. Citizens of the USA far outnumber those of any other nationality, though a very wide range of nationalities would now be found among both resident and transient foreign population.

9 Higgins's study (1974) of a poor neighbourhood in urban Oaxaca gives some idea of the present conditions of this group.

10 See Drucker (1963) for a detailed description of how clothing style, language, residence and social identity are linked in the division between 'Indian' and 'civilized people' as it occurs in the combined community of Jamiltepec, Oaxaca.

11 The festivities referred to here are among the feasts organized in many localities through the system of *mayordomiás*: the so-called *cargo* system. For a general view of the system see Cámara (1952). For a polemical interpretation see Harris (1964). For a specific study of a single system in the Chiapas highlands see Cancian (1965).

12 Nahmad (1965) found the same distribution of markets in the Mixe highlands as that described by Beals in 1933.

13 See De la Fuente (1949) for a detailed account of this region.

14 See Higgins (1974).

15 De la Fuente disagrees. The Valley was probably not normally a region which exported maize. Hamnett (1971) indicates that Oaxaca did not export maize in the colonial period but rather suffered from periodic maize shortages.

16 Warman (1977) writes that the year 1940 was the first of a series of bad harvests in the republic as a whole.

7 Market transactions under the microscope

1 On the significance of bargaining and the extent to which prices are known the following paragraphs are confusing. De la Fuente challenges Malinowski's assertion that 'the fair and correct price of each commodity is known by buyer and seller alike'. Malinowski is concerned, however, to distinguish between goods like maize for which prices change rapidly not only throughout the year but in the course of a single day, and the sale of goods for which the prices are comparatively fixed. He reckons that bargaining is significant in the first case, and compares this case (i.e. maize) with the case of other goods.

Marroquín (1957) documents the price changes of maize in the Tlaxiaco market in the course of a single day. In April 1956 I was able to observe the same phenomenon at the Tlaxiaco market. The centralized distribution and storage of maize at government warehouses may have affected such fluctuations in maize prices.

2 These are all articles which are frequently not marketed by the producers. Dried chillies and tropical fruit are brought into the Valley by specialist traders.

3 See Geertz (1979) for an analysis of the organization of a Moroccan bazaar (*suq*) which contrasts in many respects with the markets described here. Geertz argues that in the bazaar the search for information about price and quality is the essential force in organizing trade.

4 *Comadre*, literally 'co-mother', is one term of a set used by individuals linked through rituals of godparenthood. Co-parenthood (*compadrazgo*) binds the ritual sponsor of a child to the parents of that child. The relationship of co-parenthood entails 'respect' between co-parents and should, in theory at least, rule out crass cheating in market exchanges.

5 Berg (1974, p. 219) was told that in the Zapotec Highlands, prior to 1930, kindling wood and salt were used as currency due to the shortage of coin.

6 One aspect of barter in the Oaxaca market system is that it may serve as a defence against cheating. The vendor and buyer can both see the 'price' of the sale in goods rather than currency.

7 The tip (*pilón*), added to a purchase of foodstuffs and occasionally drink, was commonly given in Oaxaca markets. It might even be requested from the vendor if not offered. As an indicator of goodwill it was normally given if requested.

8 Concrete data on selling and buying

1 See Muñoz (1963). Although this work refers to the straw-weaving industry of the Mixteca in the states of Guerrero and Morelos, it is relevant to the same industry in the Mixtec Highlands of Oaxaca.

2 De la Fuente comments here on the failure of the first attempt by the central government to break the monopolistic control exercised by merchants in Tehuacan over the palm-hat industry of the states of Oaxaca and Guerrero.

According to Maurilio Muñoz (1963, p. 91) the price of palm-leaf hats fell in 1945 and the Mexican government, through the national import-export agency, CEIMSA, intervened to raise prices and organize a co-operative. The agency attempted to buy up all the hats woven by the Indian producers, and thus to force up the price paid by the Tehuacan dealers. However, 'the weavers were not helped because the Tehuacan monopolists control both the internal and the external sale of hats' (i.e. the government was unsuccessful in the competition with agents of the Tehuacan monopolists to buy up hats from the producers). Furthermore, 'the CEIMSA was obliged to act as intermediary between the Tehuacan monopolists and the weavers'. In other words, CEIMSA agents were unable to export the hats they had managed to buy and were eventually forced to sell them to the Tehuacan monopolists at a loss. Muñoz concludes:

> CEIMSA opted to retire from the enterprise. The failure of this experiment gave the Tehuacan monopolists further confidence and they continued to buy hats at the lowest prices fixed during their boycott of the government agency. Thus, the price paid to weavers has scarcely altered since 1945 and given the increase in the cost of living the poverty of the Indians has increased alarmingly. (Trans.)

Marroquín, in a course at the National School of Anthropology and History in Mexico in 1958, discussed the difficulties faced by the government agency. He explained that government agents could not compete with the local networks of intermediaries which operated between the Tehuacan merchants and the palm weavers. These trade networks were based on social relationships built up over a long period of time and often sanctioned by *compadrazgo*. He noted, as does De la Fuente, that the government agents themselves were often incorporated into the local trading networks which were thus strengthened rather than undermined by government intervention.

3 Since 1941, the outward movement of foreign population from Oaxaca City has been reversed. There is now a sizeable community of foreigners resident in Oaxaca. Population from the state of Oaxaca continues to emigrate to Mexico City and abroad to the USA and Canada. There is also some movement of intellectuals out of Mexico City, towards the provinces.

4 See Eder (1976, p. 72) for a list of major coastal crops sold in highland Oaxaca markets. In my own fieldwork in the Costa Chica (the Pacific coast) of Oaxaca in 1958, I encountered pineapple buyers from Oaxaca and Pochutla in the tiny settlement of Mechoacán. The 'market' at Mechoacán consisted only of the local Mixtec farmers who came exclusively to sell pineapples.

5 See Cook (1970, 1976) on the *metate* industry in the Oaxaca Valley. I have unfortunately been unable to consult his unpublished Ph.D. thesis, 'Teitipac and its *Metateros*: An Economic Anthropological Study of Production and Exchange in a Peasant-Artisan Stone-working Economy in the Valley of Oaxaca, Mexico', 1968; available from the University of Michigan at Ann Arbor.

6 See Chiñas (1976) for a description of market trade in the Isthmus of Tehuantepec. Chiñas notes (p. 171) that 'Isthmus traders use the Oaxaca market for selling but do not consider it a regular source for buying'. Traders now travel to and from the Isthmus by bus.

9 The maize market

1 It is certainly no longer true that 'the typical average peasant' produces sufficient maize to cover his annual needs. See Warman (1977) for data indicating that 1940 was the first harvest of a series which were extraordinarily poor; and for a description of how maize farmers in the state of Morelos reacted to the combined effects of poor harvests and devastating inflation. Berg (1974, pp. 224-5) describes the production of maize as a basic criterion of internal stratification within a highland Zapotec community, and indicates that although 'the rich' could produce more than twice as much maize as those classed as 'medium' (*medios*), there were also 'the poor' who could only produce sufficient maize to last six months or less. Berg's information refers to a period prior to 1930. Beals (1975, p. 57) writes that 'both the state and the region [of Oaxaca] are maize deficit areas' and calculates that not more than 25 per cent of the Valley villages produce a surplus.

2 The present situation of maize prices in Mexico has undoubtedly been influenced by government programmes which affect the production, storage and distribution of maize on a national scale. The prices of other staple crops, e.g. black beans, have also been affected. For a general study of changes in Mexican agriculture since 1940, see Hewitt de Alcantara (1976).

Bibliography

AGUIRRE BELTRÁN, GONZALO (1957), *El proceso de aculturación*, Universidad Nacional Autonoma de Mexico, Mexico DF. (Series: Problemas Cientificos y Filosoficos, no. 3.)

AGUIRRE BELTRÁN, GONZALO (1964), 'Introduction', in *Educación, antropología y Desaiole de la comunidad*, INI, Mexico DF. (Colección de Antropología Social, no. 6.)

AGUIRRE BELTRÁN, GONZALO (1967), *Regiones de refugio*, INI, Mexico DF, pp. 247-59.

AGUIRRE BELTRÁN, GONZALO (1976), *Obra Polémica*, La Casa Chata, Mexico DF.

BARABAS, A.M., and BARTOLOMÉ, M.A. (1974), 'Hydraulic Development and Ethnocide: The Mazatec and Chinantec People of Oaxaca, Mexico', *Critique of Anthropology*, vol. I, no. 1, pp. 74-91.

BEALS, R.L. (1970), 'Gifting, Reciprocity, Savings and Credit in Peasant Oaxaca', *Southwestern Journal of Anthropology*, vol. 26, no. 3, pp. 231-41.

BEALS, R.L. (1975), *The Peasant Marketing System of Oaxaca, Mexico*, University of California Press, Berkeley, Los Angeles, London.

BEALS, R.L. (1976), 'Oaxaca Market Study Project: Origins, Scope and Preliminary Findings', in Diskin and Cook (1976), pp. 27-43.

BENNET, WENDELL C., and ZINGG, ROBERT M. (1935), *The Tarahumara*, University of Chicago Press, Chicago, Ill.

BERG, RICHARD L. (1974), *El impacto de la economía moderna sobre la economía tradicional de Zoogocho, Oaxaca y su área circundante*, INI, Mexico DF. (Colección de Antropología Social, no. 24.)

BONFÍL BATALLA, GUILLERMO (1967), 'Andres Milina Enriquéz y la sociedad indianista Mexicana: el indigenismo en visperas de la Revolución', *Anales de antropología* (Instituto Nacional de Antropología e Historia, Mexico), vol. XVIII, pp. 217-35.

BONFÍL BATALLA, GUILLERMO (1971a), 'Introducción al ciclo de ferias de guaresma en la región de Cuantla Morelos', *Anales de antropología* (Instituto Nactional de Antropología e Historia, Mexico), vol. VIII.

BONFÍL BATALLA, GUILLERMO (1971b), *La situación del indígena en América del Sur*, Tierra Nueva, Montevideo, Uruguay.

BONFÍL BATALLA, GUILLERMO (1973), *Cholula, la ciudad sagradu en la era industrial*, Instituto de Investigaciones Historicas, Universidad Nacional Autónoma de Mexico, Mexico DF. (Serie Antropologica, no. 15.)

CALNEK, F.P. (1978), 'El sistema de mercado en Tenochtitlan', in Carrazco and Broda (1978).

CÁMARA, FERNANDO (1952), 'Religion and Political Organization' in *Heritage of Conquest*, ed. Sol Tax, The Free Press, Chicago, pp. 142-73.

CANCIAN, FRANK (1965), *Economics and Prestige in a Maya Community: The Religious Cargo System in Zinacantan*, Stanford University Press, Calif.

CANCIAN, FRANK (1972), *Change and Uncertainty in a Peasant Economy. The Maya Corn Farmers of Zinacantan*, Stanford University Press, Calif.

CARRAZCO, PEDRO (1961), 'The Civil-Religious Hierarchy in Mesoamerican Communities: Pre-Spanish Background and Colonial Development', *American Anthropologist*, no. 63, pp. 483-97.

CARRAZCO, PEDRO (1978), 'La economía del Mexico prehispánico', in Carrazco and Broda (1978).

CARRAZCO, PEDRO, and BRODA, JOHANNA (1978), *Economía política e ideología en el México prehispánico*, CIS-INAH, Nueva Imagen, Mexico.

CASO, ALFONSO (1939), 'Exploraciones en Oaxaca durante la 7ª y la 8ª temporadas (1937-1938 y 1938-1939)', *Actas del XXVII Congreso Internactional de Americanistas*, vol. 2, pp. 159-87.

CASO, ALFONSO (1950), 'Prologo' to *Densidad de la población de habla indigena en la Republica Mexicana, Morias del Instituto Nacional Indigenista*, vol. 1, INI, Mexico DF.

CASO, ALFONSO (1955), *Que es el I.N.I.*?, INI, Mexico DF.

CHANCE, J.K. (1978), *Race and Class in Colonial Oaxaca*, Stanford University Press, Calif.

CHAPMAN, ANNE (1957), 'Port of Trade Enclaves in Aztec and Maya Civilizations', in *Trade and Markets in the Early Empires*, ed. K. Polanyi, Conrad Arensberg and H.W. Pearson, The Free Press, Chicago, pp. 114-53.

CHAVEZ OROZCO, LUÍS (1943), *Las instituciones democráticas de los indígenas mexicanos en la época colonial*, Ediciones del Instituto Indigenista Interamericano, Mexico DF.

CHIÑAS, BEVERLY (1973), *The Isthmus Zapotecs*, Holt, Rinehart & Winston, New York.

CHIÑAS, BEVERLY (1976), 'Zapotec Viajeras', in Diskin and Cook (1976), pp. 169-88.

CODÉRE, HELEN (1968), 'Money Exchange Systems and a Theory of Money', *Man*, vol. 3, no. 3, pp. 557-77.

COOK, SCOTT (1970), 'Price and Output Variability in a Peasant-Artisan Stone-working Industry in Oaxaca, Mexico', *American Anthropologist*, no. 72, pp. 776-801.

COOK, SCOTT (1976), 'The "Market" as Location and Transaction: Dimensions of Marketing in a Zapotec Stoneworking Industry', in Diskin and Cook (1976), pp. 139-67.

CÓRDOVA, ARNALDO (1974), *La politica de masas del Cardenismo,* Era, Mexico DF.

DENNIS, PHILIP ADAMS (1976), *Conflictos por tierras en el Valle de Oaxaca* (An Inter-village Land Feud in the Valley of Oaxaca, Mexico), SEP-INI, Mexico DF. (Colección de Antropologia Social, no. 45.)

DISKIN, MARTIN (1969), 'Estudio estructural del sistema de plaza en el Valle de Oaxaca', *America Indígena*, vol. 29, pp. 1077-99.

DISKIN, MARTIN (1976), 'Peasant Market System Structure', in Diskin and Cook (1976).

DISKIN, MARTIN, and COOK, SCOTT, eds (1976), *Markets in Oaxaca*, University of Texas Press, Austin. First published (1975) as *Mercados de Oaxaca*, SEP-INI, Mexico DF. (Colección de Antropologia Social, no. 40.)

DRUCKER, SUSAN (1963), *Cambio de indumentaria, la estructura social y el abandono de la vestimenta indigena en la villa de Santiago Jamiltepec*, INI, Mexico DF. (Colección de Antropologia Social, no. 3.)

EDER, HERBERT M. (1976), 'Markets as Mirrors', in Diskin and Cook (1976), pp. 67-80.

FIRTH, RAYMOND, ed. (1957), *Man and Culture, An Evaluation of the Work of Bronislaw Malinowski*, Routledge & Kegan Paul, London.

FIRTH, RAYMOND (1975), 'An Appraisal of Modern Social Anthropology', *Annual Review of Anthropology*, pp. 1-25.

FORTES, MEYER (1978), 'An Anthropologist's Apprenticeship', *Annual Review of Anthropology*, vol. 4, pp. 1-25.

FOSTER, GEORGE M. (1948), 'The Folk Economy of Rural Mexico, with Special Reference to Marketing', *Journal of Marketing*, vol. 13, pp. 153-62.

FOSTER, GEORGE M. (1969), 'The Mixe, Zoque, Popuiuca', in *Handbook of Middle American Indians*, vol. 1, part 1, ed. Robert Wauchope and Evon Z. Vogt, University of Texas Press, Austin, pp. 448-88.

FUENTE, JULIO DE LA (1939), 'Gonzona agrícola and gonzona yalalteca', *El Maestro Rural* (Mexico DF), vol. XII, no. 9. Republished in La Fuente (1964), pp. 157-66.

FUENTE, JULIO DE LA (1940), 'Conflictos en la organización social y política de los zapotecos', paper presented at the Primer Congreso, Indigenista Interamericano, Patzcuaro, 1940. Republished in La Fuente (1965).

FUENTE, JULIO DE LA (1944), 'Relaciones etnicas en la Sierra Norte de Oaxaca', MS 'probably written in 1944'. Published in La Fuente (1965), pp. 33-47.

FUENTE, JULIO DE LA (1948), 'Cambios raciales y culturales en un grupo indígena', *Acta antropológica*, vol. III, pp. 389-408. Republished in La Fuente (1965), pp. 48-67.

FUENTE, JULIO DE LA (1949), *Yalalag: una villa Zapoteca Serrana*, INAH, Mexico DF.

FUENTE, JULIO DE LA (1958a), 'Cambios de indumentaria en tres áreas biculturales', *Bokín Técnico del INI* (unnumbered). Republished in La Fuente, 1965, pp. 138-61.

FUENTE, JULIO DE LA (1958b), 'La educación formal en el programa del Instituto Nacional Indigenista' (lecture). Republished in La Fuente (1964), pp. 94-107.

FUENTE, JULIO DE LA (1958c), 'Los programas de cambio dirigido', paper delivered at the 1958 Americanists' Congress. Republished in La Fuente (1964), pp. 242-9.

FUENTE, JULIO DE LA (1959), 'Integración y etnocentrismo', *La Palabra y el Hombre* (Universidad Veracruzana, Xalapa Ver.), vol. III, pp. 345-50. Republished in La Fuente (1965), pp. 131-7.

FUENTE, JULIO DE LA (1964), *Educacion, antropología y desarrollo de la comunidad*, INI, Mexico DF. (Colección de Antropologia Social, no. 6.)

FUENTE, JULIO DE LA (1965), *Relaciones Interétricas* (with introduction by Aguirre Beltrán), INI, Mexico DF. (Colección de Antropologia Social, no. 6.)

GAMIO, MANUEL (1966), *Consideraciones sobre el problema indigena*, edited, with a preface and concluding essay, by Miguel León Portilla, Instituto Indigenista Interamericano, Mexico DF. (Series: Antropología Social, no. 2.)

GAMIO, MANUEL, *et al.* (1922), *La población del Valle de Teotihuacan*, 3 vols, Dirección de Talleres Gráficos dependiente de la Secretaría de Educación, Mexico DF.

GEERTZ, CLIFFORD (1963), *Peddlers and Princes; Social Development and Economic Change in Two Indonesian Towns*, University of Chicago Press, Chicago, and London.

GEERTZ, CLIFFORD (1979), 'Suq: The Bazaar Economy in Sefron', in *Meaning and Order in Moroccan Society*, ed. C. Geertz *et al.*, Cambridge University Press, Cambridge.

GERHARD, PETER (1972), *A Guide to the Historical Geography of New Spain*, Cambridge University Press, Cambridge.

GONZÁLES CASANOVA, PABLO (1970), *Democracy in Mexico*, Oxford University Press, Oxford. First published in 1965 as *La Democracia en Mexico*, Era, Mexico DF.

GONZALEZ NAVARRO, MOISÉS (1954), 'Instituciones indigenas en Mexico independiente', in *Memorias del INI* (1954), pp. 113-69.

GOUGH, KATHLEEN (1968), 'Anthropology: Child of Imperialism', *Monthly Review*, vol. 19, no. 11.

GUDEMAN, STEPHEN (1978), 'Anthropological Economics: The Question of Distribution', *Annual Review of Anthropology*, no. 7, pp. 347-77.

HAMNETT, BRIAN R. (1971), *Politics and Trade in Southern Mexico*, Cambridge University Press, Cambridge.

HARRIS, MARVIN (1964), *Patterns of Race in the Americas*, Walker, New York.

HEWITT DE ALCANTARA, CYNTHIA (1976), *Modernizing Mexican Agriculture: Socio-economic Implications of Technological Change 1940-1970*, UN Research Institute for Social Development, Geneva.

HIGGINS, MICHAEL JAMES (1974), *Somos gente humilde, etnografía de una colonia urbana pobre de Oaxaca*, SEP-INI, Mexico DF. (Colección de Antropología Social, no. 35.)

HILL, POLLY (1966), 'Notes on Traditional Market Authority and Market Periodicity in West Africa', *Journal of African History*, vol. II, no. 2, pp. 295-311.

HUNT, E.V. (1977), *The Transformation of the Hummingbird*, Cornell University Press, Ithaca, NY, and London.

INI (1980), *Programa para el desarrollo y defensa de las culturas autoctonas*, INI, Mexico DF.

ISRAEL, J.I. (1975), *Race, Class, and Politics in Colonial Mexico 1610-1670*, Oxford Historical Monographs, Oxford University Press, Oxford.

ISZAEVICH, ABRAHAM (1973), *Modernizacion en una comunidad Oaxaqueña del valle*, Ediciones SEP-SETENTAS, no. 109, Mexico DF.

KABERRY, PHYLLIS (1968), 'Introduction' to *The Dynamics of Culture Change* by B. Malinowski, ed. Phyllis Kaberry, Yale University Press, New Haven, Conn. (2nd ed., originally published 1945), pp. i-xiii.

KAPLAN, DAVID (1965), 'The Mexican Marketplace Then and Now', *Proceedings of the 1965 Annual Spring Meeting of the American Ethnological Society*, University of Washington Press, Seattle.

K.Y. and F.E. (1974), 'Todos Somos Mexicanos, but Some are More Mexican than Others', *Critique of Anthropology*, vol. I, no. 1, pp. 93-100.

LEACH, EDMUND (1957), 'The Epistemological Background to Malinowski's Empiricism', in Firth (1957).

LEÓN PORTILLA, MIGUEL (1966), 'Algunas ideas fundamentales del Dr. Manuél Gamio', in Gamio (1966), Appendix I, pp. 241-54.

LUZ TOPETE, MARIA DE LA (1980), *Bibliografia antropologica de Oaxaca,* Instituto de Antropolgia e Historia, Oaxaca, Mexico.

MACFARLANE, ALAN (1977), 'History, Anthropology and the Study of Communities', *Journal of Social History*, vol. 5 (May), pp. 631-52.

MALINOWSKI, BRONISLAW (1921), 'The Primitive Economics of the Trobriand Islanders', *Economic Journal*, vol. XXXI, pp. 1-16. (Course of lectures given at the London School of Economics, Summer 1920.)

MALINOWSKI, BRONISLAW (1922), *Argonauts of the Western Pacific*, Routledge & Kegan Paul, London.

MALINOWSKI, BRONISLAW (1935), *Coral Gardens and Their Magic. Soil Tilling and Agricultural Rites in the Trobriand Islands*, Allen & Unwin, London.

MALINOWSKI, BRONISLAW, ed. (1938a), *Methods and Study of Culture Contact in Africa* (Memorandum XV of the International Institute of African Languages and Cultures), Oxford University Press, Oxford.

MALINOWSKI, BRONISLAW (1938b), 'The Scientific Basis of Applied Anthropology', *Transactions of the Volta Congress*, Royal Italian Academy, Rome.

MALINOWSKI, BRONISLAW (1939a), 'Culture' in *Encyclopedia of the Social Sciences*, ed. E.R. Seligman and A. Johnson, Macmillan, New York, pp. 621-45.

MALINOWSKI, BRONISLAW (1939b), 'The Group and the Individual in Functional Analysis', *American Journal of Sociology*, vol. XLIV, no. 6, pp. 938-64.

MALINOWSKI, BRONISLAW (1961), 'The Functional Theory of Culture', in *The Dynamics of Culture Change*, ed. Phyllis Kaberry, Yale University Press, New Haven, Conn. (originally published 1945).

MALINOWSKI, BRONISLAW (1963), 'Culture as a Determinant of Human Behavior', in *Sex, Culture, and Myth*, Hart-Davis, London. First published in 1937 in *Factors Determining Human Behavior*, by E.D. Adrian *et al.*, Cambridge, Mass.

MALINOWSKI, BRONISLAW (1968), 'Scientific Principles and Instruments in the Study of Culture Change', in Kaberry (1968).

MARROQUÍN, ALEJANDRO (1957), *La Ciudad Mercado: Tlaxiaco, México*, Instituto Indigenista, Imprenta Universitaria, Mexico DF.

MARTINEZ RIOS, JORGE (1964), 'Analeses funcional de la Guelaguetza Agricola', *Revista Mexicana de Sociología*, vol. 26, pp. 79-126.

MEMORIAS DEL INI (1950), vol. I, no. 1: *Densidad de la población de habla Indigena en la Republica Mexicana (por entidades federativas y municipios conforme al censo de 1940)*, Prologo de Alfonso Caso, Introducción de Manuel German Parra, INI, Mexico DF.

MEMORIAS DEL INI (1954), vol. VI, *Metodos y resultados de la política indigenista en Mexico*, by Alfonso Caso, Silvio Zavala, Jose Miranda, Moises Gonzalez Navarro, Gonzalo Aguirre Beltrán, Ricardo Pozas, INI, Mexico DF.

MUÑOZ, MAURILIO (1963), 'Mixteca Nahua Tlapaheca', in *Memorias del INI*, vol. IX, INI, Mexico DF.

NADER, LAURA (1969), 'The Zapotec of Oaxaca', in *Handbook of Middle American Indians*, vol. 7, part 1, ed. Robert Wauchope and Evon Z. Vogt, University of Texas Press, Austin, pp. 329-59.

NAHMAD, SALOMÓN (1965), 'Los Mijes', in *Memorias del INI*, vol. XI, INI, Mexico DF.

NASH, MANNING (1967), 'Indian Economics', in *Handbook of Middle American Indians*, vol. 6, ed. Robert Wauchope, University of Texas Press, Austin, pp. 87-102.

NEEDHAM, JOSEPH (1946), 'The Nazi Attack on International Science' in *History is on Our Side*, Allen & Unwin, London (written in 1940).

ORTIZ, SUTI (1967), 'Columbian Rural Market Organization: An Exploratory Model', *Man*, vol. 2, no. 3, pp. 393-414.

PADDOCK, JOHN, ed. (1966), *Ancient Oaxaca*, Stanford University Press, Calif.

PARSONS, ELSIE CLEWS (1936), *Mitla, Town of Souls*, University of Chicago.

POUDEVIDA, ANTONIO (1969), *Diccionario Porrua de la lengua Española*, revised by Francisco Monterde, Porra, Mexico DF.

REDFIELD, ROBERT (1930), *Tepoztlán, A Mexican Village*, University of Chicago Press.

REDFIELD, ROBERT (1941), *The Folk Culture of Yucatán*, University of Chicago Press.

REDFIELD, ROBERT, and SINGER, MILTON B. (1954), *City and Countryside: The Cultural Independence*, excerpts from *The Cultural Role of Cities in Economic Development and Social Change*, vol. 3, Chicago, pp. 53-73. Reprinted in *Peasants and Peasant Societies*, ed. Teodor Shanin (1971), Penguin, Harmondsworth, Middx, pp. 337-65.

ROMNEY, K., and RAVICZ, R. (1969), 'The Mixtec', in *Handbook of Middle American Indians*, vol. 7, ed. Robert Wauchope and Evon Z. Vogt, University of Texas Press, Austin, pp. 367-99.

SCHMEIDER, OSCAR (1930), *The Settlements of the Tzapotec and Mije Indians of the State of Oaxaca, Mexico*, University of California Publications in Geography, no. 4, Berkeley.

SKINNER, G.W. (1964), 'Marketing and Social Structure in Rural China', *Journal of Asian Studies*, vol. XXIII, p. 3 (part I), p. 195 (part II); vol. XXIV, pp. 363-99 (part III).

SMITH, CAROL (1976a), 'Markets in Oaxaca, Are They Really Unique?', in *Reviews in Anthropology*, July-August 1976, pp. 387-99.

SMITH, CAROL (1976b), *Regional Analysis*, vol. I, Academic Press, London.

SOLIS, LEOPOLDO (1970), *La realidad económica Mexicana retrovisión y perspectivas*, Siglo Veintiuno, Mexico DF.

SPORES, RONALD (1967), *The Mixtec Kings and Their People*, University of Oklahoma Press, Norman.

STAVENHAGEN, RODOLFO (1972), *Sociologia y Subdesarrollo*, Nuestro Tiempo, Mexico DF.

STEININGER, G.R., and VELDE, PAUL VAN DE (1935), *Three Dollars a Year*, published privately, New York. Republished in 1971 by Blaine Ethridge, Detroit.

STOLMAKER, CHARLOTTE (1976), 'Examples of Stability and Change from Santa Maria Atzompa', in Diskin and Cook (1976), pp. 189-207.

TAX, SOL (1952), 'Economy and Technology', in *Heritage of Conquest: The Ethnology of Middle America*, The Free Press, Chicago.

TAX, SOL (1935), *Penny Capitalism: A Guatemalan Indian Economy*, Smithsonian Institution Publication 16, Washington DC.

TAYLOR, WILLIAM (1972), *Landlord and Peasant in Colonial Oaxaca*, Stanford University Press, Calif.

VELDE, PAUL VAN DE, and VELDE, HENRIETTA VAN DE (1939), 'The Black Pottery of Coyotepec, Oaxaca, Mexico', Southwestern Museum Papers, no. 13, Los Angeles.

VILLA ROJAS, ALFONSO (1976), *Seis años de acción indigenista,* INI, Mexico.

VOGT, Evon 2. (ed.) (1969), *Handbook of Middle American Indians*, vol. 7, University of Texas Press, Austin.

WARMAN, ARTURO (1977), *Y Venisos a Contradecir los Campensinos de Morelos y el estado nacional*, Centro de Investigaciones Superiores del INAH, La Casa Chata, Mexico DF.

WARMAN, ARTURO, NOLAZCO, MARGARITA, BONFÍL, GUILLERMO, OLIVERA, MERCEDES, and VALENCIA, ENRIQUE (1970), *De eso que Llaman antropologiá Mexicana*, Nuestro Tiempo, Mexico DF.

WARNER, JOHN C. (1976), 'Survey of the Market System in the Nochixtlán Valley and the Mixteca Alta', in Diskin and Cook (1976), pp. 107-37.

WATERBURY, RONALD (1970), 'Urbanization and a Traditional Market System', in *The Social Anthropology of Latin America: Essays in Honor of Ralph Leon Beals*, ed. W. Goldschmidt and Harry Hoijer, Latin American Center, Los Angeles.

WATERBURY, R., and TURKENIK, C. (1976), 'Marketplace Traders of San Antonino', in Diskin and Cook (1976), pp. 209-29.

WHITECOTTON, JOSEPH W. (1977), *The Zapotecs, Princes, Priests and Peasants*, University of Oklahoma Press, Norman.

Index

abarrotes/groceries, 79, 91, 129, 131, 189
Abasolo, 56, 67, 127, 140, 170
acaparador/bulk buyer, 35-7, 87-8, 108, 179
agents, 69, 85, 108, 113, 122, 130, 136, 173
agriculture, 99; agricultural work, 98; produce, 116-18; reform, 123-4; techniques, 10
Aguirre Beltrán, Gonzalo, 6, 10, 14, 22, 49 n8 and n10, 50 n10
alfalfa, 74, 85, 87
amole, 129
aniline dyes, 167
anthropology, 1, 11, 13, 22-3, 25
artisans, 42, 69, 98, 125, 185, 191
ass, 61, 63, 74, 75, 111
atole, 88, 126, 134
Atoyac river, 93
Atzompa, 56, 103, 104, 106, 111-12, 156, 198 n4, 199 n7, 152, 154; pottery co-operative in, 158-60
Aztec, 70, 71, 192 n1

bakers, 75
bamboo, 76
bananas, 75, 81, 101, 104, 164, 186
bandstand, 96
bank, 35, 38, 82
bar/*cantina*, 75, 78, 89, 97, 100
bargaining, 36-7, 63-4, 67, 77, 103, 138-40, 142-4, 155-61, 167-8, 170, 200 n1
barter, 30, 37, 63, 102-5, 146-53, 200 n6; *see also* photo 32
basketry/baskets, 76, 99, 108
Beals, R.L., 44-6, 199 n7, n12
beans, 85, 88, 95, 97, 102, 104, 115-16, 126, 142, 146, 202 n2; broad bean/*alubia*, 131
beasts of burden, 79, 87
begging, 42, 146
Benito Juarez market, *see* Oaxaca City market
blankets/*sarape*, 100, 129, 138, 167, 179, 184; aniline dyes, 167; blanket makers, 139
booths, 100, 107, 109, 110, 104
bottles, 75
bourgeoisie, 124-5, 133, 199 n8
braziers, 76
bread, 68, 75, 79, 80, 84, 88, 97, 101, 103, 106, 128, 130, 132, 134, 143, 190
budget, 66, 122-36, 177-8, 186
bunuelo, 81
burros/donkeys, 63, 74, 95, 148
bus, 39, 63, 93, 94, 101
butchers, 51 n27, 74, 75, 79, 114, 125, 154
buying, 36, 51 n24, 87, 113, 137-73; buyers, 97, 103, 108; maize, 174-82

Cancian, F., 39, 48, 195
cantina, see bar
Cárdenas, President Lázaro, 22, 128
carpenter, 95
carriers, 131
Caso, Alfonso, 15, 19, 21-2, 62, 70, 93, 102
cattle, 69, 77, 79, 84, 90-4, 100, 114, 130, 131, 134, 139, 163, 198 n5; dealers, 113; market, 64; Ocotlán, 96-7; price, 94
Caxonos (region), 119, 161
charcoal, 88, 96, 104, 120, 128-9, 139, 186
charter, 5, 32, 183, 188
cheating, 140-1, 186, 200 n4 and n6
cheese, 33, 64, 65, 84, 103, 132, 138, 143, 198 n5

Chiapas, 48, 50 n11, 199 n11
chicharrón, 103
Chichicapa (region), 148, 149
Chilateca, 57, 99, 140
chilli, 73-4, 88, 96, 100, 115, 116, 126, 129, 138, 148, 168, 200 n2
Chinantec, 9
chocolate, 80, 114, 123, 128, 132, 189
Chontal, 119
church, 40, 61, 66, 77, 78, 79, 80, 97, 100, 104, 106, 197; Atzompa, 103; Ocotlán, 95, 99; property, 123; school, 127; selling site, 119; Tlacochahuaya, 101
clay, 111-12
clothing/clothes, 92, 101, 104, 109, 110, 125, 126, 131; dresses, 61, 88, 123, 126; huipil, 73; as indicator of status, 17-18, 199 n10; in Ocotlán, 96; ready-made, 75; *see also* photos 7-10
cochineal, 43-4, 52 n28, 135
coconut, 81, 104
coffee, 88, 91, 126, 128, 129, 131, 132, 189; government marketing, 41
coffins, 95
comales, 158
Comas, Juan, 27
commerce, 82, 84, 90, 104; in San Antonino, 98-9
community development, 7-11, 18
consumers, 68-9, 82, 87, 110, 111, 121, 124-39, 187
co-operatives, 18, 22, 159-61, 201 n2
cotton, 44
Coyotepec, 57, 93, 111, 112, 156-7
credit, 18, 145-6
Cuilapan, 103; monastery, 93
Cultural Mission, 95, 197, ch.3, n3
culture, 5, 11, 17, 50 n18, 59, 61, 98, 121-4; cultural characteristics, 83
custom, 77, 98, 122; marriage, 169-70

dairy products, 75, 119, 198 n5
demand, 122-36, 186
diffusion, cultural, 98, 122, 123
display, 95, 104, 107, 137; of earthenware, 155; market, 189
distribution, 61, 82, 111, 115, 154-74, 187
donkeys, *see* burros
drought, 84
drunkenness, 78

earthenware, 61, 62, 68, 75-9, 93, 100-5, 107, 111, 112, 118, 125, 129, 131-2; vendors in Ocotlán, 95
economic, 67, 111, 114, 121-3, 187-9; factors, 94; function, 108; motives, 68
Economics of a Mexican Market System, The, 4-7, 10-12, 18, 21, 29-32, 38-9, 44-8
education, 58, 59
eggs, 79, 88, 97, 108, 132, 136, 198 n3
ejido, 117-18
Ejutla, 70, 73, 83, 84, 85, 87, 103, 105, 113, 121, 173
electricity, 120-1, 199 n7
England, 3, 6
ethnic groups, 41, 107
ethnographer, 77, 122, 135, 140
Etla, 70, 82-4, 85-7, 90-1, 101-5, 113, 121, 177, 189; maize market, 179-80
export, 41, 103, 111-12, 116, 121, 187, 199 n1; exporters, 69, 88; from Atzompa, 159

feast, 78, 80; and food consumption, 157; personal saint, 110; *see also* saints, Virgin
festivals, 156, 197, ch.4, n3; day of the dead, 80, 90, 91, 104; day of the radish, 110; Easter (holy) week, 90-1, 104, 110; Independence Day, 105; 12 May, 104; 16 September, 105
fieldwork, 1-5, 10, 11, 29, 58-70, 77, 107, 115, 121, 154, 182
firewood/wood, 96, 103, 104, 120, 139, 147, 148, 149, 150, 152
fireworks, 122
fish, 81, 99, 100, 143, 171-3
flowers, 66, 75, 77, 80, 85, 99, 100, 169
fodder, 74, 76, 97, 100, 101, 104
food/foodstuffs, 66, 78, 80, 87, 88, 89, 103, 104, 110, 123, 131, 132, 133, 135, 200 n7
fowl, 80, 97; turkey, 80, 96
fruit, 41, 64, 75, 79, 80, 81, 87, 89, 95, 96, 100, 101, 103, 131, 138, 139, 142, 147, 152, 163, 200 n2; apples, 75, 129, 131; peaches, 129, 131, 148; pears, 129, 138

Fuente, Julio de la, on bargaining, 103; on barter, 145; on begging, 146; biographical, 1-7, 13-18, 49 n6, 50 n12; on ceramics, 104; and co-operatives, 161; and fieldwork, 55, 56, 77, 106, 128, 133; on houses, 102; on imports, 134-6; on land tenure, 116-17; on maize, 174-6; on middlemen, 153, 178; and Mixe, 131; in the Mixtec region, 130; on numeracy, 141; on prices, 138-9, 153; publications of, 16-18, 48 n3, 51 n20; and *regatones*, 87-9; on ricinus oil, 85; on salt, 114; on settlement patterns, 148; on the slack season, 90; trade journeys, 98
functionalism/function, 15, 98, 183-91; and history, 60-1

Gamio, Manuel, 15-16, 20-5, 50 n17, 58, 59, 191
garlic, 96, 116, 150, 152
Germany, 3, 51 n18
goats, 95
gold, 88
grasshoppers, 143, 147, 150
groceries, *see abarrotes*
Guatemala, 172
Guerrero, 63, 111, 114, 173, 201 n1
guitar, 89

haberdashery, *see mercerias*
haggling, 37, 113, 186
Hamnet, Brian, 43-4
hardward, 75; not supplied in market, 133
harvest, 114, 187; maize, 90-1, 179-80
hats, 75, 99, 100, 101, 104, 130
headshawls, *see rebozos*
highlands, 16, 85, 89
history/historian, 10-11, 17, 19, 43-4, 98
horses, 61, 74
hostelry/*mesón*, 63, 67, 74, 77, 88-9, 97, 100, 107, 109; fruit sales in, 164
hotels, 89
houses, 102-4, 123
household, 104, 118; production, 120; maize consumption, 134-5
Huajuapan, 84
huaraches, *see* sandals
Huila, 161
Huixtepec, 105

ices/ice-cream, 74, 103
imports, 28-9, 68, 114, 119, 121-2, 187; importer, 113; luxury goods to Oaxaca valley, 133; of textiles, 109; maize, 134-5
incense/*copal*, 80, 101, 142; burners, 113
income, 30, 85, 121-36, 178, 187, 191; of municipality, 185
Indians, 7, 9, 11, 16-19, 34, 37, 39, 40, 61, 64, 66, 70, 75, 78, 79-84, 88-9, 90, 96-7, 102, 110-13, 116, 117, 120, 122, 128-32, 177, 185, 191, 199 n6; as buyers, 155; as consumers, 157; and Republics, 7-8; welfare, 59
Indianist policy, 7-10, 22, 24
industry, 62, 95, 109-19; in Atzompa, 104, petroleum, 22; vs household production, 120-1
INI/National Indianist Institute, 6-10, 13, 15, 18, 40, 49 n9; *see also* Indianist policy
Institutio Nacional Indigenista, *see* INI
institution, 31-4, 67, 107, 123, 183
iron/ironwork, 118-19, 129; in Ocotlán, 97; *see also* photo 20
Isthmus (of Tehuantepec), 16, 84, 94, 98, 100, 114, 147, 172
ixtle, 75, 88, 96, 119, 186

Jalapa, 83
Jalisco, 63
Jamiltepec, 52 n29, 199 n10
Juquila, 84, 171, 173

kitchen, 76, 89, 129, 132; cooking utensils, 123
Kula exchange, 30, 32-3

labour, 111, 147, 190-1; agricultural, 116-18; hired, 90; time, 156
lacquered ware, 111
lamp, 79, 85, 133
land tenure, 22, 116-17, 123-4; loss of, 98-9
language, 18, 40, 125-7
Latinized, 17, 34, 40; community, 98
leather, 75, 88, 119, 129, 150; price of, 138; saddles, 119; tanneries, 104

lemons, 103, 150
lime/quicklime, 75, 96, 103, 149, 150
liquor, 78, 130, 131-2, 184, 189

maguey, 76, 129
mail, 94
maize, 37-9, 41, 47-8, 68-9, 76, 84, 87, 95, 100-2, 104, 108, 110, 113-16, 127, 129, 130, 132, 138-9, 198 n3, 202 n1 and n2; barter, 103; coba, 149-53; drying, 91; fields, 93; -market, 174-81, 187; mills, 120-1; prices, 196; shortage of, 90, 134-5; *see also* photos 23-9
Malinowska, Valetta (*née* Swann), 1, 48 n2, 56
Malinowski, Bronislaw, disagreement with de la Fuente, 29-34; influence in Mexico, 10-11; predecessors in Mexico, 19-21, 27-9; prior work, 31-4; use of terms, 34-5; *see* photo 1
marchante, 36-7, 63
market: administration of, 42, 77; as bank, 35, 38; cattle, 64, 113, 115-16; covered, 101; code, 186; daily, 83, 86, 113; duration of, 91; festival, 80, 104-5, 111, 119; gallery, 100, 101, 104; kitchens, 89; maize, 65, 112, 113; minor, 106, 107; overlapping, 85; psychology and, 189; relocation of Oaxaca, 42-3, 51 n27; routine, 88; seasonal, 87, 101; secondary, 105; small, 87, 101, 103, 105, 113; special, 90, 106-9; suburban, 78; -square, 89; yearly cycle, 90; *see also* Oaxaca City market
market day, 76, 78-9, 85-102, 105-6, 114; day following, 90; evening of, 88-9, 97; Friday, 87-9, 93, 156; Monday 86-7, 90; monthly variation in, 91; Saturday, 79, 80, 83, 90, 101; Sunday, 90, 97, 99, 101; Thursday, 87-8, 93; Tuesday, 86-7, 90
market system: centre of, 82-7; daily sequence, 86; function of, 32, 68; hierarchy of, 105-7; Michoacan, 41; middlemen in, 35-7; regional, 16; studies of, 43-7; solar, 12-13; weekly rotation, 79, 85-92
Marroquín, Alejandro, 6, 33, 38, 49, 200 n1
Marxism, 3
mats, 74, 76, 100, 107, 127
materials/textiles, 75, 78, 79, 88, 97, 101, 109, 133, 138, 150
mattresses, 74
mayordomías, 57, 110, 114, 146, 156 199 n11
measures, 176-7; almud, 85; scales, 31; *see also* photo 30
meat, 69, 74-6, 80, 88-9, 100-1, 103, 104, 114, 126, 127, 130, 131, 132, 142, 143, 147, 165-6; bacon, 143
Mechoacán, 201 n4
medicine/medicinal herbs, 63, 64, 79, 130, 170-1; patent medicines, 78
mercerias/haberdashery, 100, 101, 109, 110
merchants, 68, 75-6, 82, 85, 87, 93, 94, 98, 100, 124-39
mestizo, 34-5, 61, 62, 71, 77, 82, 91, 125
metate, 61, 169-70, 202 n5
Mexico: anthropology in, 25-51; national diet of, 88, 115; fieldwork in, 59-70; *see also* fieldwork
Mexico City: emigration to, 163; exports to, 62, 103, 114, 135
mezcal, 76, 99, 120
Miahuatlan, 55, 83, 84, 105, 154-6
Michoacán, 110
middlemen, 42, 69, 82, 87-8, 93, 97, 98, 102, 109, 113-14, 121, 155-73, 185, 188; and maize, 180; *see also* agent, *acaparador, regatón*
mining, 118; in Ejutla, 85
Mitla, 20, 59, 71, 84, 90, 95, 100, 155, 172
Mixe, 37, 40, 59, 70, 83, 84, 100, 107, 126, 130-1, 175, 199 n12
Mixtec, 21, 40, 46, 71, 83, 85, 126, 129-30
Mixteca/Mixtec region, 102, 114, 160-1, 179
money, 30, 35, 38, 78, 89, 90, 95, 103, 110, 114, 127, 129, 131, 138-9, 154, 186, 191, 200 n5; coins, 144-5; profit, 147-53
Monte Albán, 21, 50 n16, 57, 93
Morelos, 47-8, 117, 125
mountain ranges, 82, 88, 87, 103, 116, 123; southwestern range, 128-9; Northern Mixtec, 130
mules, 39, 95

municipality, 99
murder, 93-4, 127
music, 89
musical instruments, 79, 133

National Indianist Institute, *see* INI
National School of Anthropology and History (Instituto Nacional de Antropolgía a Historia), 5-6, 7, 11
natives, 77, 114, 119
Nativitas, 160
needs, 31-4, 51 n22, 91, 92, 113, 115, 122-3, 124
newspapers, 51 n27, 63
nuts, 142-3, 146, 148; peanuts, 116, 150; walnuts, 75, 85

Oaxaca, 4-7; districts, 16-17; research in, 20-1, 43-8; modernization of, 39-43; history of, 43-4, 70; Mixtec region of, 81-4; land-reform in, 116-17, 121; ethnic divisions, 125-33; palm industry, 201 n2
Oaxaca City, 62-81, 100-3; administration of, 82; bishopric of, 82; class structure, 124-5; earthenware production in, 104, 107, 112; earthenware trade from, 158; exports, 116; fruit buyers, 163; history, 70; ixtle buyers, 161; patron saint, 56; population, 39-40; transport, 39, 84, 90
Oaxaca City market, 73-9, 89; arcades, 95; *regatones* in, 88; relocation of, 42-3, 51-2 n27
Oaxaca Valley, 51 n25, 61-3, 79, 82-4, 95, 100-1, 115-17; centre for trade, 172; coastal imports, 164, 171; crafts, 119, 123; drainage, 118; research in, 20-1, 43-8
Ocotlán, 56, 63, 70, 82-4, 87, 89, 90-5, 102, 105, 106, 147-9, 189; distillery, 120; electricity, 121, flowers, 116; market, 99; maize, 180; population in 1930, 98; red-ware, 113; Santa Lucia de, 149
onions, 96, 97, 116, 131, 147, 149, 150, 152
oranges, 42, 101, 103
officials, 97-8, 108, 186
ox-carts, 39, 76, 90, 95, 100, 168; storage of, 96; *see also* photos 4 and 21
oxen, 61, 77, 94, 113, 114

Pacific Coast, 81, 164, 201 n4
palm leaf, 88, 129, 160-1, 201 n1 and n2
Parsons, Elsie Clews, 20, 59, 65, 196, ch.1, n1
peasant/s, 64, 66-7, 79, 83-4, 90, 102, 110, 112, 116, 121, 122, 125-8, 155, 175-6, 185, 191
pigs, 77, 95, 96
pineapples, 73, 104; Mixe middlemen and, 164
pixtle, 131
plastic, 199 n3
Pochutla, 84, 164, 171, 201 n4
police, 78, 196 ch.2, n2
poor, urban, 125, 132-3
porcelain, 113
potatoes, 116
potter's wheel, 112, 198 n4
price, 37-9, 41, 64-9, 75, 82, 94, 96, 100, 103, 108, 114, 187; of earthenware, 155, 166; fluctuations in, 138-41; of maize, 179-81; of medicine, 170-1; of quinces, 165; rises due to war, 85; of *sarapes*, 167
producers, 41, 62, 66, 68-9, 75, 87, 89, 97, 109, 118, 124-39, 156-7, 185, 187; of earthenware, 111-15; of maize, 175
profit, 64-5, 114, 140-8, 151, 155, 169, 171
propio, 35-9, 174; *see also* producer
prostitutes, 89
Puebla, 19, 62, 83, 84, 90, 109, 119; Atzompa pots in, 159
pulque, 74
pumpkins, 103; barter for, 149-50

quarrelling (in market), 64, 196 ch.2 n2
quinces, 132; trade from Yatareni, 164-5

radios, 89, 125
railway, 90, 114; train, 94
rebozos/head shawls, 64, 75, 97, 100, 104, 109, 139
Redfield, Robert, 15-16, 20, 59, 125, 191
reed, 74, 76

regatón/a, 35-7, 64, 87-8, 113, 140, 174, 197, ch.5, n1; wood, 148; *see also* middlemen
rent, 74
retail, 109-14
ricinus seed, 85
roads, 93-5, 101, 197 ch.3, n4 and ch.4, n2; permanent, 90; *see also* transport
robbery, 93-4
rope, 119, 139, 162, 186

Saenz, Moises, 22
saints, 77, 78, 80
salt, 100, 114, 143, 146-8
San Agustín Yatareni, 140, 164
San Antonino, 96-9; population in 1930, 98; land loss, 99; fruit producers of, 164; trade journeys to, 172
San Bartolo Yautepec, 119, 147, 148, 155, 172
San Marcos Tlapazola, 158
San Miguel (nr Ocotlán), 99, 147
San Pedro Apóstol, 83, 99, 105; maize market of, 181
San Pedro Guegoreche, 149
Santa Inez, 152
Santo Domingo del Valle, 101, 167
sandals/*huaraches*, 109, 126, 138
Santiago, 99
sarape, see blankets
science, 26, 50-1 n18, 188
seasons, 114; dry, 90-1; rainy, 90-1; variations in, 110, 114
selling, 26, 51 n24, 87-8, 109, 113-14, 154-74; seasonal, 104; sites for, 64, 101, 103, 106, 107, 110, 119, 183; of earthenware, 155; of maize, 175
sewing machine, 133
shoes, 79
shopkeepers, 98, 109, 114
shops, 66, 67, 74, 78, 100, 101, 108, 113; in Ocotlán, 96; plaza vs, 109
Sierra de Juarez, 56, 83, 84, 100, 102, 106, 161, 164
singers, 73, 79
soap, 75, 85, 127, 129
Social Defence League, 93-4
Sole de Vega, 119
soothsayer, 78
soup, 88, 126, 127
Spain, 48 n1
Spaniards, 70-3, 185, 187
Spanish, 19, 25, 34-5, 40, 43, 79, 141; Castilian, 126; colonial rule, 7-8; mill-owners, 179; translation of *Economics of a Mexican Market System*, 5-7
square/*zocalo*, 102, 103, 106
stall/*puesto*, 42, 63, 75, 79, 97; permanent, 76; eating-, 87, 88; in Ocotlán, 95; kitchen, 104
standard of living, 66, 92, 111, 121-36, 191
storage, 74, 96, 97; store rooms, 87; of pottery, 158; of maize, 175
straw, 104
subsistence, 66
sugar, 114, 128, 129, 132; brown, 78; -cane, 76, 85, 96, 101, 102, 147
sweetmeats/sweets, 74, 80, 101, 103, 106, 114; potato, 96

tailor, 109
tax, 77, 97, 108, 140, 183-4
technology, 26, 118-21
Tehuantepec, 73; *see also* Isthmus of Tehuantepec
tent, 107
Teotihuacán, San Juan, 14-15, 21, 25, 50 n16, 58
Teotitlán del Valle, 105, 167; maize-buyers of, 179, sarape makers in, 139
Tepoztlán, 14-17
testing, 77, 143; earthenware, 155
textiles, *see* materials
Tilacayapan, San Martin, 119
tin, 119, 199 n3
Tlacochahuaya, 57, 73-5; dependent on Tlacolula, 101; spice vendors in, 97
Tlacolula, 70, 83, 89-91, 93-5, 99-102, 105-7, 113, 115, 154, 161, 172, 177; All Souls market in, 120; distilleries, 121; barter in, 149; maize prices, 180-1; palm, 160; tourists, 167
Tlaxiaco, 38, 49 n5, 50 n11, 198 n3, 200 n1
tortillas, 64, 75, 88, 93, 103, 113, 126-7, 128, 134, 149, 152
Totolapan, 84, 101, 154, 172
tourists, 42, 61, 75, 76, 77, 167

townspeople, 155
toys, 62, 80, 91, 100, 110, 112, 113
trade routes/trade journeys, 60, 70, 84, 94, 147, 171-3
train, 61, 63, 104
transport, 39, 111, 114, 147, 154, 156, 157
Trobriand Islands, 3, 29-32
turkey, *see* fowl

United States of America, 19, 39, 112
urban centre, 15, 41-3, 98, 99

vegetables, 41, 64, 73, 75, 76, 79, 84, 85, 87, 91, 96, 99, 100-3, 104, 115, 116, 125, 129, 131, 132, 139, 142, 143, 150, 186; gardens, 118
vendetta, 94
vendor, 35, 42, 63, 64, 76, 95, 97, 101, 107, 108
Veracruz, 3, 63, 91
vernacular, 83
Villa Rojas, 8, 20, 59, 89, 191
village/*pueblo*, 62, 79, 82, 83, 85, 89, 97, 103, 106; communities, 15-16; land holding, 116-17; ownership of mountain land, 120; source of raw materials, 119; vendors in, 107
villager, 34, 83, 84, 87, 93, 94, 100, 103
Virgin, 77, 80, 81; de la Soledad, 81; Juquila, 81; Guadalupe, 104; de la Asuncion, 99
votive offerings, 19, 80, 96, 119

war, 19, 26-7, 31, 85; revolution, 23
Warman, Arturo, 47-8, 50 n10
waters, 70, 74, 75, 118, 146, 155
Waterbury, Ronald, 41, 197 ch.5, n1
wheat, 84, 115, 121, 131, 134
wheelwright, 119
women, 17, 103, 109, 111, 112
wool, 75, 104, 129, 130; weaving, 119

Yalalag, 14, 16-17, 23-4
Yale University, 4, 15, 19, 22, 56, 196 ch.1, n2
Yucatań, 20

Zaachila, 57, 63, 70, 84, 87, 91, 93, 102, 103, 105, 124, 152, 164, 189; marshes of, 90; flowers of, 116; school in, 127
Zimatlán, 70, 84, 85, 90, 91, 93, 102, 105, 113, 116, 149, 152, 164, 181, 189
Zapotec, 13, 16, 18, 21, 23, 40, 59, 62, 67, 83, 99, 126, 131-2, 140; culture, 98; villages of, 85

Routledge Social Science Series

Routledge & Kegan Paul London, Henley and Boston

39 Store Street,
London WC1E 7DD
Broadway House,
Newtown Road,
Henley-on-Thames,
Oxon RG9 1EN
9 Park Street,
Boston, Mass. 02108

Contents

International Library of Sociology 2
General Sociology 2
Foreign Classics of Sociology 2
Social Structure 3
Sociology and Politics 3
Criminology 4
Social Psychology 4
Sociology of the Family 5
Social Services 5
Sociology of Education 5
Sociology of Culture 6
Sociology of Religion 6
Sociology of Art and Literature 6
Sociology of Knowledge 6
Urban Sociology 7
Rural Sociology 7
Sociology of Industry and Distribution 7
Anthropology 8
Sociology and Philosophy 8
International Library of Anthropology 9
International Library of Phenomenology and Moral Sciences 9
International Library of Social Policy 9
International Library of Welfare and Philosophy 10
Library of Social Work 10
Primary Socialization, Language and Education 12
Reports of the Institute of Community Studies 12
Reports of the Institute for Social Studies in Medical Care 13
Medicine, Illness and Society 13
Monographs in Social Theory 13
Routledge Social Science Journals 13
Social and Psychological Aspects of Medical Practice 14

Authors wishing to submit manuscripts for any series in this catalogue should send them to the Social Science Editor, Routledge & Kegan Paul Ltd, 39 Store Street, London WC1E 7DD.

● *Books so marked are available in paperback.*

○ *Books so marked are available in paperback only.*

All books are in metric Demy 8vo format (216 × 138mm approx.) unless otherwise stated.

International Library of Sociology
General Editor John Rex

GENERAL SOCIOLOGY

Barnsley, J. H. The Social Reality of Ethics. *464 pp.*
Brown, Robert. Explanation in Social Science. *208 pp.*
● Rules and Laws in Sociology. *192 pp.*
Bruford, W. H. Chekhov and His Russia. *A Sociological Study. 244 pp.*
Burton, F. and **Carlen, P.** Official Discourse. *On Discourse Analysis, Government Publications, Ideology. About 140 pp.*
Cain, Maureen E. Society and the Policeman's Role. *326 pp.*
● **Fletcher, Colin.** Beneath the Surface. *An Account of Three Styles of Sociological Research. 221 pp.*
Gibson, Quentin. The Logic of Social Enquiry. *240 pp.*
Glassner, B. Essential Interactionism. *208 pp.*
Glucksmann, M. Structuralist Analysis in Contemporary Social Thought. *212 pp.*
Gurvitch, Georges. Sociology of Law. *Foreword by Roscoe Pound. 264 pp.*
Hinkle, R. Founding Theory of American Sociology 1881–1913. *About 350 pp.*
Homans, George C. Sentiments and Activities. *336 pp.*
Johnson, Harry M. Sociology: *A Systematic Introduction. Foreword by Robert K. Merton. 710 pp.*
● **Keat, Russell** and **Urry, John.** Social Theory as Science. *278 pp.*
Mannheim, Karl. Essays on Sociology and Social Psychology. *Edited by Paul Keckskemeti. With Editorial Note by Adolph Lowe. 344 pp.*
Martindale, Don. The Nature and Types of Sociological Theory. *292 pp.*
● **Maus, Heinz.** A Short History of Sociology. *234 pp.*
Myrdal, Gunnar. Value in Social Theory: *A Collection of Essays on Methodology. Edited by Paul Streeten. 332 pp.*
Ogburn, William F. and **Nimkoff, Meyer F.** A Handbook of Sociology. *Preface by Karl Mannheim. 656 pp. 46 figures. 35 tables.*
Parsons, Talcott and **Smelser, Neil J.** Economy and Society: *A Study in the Integration of Economic and Social Theory. 362 pp.*
Payne, G., Dingwall, R., Payne, J. and **Carter, M.** Sociology and Social Research. *About 250 pp.*
Podgórecki, A. Practical Social Sciences. *About 200 pp.*
Podgórecki, A. and **Łos, M.** Multidimensional Sociology. *268 pp.*
Raffel, S. Matters of Fact. *A Sociological Inquiry. 152 pp.*
● **Rex, John.** Key Problems of Sociological Theory. *220 pp.*
Sociology and the Demystification of the Modern World. *282 pp.*
● **Rex, John.** (Ed.) Approaches to Sociology. *Contributions by Peter Abell, Frank Bechhofer, Basil Bernstein, Ronald Fletcher, David Frisby, Miriam Glucksmann, Peter Lassman, Herminio Martins, John Rex, Roland Robertson, John Westergaard and Jock Young. 302 pp.*
Rigby, A. Alternative Realities. *352 pp.*
Roche, M. Phenomenology, Language and the Social Sciences. *374 pp.*
Sahay, A. Sociological Analysis. *220 pp.*
Strasser, Hermann. The Normative Structure of Sociology. *Conservative and Emancipatory Themes in Social Thought. About 340 pp.*
Strong, P. Ceremonial Order of the Clinic. *267 pp.*
Urry, John. Reference Groups and the Theory of Revolution. *244 pp.*
Weinberg, E. Development of Sociology in the Soviet Union. *173 pp.*

FOREIGN CLASSICS OF SOCIOLOGY

● **Gerth, H. H.** and **Mills, C. Wright.** From Max Weber: *Essays in Sociology. 502 pp.*

● **Tönnies, Ferdinand.** Community and Association *(Gemeinschaft und Gesellschaft). Translated and Supplemented by Charles P. Loomis. Foreword by Pitirim A. Sorokin. 334 pp.*

SOCIAL STRUCTURE

Andreski, Stanislav. Military Organization and Society. *Foreword by Professor A. R. Radcliffe-Brown. 226 pp. 1 folder.*

Broom, L., Lancaster Jones, F., McDonnell, P. and **Williams, T.** The Inheritance of Inequality. *About 180 pp.*

Carlton, Eric. Ideology and Social Order. *Foreword by Professor Philip Abrahams. About 320 pp.*

Clegg, S. and **Dunkerley, D.** Organization, Class and Control. *614 pp.*

Coontz, Sydney H. Population Theories and the Economic Interpretation. *202 pp.*

Coser, Lewis. The Functions of Social Conflict. *204 pp.*

Crook, I. and **D.** The First Years of the Yangyi Commune. *304 pp., illustrated.*

Dickie-Clark, H. F. Marginal Situation: *A Sociological Study of a Coloured Group. 240 pp. 11 tables.*

Giner, S. and **Archer, M. S.** (Eds) Contemporary Europe: *Social Structures and Cultural Patterns, 336 pp.*

● **Glaser, Barney** and **Strauss, Anselm L.** Status Passage: *A Formal Theory. 212 pp.*

Glass, D. V. (Ed.) Social Mobility in Britain. *Contributions by J. Berent, T. Bottomore, R. C. Chambers, J. Floud, D. V. Glass, J. R. Hall, H. T. Himmelweit, R. K. Kelsall, F. M. Martin, C. A. Moser, R. Mukherjee and W. Ziegel. 420 pp.*

Kelsall, R. K. Higher Civil Servants in Britain: *From 1870 to the Present Day. 268 pp. 31 tables.*

● **Lawton, Denis.** Social Class, Language and Education. *192 pp.*

McLeish, John. The Theory of Social Change: *Four Views Considered. 128 pp.*

● **Marsh, David C.** The Changing Social Structure of England and Wales, 1871–1961. *Revised edition. 288 pp.*

Menzies, Ken. Talcott Parsons and the Social Image of Man. *About 208 pp.*

● **Mouzelis, Nicos.** Organization and Bureaucracy. *An Analysis of Modern Theories. 240 pp.*

● **Ossowski, Stanislaw.** Class Structure in the Social Consciousness. *210 pp.*

● **Podgórecki, Adam.** Law and Society. *302 pp.*

Renner, Karl. Institutions of Private Law and Their Social Functions. *Edited, with an Introduction and Notes, by O. Kahn-Freud. Translated by Agnes Schwarzschild. 316 pp.*

Rex, J. and **Tomlinson, S.** Colonial Immigrants in a British City. *A Class Analysis. 368 pp.*

Smooha, S. Israel: Pluralism and Conflict. *472 pp.*

Wesolowski, W. Class, Strata and Power. *Trans. and with Introduction by G. Kolankiewicz. 160 pp.*

Zureik, E. Palestinians in Israel. *A Study in Internal Colonialism. 264 pp.*

SOCIOLOGY AND POLITICS

Acton, T. A. Gypsy Politics and Social Change. *316 pp.*

Burton, F. Politics of Legitimacy. *Struggles in a Belfast Community. 250 pp.*

Crook, I. and **D.** Revolution in a Chinese Village. *Ten Mile Inn. 216 pp., illustrated.*

Etzioni-Halevy, E. Political Manipulation and Administrative Power. *A Comparative Study. About 200 pp.*

Fielding, N. The National Front. *About 250 pp.*

● **Hechter, Michael.** Internal Colonialism. *The Celtic Fringe in British National Development, 1536–1966. 380 pp.*

Kornhauser, William. The Politics of Mass Society. *272 pp. 20 tables.*

Korpi, W. The Working Class in Welfare Capitalism. *Work, Unions and Politics in Sweden. 472 pp.*
Kroes, R. Soldiers and Students. *A Study of Right- and Left-wing Students. 174 pp.*
Martin, Roderick. Sociology of Power. *About 272 pp.*
Merquior, J. G. Rousseau and Weber. *A Study in the Theory of Legitimacy. About 288 pp.*
Myrdal, Gunnar. The Political Element in the Development of Economic Theory. *Translated from the German by Paul Streeten. 282 pp.*
Varma, B. N. The Sociology and Politics of Development. *A Theoretical Study. 236 pp.*
Wong, S.-L. Sociology and Socialism in Contemporary China. *160 pp.*
Wootton, Graham. Workers, Unions and the State. *188 pp.*

CRIMINOLOGY

Ancel, Marc. Social Defence: *A Modern Approach to Criminal Problems. Foreword by Leon Radzinowicz. 240 pp.*
Athens, L. Violent Criminal Acts and Actors. *104 pp.*
Cain, Maureen E. Society and the Policeman's Role. *326 pp.*
Cloward, Richard A. and **Ohlin, Lloyd E.** Delinquency and Opportunity: *A Theory of Delinquent Gangs. 248 pp.*
Downes, David M. The Delinquent Solution. *A Study in Subcultural Theory. 296 pp.*
Friedlander, Kate. The Psycho-Analytical Approach to Juvenile Delinquency: *Theory, Case Studies, Treatment. 320 pp.*
Gleuck, Sheldon and **Eleanor.** Family Environment and Delinquency. *With the statistical assistance of Rose W. Kneznek. 340 pp.*
Lopez-Rey, Manuel. Crime. *An Analytical Appraisal. 288 pp.*
Mannheim, Hermann. Comparative Criminology: *A Text Book. Two volumes. 442 pp. and 380 pp.*
Morris, Terence. The Criminal Area: *A Study in Social Ecology. Foreword by Hermann Mannheim. 232 pp. 25 tables. 4 maps.*
Rock, Paul. Making People Pay. *338 pp.*
● **Taylor, Ian, Walton, Paul** and **Young, Jock.** The New Criminology. *For a Social Theory of Deviance. 325 pp.*
● **Taylor, Ian, Walton, Paul** and **Young, Jock.** (Eds) Critical Criminology. *268 pp.*

SOCIAL PSYCHOLOGY

Bagley, Christopher. The Social Psychology of the Epileptic Child. *320 pp.*
Brittan, Arthur. Meanings and Situations. *224 pp.*
Carroll, J. Break-Out from the Crystal Palace. *200 pp.*
● **Fleming, C. M.** Adolescence: Its Social Psychology. *With an Introduction to recent findings from the fields of Anthropology, Physiology, Medicine, Psychometrics and Sociometry. 288 pp.*
● The Social Psychology of Education: *An Introduction and Guide to Its Study. 136 pp.*
Linton, Ralph. The Cultural Background of Personality. *132 pp.*
● **Mayo, Elton.** The Social Problems of an Industrial Civilization. *With an Appendix on the Political Problem. 180 pp.*
Ottaway, A. K. C. Learning Through Group Experience. *176 pp.*
Plummer, Ken. Sexual Stigma. *An Interactionist Account. 254 pp.*
● **Rose, Arnold M.** (Ed.) Human Behaviour and Social Processes: *an Interactionist Approach. Contributions by Arnold M. Rose, Ralph H. Turner, Anselm Strauss, Everett C. Hughes, E. Franklin Frazier, Howard S. Becker et al. 696 pp.*
Smelser, Neil J. Theory of Collective Behaviour. *448 pp.*
Stephenson, Geoffrey M. The Development of Conscience. *128 pp.*
Young, Kimball. Handbook of Social Psychology. *658 pp. 16 figures. 10 tables.*

SOCIOLOGY OF THE FAMILY

Bell, Colin R. Middle Class Families: *Social and Geographical Mobility. 224 pp.*
Burton, Lindy. Vulnerable Children. *272 pp.*
Gavron, Hannah. The Captive Wife: *Conflicts of Household Mothers. 190 pp.*
George, Victor and **Wilding, Paul.** Motherless Families. *248 pp.*
Klein, Josephine. Samples from English Cultures.
1. Three Preliminary Studies and Aspects of Adult Life in England. *447 pp.*
2. Child-Rearing Practices and Index. *247 pp.*

Klein, Viola. The Feminine Character. *History of an Ideology. 244 pp.*
McWhinnie, Alexina M. Adopted Children. *How They Grow Up. 304 pp.*
● **Morgan, D. H. J.** Social Theory and the Family. *About 320 pp.*
● **Myrdal, Alva** and **Klein, Viola.** Women's Two Roles: *Home and Work. 238 pp. 27 tables.*
Parsons, Talcott and **Bales, Robert F.** Family: Socialization and Interaction Process. *In collaboration with James Olds, Morris Zelditch and Philip E. Slater. 456 pp. 50 figures and tables.*

SOCIAL SERVICES

Bastide, Roger. The Sociology of Mental Disorder. *Translated from the French by Jean McNeil. 260 pp.*
Carlebach, Julius. Caring For Children in Trouble. *266 pp.*
George, Victor. Foster Care. *Theory and Practice. 234 pp.*
Social Security: *Beveridge and After. 258 pp.*
George, V. and **Wilding, P.** Motherless Families. *248 pp.*
● **Goetschius, George W.** Working with Community Groups. *256 pp.*
Goetschius, George W. and **Tash, Joan.** Working with Unattached Youth. *416 pp.*
Heywood, Jean S. Children in Care. *The Development of the Service for the Deprived Child. Third revised edition. 284 pp.*
King, Roy D., Ranes, Norma V. and **Tizard, Jack.** Patterns of Residential Care. *356 pp.*
Leigh, John. Young People and Leisure. *256 pp.*
● **Mays, John.** (Ed.) Penelope Hall's Social Services of England and Wales. *368 pp.*
Morris, Mary. Voluntary Work and the Welfare State. *300 pp.*
Nokes, P. L. The Professional Task in Welfare Practice. *152 pp.*
Timms, Noel. Psychiatric Social Work in Great Britain (1939–1962). *280 pp.*
● Social Casework: *Principles and Practice. 256 pp.*

SOCIOLOGY OF EDUCATION

Banks, Olive. Parity and Prestige in English Secondary Education: a Study in Educational Sociology. *272 pp.*
● **Blyth, W. A. L.** English Primary Education. *A Sociological Description.*
2. Background. *168 pp.*

Collier, K. G. The Social Purposes of Education: *Personal and Social Values in Education. 268 pp.*
Evans, K. M. Sociometry and Education. *158 pp.*
● **Ford, Julienne.** Social Class and the Comprehensive School. *192 pp.*
Foster, P. J. Education and Social Change in Ghana. *336 pp. 3 maps.*
Fraser, W. R. Education and Society in Modern France. *150 pp.*
Grace, Gerald R. Role Conflict and the Teacher. *150 pp.*
Hans, Nicholas. New Trends in Education in the Eighteenth Century. *278 pp. 19 tables.*
● Comparative Education: *A Study of Educational Factors and Traditions. 360 pp.*
● **Hargreaves, David.** Interpersonal Relations and Education. *432 pp.*
● Social Relations in a Secondary School. *240 pp.*
School Organization and Pupil Involvement. *A Study of Secondary Schools.*

● **Mannheim, Karl** and **Stewart, W. A. C.** An Introduction to the Sociology of Education. *206 pp.*
● **Musgrove, F.** Youth and the Social Order. *176 pp.*
● **Ottaway, A. K. C.** Education and Society: An Introduction to the Sociology of Education. *With an Introduction by W. O. Lester Smith. 212 pp.*
Peers, Robert. Adult Education: *A Comparative Study. Revised edition. 398 pp.*
Stratta, Erica. The Education of Borstal Boys. *A Study of their Educational Experiences prior to, and during, Borstal Training. 256 pp.*
● **Taylor, P. H., Reid, W. A.** and **Holley, B. J.** The English Sixth Form. *A Case Study in Curriculum Research. 198 pp.*

SOCIOLOGY OF CULTURE

Eppel, E. M. and **M.** Adolescents and Morality: *A Study of some Moral Values and Dilemmas of Working Adolescents in the Context of a changing Climate of Opinion. Foreword by W. J. H. Sprott. 268 pp. 39 tables.*
● **Fromm, Erich.** The Fear of Freedom. *286 pp.*
● The Sane Society. *400 pp.*
Johnson, L. The Cultural Critics. *From Matthew Arnold to Raymond Williams. 233 pp.*
Mannheim, Karl. Essays on the Sociology of Culture. *Edited by Ernst Mannheim in co-operation with Paul Kecskemeti. Editorial Note by Adolph Lowe. 280 pp.*
Merquior, J. G. The Veil and the Mask. *Essays on Culture and Ideology. Foreword by Ernest Gellner. 140 pp.*
Zijderfeld, A. C. On Clichés. *The Supersedure of Meaning by Function in Modernity. 150 pp.*

SOCIOLOGY OF RELIGION

Argyle, Michael and **Beit-Hallahmi, Benjamin.** The Social Psychology of Religion. *256 pp.*
Glasner, Peter E. The Sociology of Secularisation. *A Critique of a Concept. 146 pp.*
Hall, J. R. The Ways Out. *Utopian Communal Groups in an Age of Babylon. 280 pp.*
Ranson, S., Hinings, B. and **Bryman, A.** Clergy, Ministers and Priests. *216 pp.*
Stark, Werner. The Sociology of Religion. *A Study of Christendom.*
Volume II. *Sectarian Religion. 368 pp.*
Volume III. *The Universal Church. 464 pp.*
Volume IV. *Types of Religious Man. 352 pp.*
Volume V. *Types of Religious Culture. 464 pp.*
Turner, B. S. Weber and Islam. *216 pp.*
Watt, W. Montgomery. Islam and the Integration of Society. *320 pp.*

SOCIOLOGY OF ART AND LITERATURE

Jarvie, Ian C. Towards a Sociology of the Cinema. *A Comparative Essay on the Structure and Functioning of a Major Entertainment Industry. 405 pp.*
Rust, Frances S. Dance in Society. *An Analysis of the Relationships between the Social Dance and Society in England from the Middle Ages to the Present Day. 256 pp. 8 pp. of plates.*
Schücking, L. L. The Sociology of Literary Taste. *112 pp.*
Wolff, Janet. Hermeneutic Philosophy and the Sociology of Art. *150 pp.*

SOCIOLOGY OF KNOWLEDGE

Diesing, P. Patterns of Discovery in the Social Sciences. *262 pp.*

● **Douglas, J. D.** (Ed.) Understanding Everyday Life. *370 pp.*
● **Hamilton, P.** Knowledge and Social Structure. *174 pp.*
Jarvie, I. C. Concepts and Society. *232 pp.*
Mannheim, Karl. Essays on the Sociology of Knowledge. *Edited by Paul Kecskemeti. Editorial Note by Adolph Lowe. 353 pp.*
Remmling, Gunter W. The Sociology of Karl Mannheim. *With a Bibliographical Guide to the Sociology of Knowledge, Ideological Analysis, and Social Planning. 255 pp.*
Remmling, Gunter W. (Ed.) Towards the Sociology of Knowledge. *Origin and Development of a Sociological Thought Style. 463 pp.*
Scheler, M. Problems of a Sociology of Knowledge. *Trans. by M. S. Frings. Edited and with an Introduction by K. Stikkers. 232 pp.*

URBAN SOCIOLOGY

Aldridge, M. The British New Towns. *A Programme Without a Policy. 232 pp.*
Ashworth, William. The Genesis of Modern British Town Planning: *A Study in Economic and Social History of the Nineteenth and Twentieth Centuries. 288 pp.*
Brittan, A. The Privatised World. *196 pp.*
Cullingworth, J. B. Housing Needs and Planning Policy: *A Restatement of the Problems of Housing Need and 'Overspill' in England and Wales. 232 pp. 44 tables. 8 maps.*
Dickinson, Robert E. City and Region: *A Geographical Interpretation. 608 pp. 125 figures.*
The West European City: *A Geographical Interpretation. 600 pp. 129 maps. 29 plates.*
Humphreys, Alexander J. New Dubliners: *Urbanization and the Irish Family. Foreword by George C. Homans. 304 pp.*
Jackson, Brian. Working Class Community: *Some General Notions raised by a Series of Studies in Northern England. 192 pp.*
● **Mann, P. H.** An Approach to Urban Sociology. *240 pp.*
Mellor, J. R. Urban Sociology in an Urbanized Society. *326 pp.*
Morris, R. N. and **Mogey, J.** The Sociology of Housing. *Studies at Berinsfield. 232 pp. 4 pp. plates.*
Mullan, R. Stevenage Ltd. *About 250 pp.*
Rex, J. and **Tomlinson, S.** Colonial Immigrants in a British City. *A Class Analysis. 368 pp.*
Rosser, C. and **Harris, C.** The Family and Social Change. *A Study of Family and Kinship in a South Wales Town. 352 pp. 8 maps.*
● **Stacey, Margaret, Batsone, Eric, Bell, Colin** and **Thurcott, Anne.** Power, Persistence and Change. *A Second Study of Banbury. 196 pp.*

RURAL SOCIOLOGY

Mayer, Adrian C. Peasants in the Pacific. *A Study of Fiji Indian Rural Society. 248 pp. 20 plates.*
Williams, W. M. The Sociology of an English Village: *Gosforth. 272 pp. 12 figures. 13 tables.*

SOCIOLOGY OF INDUSTRY AND DISTRIBUTION

Dunkerley, David. The Foreman. *Aspects of Task and Structure. 192 pp.*
Eldridge, J. E. T. Industrial Disputes. *Essays in the Sociology of Industrial Relations. 288 pp.*
Hollowell, Peter G. The Lorry Driver. *272 pp.*
● **Oxaal, I., Barnett, T.** and **Booth, D.** (Eds) Beyond the Sociology of Development.

Economy and Society in Latin America and Africa. 295 pp.

Smelser, Neil J. Social Change in the Industrial Revolution: *An Application of Theory to the Lancashire Cotton Industry, 1770–1840. 468 pp. 12 figures. 14 tables.*

Watson, T. J. The Personnel Managers. *A Study in the Sociology of Work and Employment, 262 pp.*

ANTHROPOLOGY

Brandel-Syrier, Mia. Reeftown Elite. *A Study of Social Mobility in a Modern African Community on the Reef. 376 pp.*

Dickie-Clark, H. F. The Marginal Situation. *A Sociological Study of a Coloured Group. 236 pp.*

Dube, S. C. Indian Village. *Foreword by Morris Edward Opler. 276 pp. 4 plates.*
India's Changing Villages: *Human Factors in Community Development. 260 pp. 8 plates. 1 map.*

Fei, H.-T. Peasant Life in China. *A Field Study of Country Life in the Yangtze Valley. With a foreword by Bronislaw Malinowski. 328 pp. 16 pp. plates.*

Firth, Raymond. Malay Fishermen. *Their Peasant Economy. 420 pp. 17 pp. plates.*

Gulliver, P. H. Social Control in an African Society: a Study of the Arusha, Agricultural Masai of Northern Tanganyika. *320 pp. 8 plates. 10 figures.*
Family Herds. *288 pp.*

Jarvie, Ian C. The Revolution in Anthropology. *268 pp.*

Little, Kenneth L. Mende of Sierra Leone. *308 pp. and folder.*
Negroes in Britain. *With a New Introduction and Contemporary Study by Leonard Bloom. 320 pp.*

Tambs-Lyche, H. London Patidars. *About 180 pp.*

Madan, G. R. Western Sociologists on Indian Society. *Marx, Spencer, Weber, Durkheim, Pareto. 384 pp.*

Mayer, A. C. Peasants in the Pacific. *A Study of Fiji Indian Rural Society. 248 pp.*

Meer, Fatima. Race and Suicide in South Africa. *325 pp.*

Smith, Raymond T. The Negro Family in British Guiana: *Family Structure and Social Status in the Villages. With a Foreword by Meyer Fortes. 314 pp. 8 plates. 1 figure. 4 maps.*

SOCIOLOGY AND PHILOSOPHY

Adriaansens, H. Talcott Parsons and the Conceptual Dilemma. *About 224 pp.*

Barnsley, John H. The Social Reality of Ethics. *A Comparative Analysis of Moral Codes. 448 pp.*

Diesing, Paul. Patterns of Discovery in the Social Sciences. *362 pp.*

● **Douglas, Jack D.** (Ed.) Understanding Everyday Life. *Toward the Reconstruction of Sociological Knowledge. Contributions by Alan F. Blum, Aaron W. Cicourel, Norman K. Denzin, Jack D. Douglas, John Heeren, Peter McHugh, Peter K. Manning, Melvin Power, Matthew Speier, Roy Turner, D. Lawrence Wieder, Thomas P. Wilson and Don H. Zimmerman. 370 pp.*

Gorman, Robert A. The Dual Vision. *Alfred Schutz and the Myth of Phenomenological Social Science. 240 pp.*

Jarvie, Ian C. Concepts and Society. *216 pp.*

Kilminster, R. Praxis and Method. *A Sociological Dialogue with Lukács, Gramsci and the Early Frankfurt School. 334 pp.*

● **Pelz, Werner.** The Scope of Understanding in Sociology. *Towards a More Radical Reorientation in the Social Humanistic Sciences. 283 pp.*

Roche, Maurice. Phenomenology, Language and the Social Sciences. *371 pp.*

Sahay, Arun. Sociological Analysis. *212 pp.*

● **Slater, P.** Origin and Significance of the Frankfurt School. *A Marxist Perspective. 185 pp.*

Spurling, L. Phenomenology and the Social World. *The Philosophy of Merleau-Ponty and its Relation to the Social Sciences. 222 pp.*
Wilson, H. T. The American Ideology. *Science, Technology and Organization as Modes of Rationality. 368 pp.*

International Library of Anthropology
General Editor Adam Kuper

● **Ahmed, A. S.** Millennium and Charisma Among Pathans. *A Critical Essay in Social Anthropology. 192 pp.*
Pukhtun Economy and Society. *Traditional Structure and Economic Development. About 360 pp.*
Barth, F. Selected Essays. *Volume I. About 250 pp.* Selected Essays. *Volume II. About 250 pp.*
Brown, Paula. The Chimbu. *A Study of Change in the New Guinea Highlands. 151 pp.*
Foner, N. Jamaica Farewell. *200 pp.*
Gudeman, Stephen. Relationships, Residence and the Individual. *A Rural Panamanian Community. 288 pp. 11 plates, 5 figures, 2 maps, 10 tables.*
The Demise of a Rural Economy. *From Subsistence to Capitalism in a Latin American Village. 160 pp.*
Hamnett, Ian. Chieftainship and Legitimacy. *An Anthropological Study of Executive Law in Lesotho. 163 pp.*
Hanson, F. Allan. Meaning in Culture. *127 pp.*
Hazan, H. The Limbo People. *A Study of the Constitution of the Time Universe Among the Aged. About 192 pp.*
Humphreys, S. C. Anthropology and the Greeks. *288 pp.*
Karp, I. Fields of Change Among the Iteso of Kenya. *140 pp.*
Lloyd, P. C. Power and Independence. *Urban Africans' Perception of Social Inequality. 264 pp.*
Parry, J. P. Caste and Kinship in Kangra. *352 pp. Illustrated.*
Pettigrew, Joyce. Robber Noblemen. *A Study of the Political System of the Sikh Jats. 284 pp.*
Street, Brian V. The Savage in Literature. *Representations of 'Primitive' Society in English Fiction, 1858–1920. 207 pp.*
Van Den Berghe, Pierre L. Power and Privilege at an African University. *278 pp.*

International Library of Phenomenology and Moral Sciences
General Editor John O'Neill

Apel, K.-O. Towards a Transformation of Philosophy. *308 pp.*
Bologh, R. W. Dialectical Phenomenology. *Marx's Method. 287 pp.*
Fekete, J. The Critical Twilight. *Explorations in the Ideology of Anglo-American Literary Theory from Eliot to McLuhan. 300 pp.*
Medina, A. Reflection, Time and the Novel. *Towards a Communicative Theory of Literature. 143 pp.*

International Library of Social Policy
General Editor Kathleen Jones

Bayley, M. Mental Handicap and Community Care. *426 pp.*
Bottoms, A. E. and **McClean, J. D.** Defendants in the Criminal Process. *284 pp.*
Bradshaw, J. The Family Fund. *An Initiative in Social Policy. About 224 pp.*

Butler, J. R. Family Doctors and Public Policy. *208 pp.*
Davies, Martin. Prisoners of Society. *Attitudes and Aftercare. 204 pp.*
Gittus, Elizabeth. Flats, Families and the Under-Fives. *285 pp.*
Holman, Robert. Trading in Children. *A Study of Private Fostering. 355 pp.*
Jeffs, A. Young People and the Youth Service. *160 pp.*
Jones, Howard and Cornes, Paul. Open Prisons. *288 pp.*
Jones, Kathleen. History of the Mental Health Service. *428 pp.*
Jones, Kathleen with **Brown, John, Cunningham, W. J., Roberts, Julian** and **Williams, Peter.** Opening the Door. *A Study of New Policies for the Mentally Handicapped. 278 pp.*
Karn, Valerie. Retiring to the Seaside. *400 pp. 2 maps. Numerous tables.*
King, R. D. and **Elliot, K. W.** Albany: Birth of a Prison—End of an Era. *394 pp.*
Thomas, J. E. The English Prison Officer since 1850: *A Study in Conflict. 258 pp.*
Walton, R. G. Women in Social Work. *303 pp.*
● **Woodward, J.** To Do the Sick No Harm. *A Study of the British Voluntary Hospital System to 1875. 234 pp.*

International Library of Welfare and Philosophy
General Editors Noel Timms and David Watson

● **McDermott, F. E.** (Ed.) Self-Determination in Social Work. *A Collection of Essays on Self-determination and Related Concepts by Philosophers and Social Work Theorists. Contributors: F. P. Biestek, S. Bernstein, A. Keith-Lucas, D. Sayer, H. H. Perelman, C. Whittington, R. F. Stalley, F. E. McDermott, I. Berlin, H. J. McCloskey, H. L. A. Hart, J. Wilson, A. I. Melden, S. I. Benn. 254 pp.*
● **Plant, Raymond.** Community and Ideology. *104 pp.*
Ragg, Nicholas M. People Not Cases. *A Philosophical Approach to Social Work. 168 pp.*
● **Timms, Noel** and **Watson, David.** (Eds) Talking About Welfare. *Readings in Philosophy and Social Policy. Contributors: T. H. Marshall, R. B. Brandt, G. H. von Wright, K. Nielsen, M. Cranston, R. M. Titmuss, R. S. Downie, E. Telfer, D. Donnison, J. Benson, P. Leonard, A. Keith-Lucas, D. Walsh, I. T. Ramsey. 320 pp.*
● Philosophy in Social Work. *250 pp.*
● **Weale, A.** Equality and Social Policy. *164 pp.*

Library of Social Work
General Editor Noel Timms

● **Baldock, Peter.** Community Work and Social Work. *140 pp.*
○ **Beedell, Christopher.** Residential Life with Children. *210 pp. Crown 8vo.*
● **Berry, Juliet.** Daily Experience in Residential Life. *A Study of Children and their Care-givers. 202 pp.*
○ Social Work with Children. *190 pp. Crown 8vo.*
● **Brearley, C. Paul.** Residential Work with the Elderly. *116 pp.*
● Social Work, Ageing and Society. *126 pp.*
● **Cheetham, Juliet.** Social Work with Immigrants. *240 pp. Crown 8vo.*
● **Cross, Crispin P.** (Ed.) Interviewing and Communication in Social Work. *Contributions by C. P. Cross, D. Laurenson, B. Strutt, S. Raven. 192 pp. Crown 8vo.*

- ● **Curnock, Kathleen** and **Hardiker, Pauline.** Towards Practice Theory. *Skills and Methods in Social Assessments. 208 pp.*
- ● **Davies, Bernard.** The Use of Groups in Social Work Practice. *158 pp.*
- ● **Davies, Martin.** Support Systems in Social Work. *144 pp.*
- **Ellis, June.** (Ed.) West African Families in Britain. *A Meeting of Two Cultures. Contributions by Pat Stapleton, Vivien Biggs. 150 pp. 1 Map.*
- ● **Hart, John.** Social Work and Sexual Conduct. *230 pp.*
- ● **Hutten, Joan M.** Short-Term Contracts in Social Work. *Contributions by Stella M. Hall, Elsie Osborne, Mannie Sher, Eva Sternberg, Elizabeth Tuters. 134 pp.*
- **Jackson, Michael P.** and **Valencia, B. Michael.** Financial Aid Through Social Work. *140 pp.*
- ● **Jones, Howard.** The Residential Community. *A Setting for Social Work. 150 pp.*
- ● (Ed.) Towards a New Social Work. *Contributions by Howard Jones, D. A. Fowler, J. R. Cypher, R. G. Walton, Geoffrey Mungham, Philip Priestley, Ian Shaw, M. Bartley, R. Deacon, Irwin Epstein, Geoffrey Pearson. 184 pp.*
- **Jones, Ray** and **Pritchard, Colin.** (Eds) Social Work With Adolescents. *Contributions by Ray Jones, Colin Pritchard, Jack Dunham, Florence Rossetti, Andrew Kerslake, John Burns, William Gregory, Graham Templeman, Kenneth E. Reid, Audrey Taylor. About 170 pp.*
- ○ **Jordon, William.** The Social Worker in Family Situations. *160 pp. Crown 8vo.*
- ● **Laycock, A. L.** Adolescents and Social Work. *128 pp. Crown 8vo.*
- ● **Lees, Ray.** Politics and Social Work. *128 pp. Crown 8vo.*
- ● Research Strategies for Social Welfare. *112 pp. Tables.*
- ○ **McCullough, M. K.** and **Ely, Peter J.** Social Work with Groups. *127 pp. Crown 8vo.*
- ● **Moffett, Jonathan.** Concepts in Casework Treatment. *128 pp. Crown 8vo.*
- **Parsloe, Phyllida.** Juvenile Justice in Britain and the United States. *The Balance of Needs and Rights. 336 pp.*
- ● **Plant, Raymond.** Social and Moral Theory in Casework. *112 pp. Crown 8vo.*
- **Priestley, Philip, Fears, Denise** and **Fuller, Roger.** Justice for Juveniles. *The 1969 Children and Young Persons Act: A Case for Reform? 128 pp.*
- ● **Pritchard, Colin** and **Taylor, Richard.** Social Work: Reform or Revolution? *170 pp.*
- ○ **Pugh, Elisabeth.** Social Work in Child Care. *128 pp. Crown 8vo.*
- ● **Robinson, Margaret.** Schools and Social Work. *282 pp.*
- ○ **Ruddock, Ralph.** Roles and Relationships. *128 pp. Crown 8vo.*
- ● **Sainsbury, Eric.** Social Diagnosis in Casework. *118 pp. Crown 8vo.*
- ● Social Work with Families. *Perceptions of Social Casework among Clients of a Family Service. 188 pp.*
- **Seed, Philip.** The Expansion of Social Work in Britain. *128 pp. Crown 8vo.*
- ● **Shaw, John.** The Self in Social Work. *124 pp.*
- **Smale, Gerald G.** Prophecy, Behaviour and Change. *An Examination of Self-fulfilling Prophecies in Helping Relationships. 116 pp. Crown 8vo.*
- **Smith, Gilbert.** Social Need. *Policy, Practice and Research. 155 pp.*
- ● Social Work and the Sociology of Organisations. *124 pp. Revised edition.*
- ● **Sutton, Carole.** Psychology for Social Workers and Counsellors. *An Introduction. 248 pp.*
- ● **Timms, Noel.** Language of Social Casework. *122 pp. Crown 8vo.*
- ● Recording in Social Work. *124 pp. Crown 8vo.*
- ● **Todd, F. Joan.** Social Work with the Mentally Subnormal. *96 pp. Crown 8vo.*
- ● **Walrond-Skinner, Sue.** Family Therapy. *The Treatment of Natural Systems. 172 pp.*
- ● **Warham, Joyce.** An Introduction to Administration for Social Workers. *Revised edition. 112 pp.*
- ● An Open Case. *The Organisational Context of Social Work. 172 pp.*
- ○ **Wittenberg, Isca Salzberger.** Psycho-Analytic Insight and Relationships. *A Kleinian Approach. 196 pp. Crown 8vo.*

Primary Socialization, Language and Education
General Editor Basil Bernstein

Adlam, Diana S., *with the assistance of Geoffrey Turner and Lesley Lineker.* Code in *Context. 272 pp.*

Bernstein, Basil. Class, Codes and Control. *3 volumes.*

● 1. *Theoretical Studies Towards a Sociology of Language. 254 pp.*

2. *Applied Studies Towards a Sociology of Language. 377 pp.*

● 3. *Towards a Theory of Educational Transmission. 167 pp.*

Brandis, W. and **Bernstein, B.** Selection and Control. *176 pp.*

Brandis, Walter and **Henderson, Dorothy.** Social Class, Language and Communication. *288 pp.*

Cook-Gumperz, Jenny. Social Control and Socialization. *A Study of Class Differences in the Language of Maternal Control. 290 pp.*

● **Gahagan, D. M.** and **G. A.** Talk Reform. *Exploration in Language for Infant School Children. 160 pp.*

Hawkins, P. R. Social Class, the Nominal Group and Verbal Strategies. *About 220 pp.*

Robinson, W. P. and **Rackstraw, Susan D. A.** A Question of Answers. *2 volumes. 192 pp. and 180 pp.*

Turner, Geoffrey J. and **Mohan, Bernard A.** A Linguistic Description and Computer Programme for Children's Speech. *208 pp.*

Reports of the Institute of Community Studies

Baker, J. The Neighbourhood Advice Centre. A Community Project in Camden. *320 pp.*

● **Cartwright, Ann.** Patients and their Doctors. *A Study of General Practice. 304 pp.*

Dench, Geoff. Maltese in London. *A Case-study in the Erosion of Ethnic Consciousness. 302 pp.*

Jackson, Brian and **Marsden, Dennis.** Education and the Working Class: *Some General Themes Raised by a Study of 88 Working-class Children in a Northern Industrial City. 268 pp. 2 folders.*

Marris, Peter. The Experience of Higher Education. *232 pp. 27 tables.*

● Loss and Change. *192 pp.*

Marris, Peter and **Rein, Martin.** Dilemmas of Social Reform. *Poverty and Community Action in the United States. 256 pp.*

Marris, Peter and **Somerset, Anthony.** African Businessmen. *A Study of Entrepreneurship and Development in Kenya. 256 pp.*

Mills, Richard. Young Outsiders: *a Study in Alternative Communities. 216 pp.*

Runciman, W. G. Relative Deprivation and Social Justice. *A Study of Attitudes to Social Inequality in Twentieth-Century England. 352 pp.*

Willmott, Peter. Adolescent Boys in East London. *230 pp.*

Willmott, Peter and **Young, Michael.** Family and Class in a London Suburb. *202 pp. 47 tables.*

Young, Michael and **McGeeney, Patrick.** Learning Begins at Home. *A Study of a Junior School and its Parents. 128 pp.*

Young, Michael and **Willmott, Peter.** Family and Kinship in East London. *Foreword by Richard M. Titmuss. 252 pp. 39 tables.*

The Symmetrical Family. *410 pp.*

Reports of the Institute for Social Studies in Medical Care

Cartwright, Ann, Hockey, Lisbeth and **Anderson, John J.** Life Before Death. *310 pp.*
Dunnell, Karen and **Cartwright, Ann.** Medicine Takers, Prescribers and Hoarders. *190 pp.*
Farrell, C. My Mother Said. . . *A Study of the Way Young People Learned About Sex and Birth Control. 288 pp.*

Medicine, Illness and Society
General Editor W. M. Williams

Hall, David J. Social Relations & Innovation. *Changing the State of Play in Hospitals. 232 pp.*
Hall, David J. and **Stacey, M.** (Eds) Beyond Separation. *234 pp.*
Robinson, David. The Process of Becoming Ill. *142 pp.*
Stacey, Margaret *et al.* Hospitals, Children and Their Families. *The Report of a Pilot Study. 202 pp.*
Stimson, G. V. and **Webb, B.** Going to See the Doctor. *The Consultation Process in General Practice. 155 pp.*

Monographs in Social Theory
General Editor Arthur Brittan

● **Barnes, B.** Scientific Knowledge and Sociological Theory. *192 pp.*
Bauman, Zygmunt. Culture as Praxis. *204 pp.*
● **Dixon, Keith.** Sociological Theory. *Pretence and Possibility. 142 pp.*
The Sociology of Belief. *Fallacy and Foundation. About 160 pp.*
Goff, T. W. Marx and Mead. *Contributions to a Sociology of Knowledge. 176 pp.*
Meltzer, B. N., Petras, J. W. and **Reynolds, L. T.** Symbolic Interactionism. *Genesis, Varieties and Criticisms. 144 pp.*
● **Smith, Anthony D.** The Concept of Social Change. *A Critique of the Functionalist Theory of Social Change. 208 pp.*

Routledge Social Science Journals

The British Journal of Sociology. *Editor – Angus Stewart; Associate Editor – Leslie Sklair. Vol. 1, No. 1 – March 1950 and Quarterly. Roy. 8vo. All back issues available. An international journal publishing original papers in the field of sociology and related areas.*
Community Work. *Edited by David Jones and Marjorie Mayo. 1973. Published annually.*
Economy and Society. *Vol. 1, No. 1. February 1972 and Quarterly. Metric Roy. 8vo. A journal for all social scientists covering sociology, philosophy, anthropology, economics and history. All back numbers available.*

Ethnic and Racial Studies. *Editor – John Stone. Vol. 1 – 1978. Published quarterly.*
Religion. Journal of Religion and Religions. *Chairman of Editorial Board, Ninian Smart. Vol. 1, No. 1, Spring 1971. A journal with an inter-disciplinary approach to the study of the phenomena of religion. All back numbers available.*
Sociology of Health and Illness. *A Journal of Medical Sociology. Editor – Alan Davies; Associate Editor – Ray Jobling. Vol. 1, Spring 1979. Published 3 times per annum.*
Year Book of Social Policy in Britain. *Edited by Kathleen Jones. 1971. Published annually.*

Social and Psychological Aspects of Medical Practice
Editor Trevor Silverstone

Lader, Malcolm. Psychophysiology of Mental Illness. *280 pp.*
● **Silverstone, Trevor** and **Turner, Paul.** Drug Treatment in Psychiatry. *Revised edition. 256 pp.*
Whiteley, J. S. and **Gordon, J.** Group Approaches in Psychiatry. *240 pp.*

Printed and bound in Great Britain by
Redwood Burn Limited, Trowbridge & Esher

1279